Toyota
Starlet
Owners
Workshop
Manual

by J H Haynes
Member of the Guild of Motoring Writers
and A K Legg T Eng (CEI), AMIMI

Models covered
Toyota Starlet 1.0 GL; 993 cc
Toyota Starlet 1.2 S & GL; 1166 cc
Toyota Starlet 1.3 GL; 1290 cc

Does not cover automatic transmission

ISBN 1 85010 305 4

Printed in England *(462–9N4)*

ABCDE
FGHIJ
KL

THE BOOK

Haynes Publishing Group
Sparkford Nr Yeovil
Somerset BA22 7JJ England

Haynes Publications, Inc
861 Lawrence Drive
Newbury Park
California 91320 USA

British Library Cataloguing in Publication Data

Legg, A. K.
   Toyota Starlet ('78 to Jan '85) owners workshop manual.
  –(Owners Workshop Manuals)
  1. Toyota Starlet automobile
I. Title   II. Series
629.28'722   TL215.T64
ISBN 1-85010-305-4

Acknowledgements

Thanks are due to Toyota Motor Sales Company Limited for the provision of technical information and certain illustrations. Castrol Limited provided lubrication data and the Champion Sparking Plug Company provided the illustrations showing the various spark plug conditions.

Lastly, thanks are due to all those people at Sparkford who helped in the production of this manual.

About this manual

Its aim

The aim of this manual is to help you get the best value from your vehicle. It can do so in several ways. It can help you decide what work must be done (even should you choose to get it done by a garage), provide information on routine maintenance and servicing, and give a logical course of action and diagnosis when random faults occur. However, it is hoped that you will use the manual by tackling the work yourself. On simpler jobs it may even be quicker than booking the car into a garage and going there twice, to leave and collect it. Perhaps most important, a lot of money can be saved by avoiding the costs a garage must charge to cover its labour and overheads.

The manual has drawings and descriptions to show the function of the various components so that their layout can be understood. Then the tasks are described and photographed in a step-by-step sequence so that even a novice can do the work.

Its arrangement

The manual is divided into thirteen Chapters, each covering a logical sub-division of the vehicle. The Chapters are each divided into Sections, numbered with single figures, eg 5; and the Sections into paragraphs (or sub-sections), with decimal numbers following on from the Section they are in, eg 5.1, 5.2, 5.3 etc.

It is freely illustrated, especially in those parts where there is a detailed sequence of operations to be carried out. There are two forms of illustration: figures and photographs. The figures are numbered in sequence with decimal numbers, according to their position in the Chapter – eg Fig. 6.4 is the fourth drawing/illustration in Chapter 6. Photographs carry the same number (either individually or in related groups) as the Section or sub-section to which they relate.

There is an alphabetical index at the back of the manual as well as a contents list at the front. Each Chapter is also preceded by its own individual contents list.

References to the 'left' or 'right' of the vehicle are in the sense of a person in the driver's seat facing forwards.

Unless otherwise stated, nuts and bolts are removed by turning anti-clockwise, and tightened by turning clockwise.

Vehicle manufacturers continually make changes to specifications and recommendations, and these, when notified, are incorporated into our manuals at the earliest opportunity.

Whilst every care is taken to ensure that the information in this manual is correct, no liability can be accepted by the authors or publishers for loss, damage or injury caused by any errors in, or omissions from, the information given.

Introduction to the Toyota Starlet

The Toyota Starlet succeeds the Toyota 1000 and is now the smallest car marketed in the UK by Toyota. It is an excellent example of a reliable, robust and economical small car at a very reasonable price.

The mechanical layout of the car is conventional, with a front-mounted engine and rear wheel drive. The body is of three or five-door hatchback type. A four or five-speed gearbox is available according to model; the fifth speed gear is in effect an overdrive.

The overhead valve engine is over-square (ie the stroke measures less than the bore) and is extremely sturdy, the crankshaft being supported in five bearings. Both the 993 cc and the 1166 cc engines are economical to run and, with a compression ratio of 9 : 1, two star petrol can be used.

Toyota engineers have taken considerable measures to ensure passenger comfort by fitting sound deadening material and reducing wind noise. The bodywork is also adequately rust-proofed and a particularly good point is the fitting of galvanised panels beneath the front wings.

Although the Starlet is relatively inexpensive, it comes equipped with fully reclining front seats, adjustable headrests, fabric trim, push-button radio, electric clock, carpets, tinted glass all round, and many other refinements usually associated with more expensive models.

Contents

Toyota Starlet GL (3-door)

Toyota Starlet GL (5-door)

Toyota Starlet 1.2 GL

General dimensions, weights and capacities

For modifications, and information applicable to later models, see Supplement at end of manual

Dimensions
Overall length
With small bumper . . . . 143.5 in (3.68 m)
With large bumper . . . . 145.3 in (3.73 m)

Overall width
With small bumper . . . . 60.0 in (1.53 m)
With large bumper . . . . 60.4 in (1.54 m)

Overall height
With 12 inch tyres . . . . 54.3 in (1.38 m)
With 13 inch tyres . . . . 54.5 in (1.39 m)

Ground clearance
With 12 inch tyres . . . . 6.5 in (165 mm)
With 13 inch tyres . . . . 6.7 in (170 mm)

Wheelbase . . . . 90.6 in (2.3 m)

Track
Front . . . . 50.8 in (1.29 m)
Rear . . . . 50.2 in (1.28 m)

Turning circle . . . . 30.2 ft (9.2 m)

Weights
Kerb weight
993 cc 3-door . . . . 1529 lb (695 kg)
993 cc 5-door . . . . 1570 lb (710 kg)
1166 cc 3-door . . . . 1545 lb (700 kg)
1166 cc 5-door . . . . 1580 lb (715 kg)

Towing capacity
With braked trailer . . . . 1545 lb (700 kg)
With unbraked trailer . . . . 880 lb (400 kg)

Capacities
Cooling system capacity . . . . 9.2 Imp pints (5.3 litres)

Engine oil capacity
With filter . . . . 6.6 Imp pints (3.5 litres)
Without filter . . . . 4.8 Imp pints (2.7 litres)

Gearbox oil capacity
4-speed . . . . 3.0 Imp pints (1.7 litres)
5-speed . . . . 4.2 Imp pints (2.45 litres)

Rear axle oil capacity . . . . 1.8 Imp pints (1.0 litres)

Fuel tank capacity . . . . 8.8 Imp gallons (40.0 litres)

Buying spare parts
and vehicle identification numbers

Buying spare parts

Spare parts are available from many sources, for example: Toyota garages, other garages and accessory shops, and motor factors. Our advice regarding spare part sources is as follows:

Officially appointed Toyota garages – This is the best source of parts which are peculiar to your car and are otherwise not generally available (eg complete cylinder heads, internal gearbox components, badges, interior trim, etc). It is also the only place at which you should buy parts if your car is still under warranty – non-Toyota components may invalidate the warranty. To be sure of obtaining the correct parts it will always be necessary to give the storeman your car's engine and chassis number, and if possible, to take the 'old' part along for positive identification. Remember that many parts are available on a factory exchange scheme – any parts returned should always be clean! It obviously makes good sense to go straight to the specialist on your car for this type of part for they are best equipped to supply you.

Other garages and accessory shops – These are often very good places to buy materials and components needed for the maintenance of your car (eg oil filters, spark plugs, bulbs, fan belts, oils and greases, touch-up paint, filler paste etc). They also sell general accessories, usually have convenient opening hours, charge lower prices and can often be found not far from home.

Motor factors – Good factors will stock all of the more important components which wear out relatively quickly (eg clutch components, pistons, valves, exhaust systems, brake cylinders/pipes/hoses/seals/shoes and pads etc. Motor factors will often provide new or reconditioned components on a part exchange basis – this can save a considerable amount of money.

Vehicle identification numbers

Always have details of the car, its serial and engine numbers available, when ordering parts. If you can take along the part to be renewed, it is helpful. Modifications were and are being continually made and often are not generally publicised. A storeman in a parts department is quite justified in saying that he cannot guarantee the correctness of a part unless these important numbers are available.

The engine number is stamped on the right-hand side of the cylinder block.

The serial number is stamped on a plate on the engine compartment rear bulkhead.

The gearbox number is stamped on the bottom of the clutch bellhousing.

Engine number

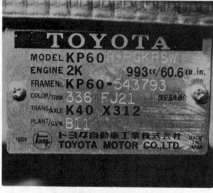

Car serial number plate

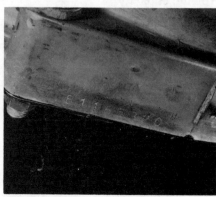

Gearbox serial number

Tools and working facilities

Introduction

A selection of good tools is a fundamental requirement for anyone contemplating the maintenance and repair of a motor vehicle. For the owner who does not possess any, their purchase will prove a considerable expense, offsetting some of the savings made by doing-it-yourself. However, provided that the tools purchased meet the relevant national safety standards and are of good quality, they will last for many years and prove an extremely worthwhile investment.

To help the average owner to decide which tools are needed to carry out the various tasks detailed in this manual, we have compiled three lists of tools under the following headings: *Maintenance and minor repair, Repair and overhaul,* and *Special.* The newcomer to practical mechanics should start off with the *Maintenance and minor repair* tool kit and confine himself to the simpler jobs around the vehicle. Then, as his confidence and experience grows, he can undertake more difficult tasks, buying extra tools as, and when, they are needed. In this way, a *Maintenance and minor repair* tool kit can be built-up into a *Repair and overhaul* tool kit over a considerable period of time without any major cash outlays. The experienced do-it-yourselfer will have a tool kit good enough for most repair and overhaul procedures and will add tools from the *Special* category when he feels the expense is justified by the amount of use to which these tools will be put.

It is obviously not possible to cover the subject of tools fully here. For those who wish to learn more about tools and their use there is a book entitled *How to Choose and Use Car Tools* available from the publishers of this manual.

Maintenance and minor repair tool kit

The tools given in this list should be considered as a minimum requirement if routine maintenance, servicing and minor repair operations are to be undertaken. We recommend the purchase of combination spanners (ring one end, open-ended the other); although more expensive than open-ended ones, they do give the advantages of both types of spanner. All nuts, bolts screws and threads on the Starlet are to metric standards.

Combination spanners - 10, 11, 13, 14, 17 mm
Adjustable spanner - 9 inch
Engine sump/gearbox/rear axle drain plug key (where applicable)
Spark plug spanner (with rubber insert)
Spark plug gap adjustment tool
Set of feeler gauges
Brake adjuster spanner (where applicable)
Brake bleed nipple spanner
Screwdriver - 4 in long x $\frac{1}{4}$ in dia (flat blade)
Screwdriver - 4 in long x $\frac{1}{4}$ in dia (cross blade)
Combination pliers - 6 inch
Hacksaw, junior
Tyre pump
Tyre pressure gauge
Grease gun (where applicable)
Oil can
Fine emery cloth (1 sheet)
Wire brush (small)
Funnel (medium size)

Repair and overhaul tool kit

These tools are virtually essential for anyone undertaking any major repairs to a motor vehicle, and are additional to those given in the *Maintenance and minor repair* list. Included in this list is a comprehensive set of sockets. Although these are expensive they will be found invaluable as they are so versatile - particularly if various drives are included in the set. We recommend the $\frac{1}{2}$ in square-drive type, as this can be used with most proprietary torque wrenches. If you cannot afford a socket set, even bought piecemeal, then inexpensive tubular box spanners are a useful alternative.

The tools in this list will occasionally need to be supplemented by tools from the *Special* list.

Sockets (or box spanners) to cover range in previous list
Reversible ratchet drive (for use with sockets)·
Extension piece, 10 inch (for use with sockets)
Universal joint (for use with sockets)
Torque wrench (for use with sockets)
'Mole' wrench - 8 inch
Ball pein hammer
Soft-faced hammer, plastic or rubber
Screwdriver - 6 in long x $\frac{5}{16}$ in dia (flat blade)
Screwdriver - 2 in long x $\frac{5}{16}$ in square (flat blade)
Screwdriver - 1$\frac{1}{2}$ in long x $\frac{1}{4}$ in dia (cross blade)
Screwdriver - 3 in long x $\frac{1}{8}$ in dia (electricians)
Pliers - electricians side cutters
Pliers - needle nosed
Pliers - circlip (internal and external)
Cold chisel - $\frac{1}{2}$ inch
Scriber (this can be made by grinding the end of a broken hacksaw blade)
Scraper (this can be made by flattening and sharpening one end of a piece of copper pipe)
Centre punch
Pin punch
Hacksaw
Valve grinding tool
Steel rule/straight edge
Allen keys
Selection of files
Wire brush (large)
Axle-stands
Jack (strong scissor or hydraulic type)

Special tools

The tools in this list are those which are not used regularly, are expensive to buy, or which need to be used in accordance with their manufacturers' instructions. Unless relatively difficult mechanical jobs are undertaken frequently, it will not be economic to buy many of these tools. Where this is the case, you could consider clubbing together with friends (or a motorists' club) to make a joint purchase, or borrowing the tools against a deposit from a local garage or tool hire specialist.

The following list contains only those tools and instruments freely available to the public, and not those special tools produced by the vehicle manufacturer specifically for its dealer network. You will find occasional references to these manufacturers' special tools in the text of this manual. Generally, an alternative method of doing the job without the vehicle manufacturer's special tool is given. However, sometimes, there is no alternative to using them. Where this is the case and the relevant tool cannot be bought or borrowed you will have to entrust the work to a franchised garage.

> *Valve spring compressor*
> *Piston ring compressor*
> *Balljoint separator*
> *Universal hub/bearing puller*
> *Impact screwdriver*
> *Micrometer and/or vernier gauge*
> *Dial gauge*
> *Stroboscopic timing light*
> *Dwell angle meter/tachometer*
> *Universal electrical multi-meter*
> *Cylinder compression gauge*
> *Lifting tackle*
> *Trolley jack*
> *Light with extension lead*

Buying tools

For practically all tools, a tool factor is the best source since he will have a very comprehensive range compared with the average garage or accessory shop. Having said that, accessory shops often offer excellent quality tools at discount prices, so it pays to shop around.

There are plenty of good tools around at reasonable prices, but always aim to purchase items which meet the relevant national safety standards. If in doubt, ask the proprietor or manager of the shop for advice before making a purchase.

Care and maintenance of tools

Having purchased a reasonable tool kit, it is necessary to keep the tools in a clean serviceable condition. After use, always wipe off any dirt, grease and metal particles using a clean, dry cloth, before putting the tools away. Never leave them lying around after they have been used. A simple tool rack on the garage or workshop wall, for items such as screwdrivers and pliers is a good idea. Store all normal spanners and sockets in a metal box. Any measuring instruments, gauges, meters, etc, must be carefully stored where they cannot be damaged or become rusty.

Take a little care when tools are used. Hammer heads inevitably become marked and screwdrivers lose the keen edge on their blades from time to time. A little timely attention with emery cloth or a file will soon restore items like this to a good serviceable finish.

Working facilities

Not to be forgotten when discussing tools, is the workshop itself. If anything more than routine maintenance is to be carried out, some form of suitable working area becomes essential.

It is appreciated that many an owner mechanic is forced by circumstances to remove an engine or similar item, without the benefit of a garage or workshop. Having done this, any repairs should always be done under the cover of a roof.

Wherever possible, any dismantling should be done on a clean flat workbench or table at a suitable working height.

Any workbench needs a vice: one with a jaw opening of 4 in (100 mm) is suitable for most jobs. As mentioned previously, some clean dry storage space is also required for tools, as well as the lubricants, cleaning fluids, touch-up paints and so on which become necessary.

Another item which may be required, and which has a much more general usage, is an electric drill with a chuck capacity of at least $\frac{5}{16}$ in (8 mm). This, together with a good range of twist drills, is virtually essential for fitting accessories such as wing mirrors and reversing lights.

Last, but not least, always keep a supply of old newspapers and clean, lint-free rags available, and try to keep any working area as clean as possible.

Spanner jaw gap comparison table

Jaw gap (in)	Spanner size
0·250	$\frac{1}{4}$ in AF
0·277	7 mm
0·313	$\frac{5}{16}$ in AF
0·315	8 mm
0·344	$\frac{11}{32}$ in AF; $\frac{1}{8}$ in Whitworth
0·354	9 mm
0·375	$\frac{3}{8}$ in AF
0·394	10 mm
0·433	11 mm
0·438	$\frac{7}{16}$ in AF
0·445	$\frac{3}{16}$ in Whitworth; $\frac{1}{4}$ in BSF
0·472	12 mm
0·500	$\frac{1}{2}$ in AF
0·512	13 mm
0·525	$\frac{1}{4}$ in Whitworth; $\frac{5}{16}$ in BSF
0·551	14 mm
0·563	$\frac{9}{16}$ in AF
0·591	15 mm
0·600	$\frac{5}{16}$ in Whitworth; $\frac{3}{8}$ in BSF
0·625	$\frac{5}{8}$ in AF
0·630	16 mm
0·669	17 mm
0·686	$\frac{11}{16}$ in AF
0·709	18 mm
0·710	$\frac{3}{8}$ in Whitworth; $\frac{7}{16}$ in BSF
0·748	19 mm
0·750	$\frac{3}{4}$ in AF
0·813	$\frac{13}{16}$ in AF
0·820	$\frac{7}{16}$ in Whitworth; $\frac{1}{2}$ in BSF
0·866	22 mm
0·875	$\frac{7}{8}$ in AF
0·920	$\frac{1}{2}$ in Whitworth; $\frac{9}{16}$ in BSF
0·938	$\frac{15}{16}$ in AF
0·945	24 mm
1·000	1 in AF
1·010	$\frac{9}{16}$ in Whitworth; $\frac{5}{8}$ in BSF
1·024	26 mm
1·063	$1\frac{1}{16}$ in AF; 27 mm
1·100	$\frac{5}{8}$ in Whitworth; $\frac{11}{16}$ in BSF
1·125	$1\frac{1}{8}$ in AF
1·181	30 mm
1·200	$\frac{11}{16}$ in Whitworth; $\frac{3}{4}$ in BSF
1·250	$1\frac{1}{4}$ in AF
1·260	32 mm
1·300	$\frac{3}{4}$ in Whitworth; $\frac{7}{8}$ in BSF
1·313	$1\frac{5}{16}$ in AF
1·390	$\frac{13}{16}$ in Whitworth; $\frac{15}{16}$ in BSF
1·417	36 mm
1·438	$1\frac{7}{16}$ in AF
1·480	$\frac{7}{8}$ in Whitworth; 1 in BSF
1·500	$1\frac{1}{2}$ in AF
1·575	40 mm; $\frac{15}{16}$ in Whitworth
1·614	41 mm
1·625	$1\frac{5}{8}$ in AF
1·670	1 in Whitworth; $1\frac{1}{8}$ in BSF
1·688	$1\frac{11}{16}$ in AF
1·811	46 mm
1·813	$1\frac{13}{16}$ in AF
1·860	$1\frac{1}{8}$ in Whitworth; $1\frac{1}{4}$ in BSF
1·875	$1\frac{7}{8}$ in AF
1·969	50 mm
2·000	2 in AF
2·050	$1\frac{1}{4}$ in Whitworth; $1\frac{3}{8}$ in BSF
2·165	55 mm
2·362	60 mm

Jacking and towing

The jack supplied in the car tool kit is intended for roadside emergency wheel changing only. Make sure that the jack is fully engaged in the sill recesses before raising the car and use the chock supplied against the roadwheel diagonally opposite the wheel being removed.

To raise the car for maintenance or overhaul, use a trolley, hydraulic or screw type jack. To raise the front of the car, place the jack under the crossmember. To raise the rear of the car, place the jack under the differential housing.

Always supplement the jack by placing axle stands under the bodysill jacking brackets.

Towing another vehicle is not recommended at all. The rear 'towing' hook is in fact a lashing eye for use during transportation on a vehicle carrier.

If your car must be towed in an emergency, use a proper towing rope attached to the front towing eye (photo). Unlock the steering column before moving and remember that after the first few brake applications, the servo assistance will not be available and harder than normal foot pedal pressures will be required.

Front crossmember jacking point

Rear axle jacking point

Jack location

Jack in position

Rear lash-down hook

Front lash-down/towing eye

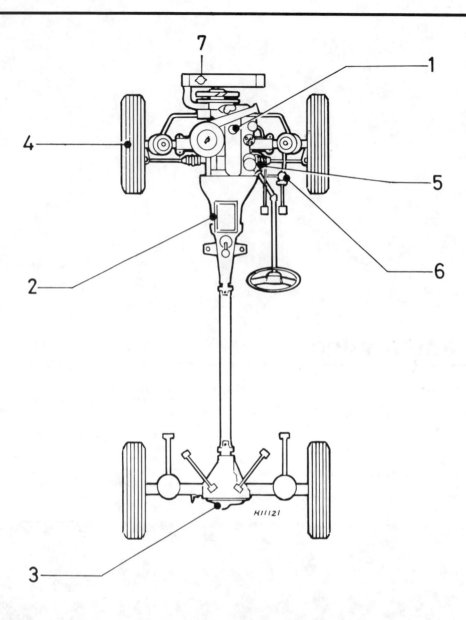

Recommended lubricants and fluids

Component or system	Lubricant type or specification
1 Engine	Multigrade engine oil to SAE 10W/30, 10W/40 or 10W/50

2 Transmission
  Manual
  Automatic
	Gear oil to API GL-4 or GL-5
	Dexron® II automatic transmission fluid

3 Differential	Gear oil to API GL-5
4 Wheel bearings	Multi-purpose lithium based grease (NLGI No 2)
5 Steering rack	Multi-purpose lithium based grease (NLGI No 2)
6 Braking system	Hydraulic fluid to SAE J1703 or DOT 3
7 Cooling system	Ethylene glycol based antifreeze solution, with corrosion inhibitors

Note: *these are recommendations only. Lubrication requirements vary from climate to climate and conditions of use. Consult your handbook or local dealer for extreme conditions.*

Routine maintenance

For additional service requirements see Supplement at end of manual

Introduction

Maintenance is essential for ensuring safety and desirable for the purpose of getting the best in terms of performance and economy from the vehicle. Over the years the need for periodical lubrication – oiling, greasing and so on – has been drastically reduced if not toally eliminated. This has unfortunately tended to lead some owners to think that because no such action is required the items either no longer exist or will last for ever. This is a serious delusion. It follows therefore that the largest initial element of maintenance is visual examination. This may lead to repairs or renewals.

Every 250 miles (400 km) travelled or weekly – whichever comes first

Check the engine oil level and top-up if necessary (photo).
Check the battery electrolyte level and top-up if necessary.
Check the windshield washer fluid level and top-up if necessary.
Check the tyre pressures including the spare wheel (when cold).
Examine tyres for wear or damage.
Check the brake reservoir fluid level and top-up if necessary.
Check the radiator coolant level and top up if necessary.
Check that the brake operation is satisfactory.
Check the operation of all lights, instruments, warning devices, accessories, controls etc.

Every 6000 miles (10 000 km) travelled, or 6 months – whichever comes first

Engine
Drain the engine oil when warm, and refill with the correct quantity and grade of oil. Renew oil filter.

Ignition system
Check the spark plugs; clean and adjust as necessary.
Check the contact breaker points; clean and adjust as necessary.

Chassis and body
Check the condition of the seat belts and their anchorage points; renew any belts which are frayed or damaged. Lubricate all controls, linkages, pedals, door locks and hinges.
Check disc pads for wear; renew as necessary.
Check brake hydraulic system for leaks, damaged pipes etc.
Check for wear in steering gear and balljoints; check condition of rubber bellows and dust excluders.
Check and if necessary top-up gearbox oil level.
Check and if necessary top-up rear axle oil level
Adjust clutch free travel.

Every 12 000 miles (20 000 km) travelled, or 12 months – whichever comes first

Engine
Adjust valve clearances.
Check drivebelt tension and adjust if necessary.

Cooling system
Check cooling system hoses for leaks and damage; renew as necessary.

Ignition system
Renew contact breaker points and spark plugs.
Check and adjust ignition timing and dwell angle.
Examine the distributor cap, rotor and advance mechanism. Clean or renew as necessary.

Fuel and exhaust system
Examine exhaust system for corrosion and leakage.
Adjust engine idle speed and mixture.
Lubricate accelerator and choke controls; adjust if necessary.
Clean air filter element.
Check fuel pipes and connections for leaks and damage.
Clean and inspect PCV valve and hoses.

Chassis and body
Check brake servo hose for deterioration.
Check brake servo operation.
Inspect brake shoes for wear, renew if necessary.
Renew brake hydraulic fluid.
Check front wheel alignment; adjust if necessary.
Inspect suspension bushes and components; renew if necessary.
Check tightness of suspension nuts and bolts.
Check operation of shock absorbers; renew if necessary.
Inspect wiper blades; renew if necessary.
Clean battery terminals and apply petroleum jelly.

Every 24 000 (40 000 km) travelled, or two years – whichever comes first

Engine
Renew the drivebelt.

Cooling system
Drain, flush and refill the cooling system, using new antifreeze.

Fuel and exhaust system
Renew in-line fuel filter and clean fuel pump.
Renew air cleaner element
Renew fuel tank filler cap gasket.

Chassis and body
Change gearbox oil
Change rear axle oil
Renew front wheel bearing grease; adjust bearings.
Grease front suspension upper support bearings (photo).
Check headlamp alignment; adjust if necessary.

Every 48 000 miles (80 000 km) travelled, or four years – whichever comes first

Fuel and exhaust system
Renew PCV valve

Chassis and body
Renew brake hydraulic system rubber seals.
Check propeller shaft joints for wear; renew if necessary.
Check underbody for rust or corrosion; clean and apply new sealant as necessary.

Checking a tyre pressure

Location of the spare wheel

Windscreen washer reservoir

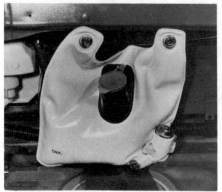

Rear screen washer reservoir

Engine oil dipstick

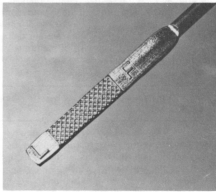

Dipstick markings

Topping-up with engine oil

Sump drain plug

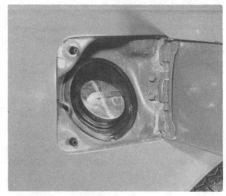

Fuel filler cap

Gearbox drain plug

Rear axle drain and filler plugs

A front strut upper bearing cap

Chapter 1 Engine

For modifications, and information applicable to later models, see Supplement at end of manual

Contents

Specifications

General

Type	4-cylinder in-line, ohv, inclined
Displacement:	
2K series	993 cc (60.6 cu in)
3K series	1166 cc (71.2 cu in)
Bore and stroke:	
2K series	2.83 x 2.40 in (72.0 x 61.0 mm)
3K series	2.95 x 2.60 in (75.0 x 66.0 mm)
Firing order	1 – 3 – 4 – 2
Compression ratio	9.0:1
Maximum power (DIN):	
2K series	47 bhp at 5800 rpm
3K series	56 bhp at 6000 rpm
Maximum torque (DIN):	
2K series	47 lbf ft at 3800 rpm
3K series	62 lbf ft at 3800 rpm
Compression pressure:	
Normal	156 lbf/in^2 (11.0 kgf/cm^2)
Minimum	128 lbf/in^2 (9.0 kgf/cm^2)
Difference between cylinders	Less than 14.2 lbf/in^2 (1.0 kgf/cm^2)

Cylinder head

Material	Aluminium alloy
Warpage limit	0.002 in (0.05 mm)

Valves

Seat width	0.047 to 0.063 in (1.2 to 1.6 mm)
Face angle	45°
Stem diameter:	
Inlet	0.3136 to 0.3140 in (7.965 to 7.975 mm)
Exhaust	0.3134 to 0.3140 in (7.960 to 7.975 mm)
Valve stem oil clearance (normal):	
Inlet	0.0014 to 0.0026 in (0.035 to 0.065 mm)
Exhaust	0.0014 to 0.0028 in (0.035 to 0.070 mm)
Valve stem oil clearance (maximum):	
Inlet	0.0031 in (0.08 mm)
Exhaust	0.0039 in (0.10 mm)
Minimum valve head thickness:	
Inlet	0.031 in (0.8 mm)
Exhaust	0.035 in (0.9 mm)
Valve guide protrusion from cylinder head	0.71 in (18.0 mm)
Valve guide oversize available	+ 0.002 in (0.05 mm)
Valve spring free length	1.831 in (46.5 mm)
Maximum rocker arm to shaft clearance	0.0024 in (0.06 mm)
Maximum cam follower clearance in block	0.004 in (0.1 mm)
Valve timing:	
Inlet opens	16° BTDC
Inlet closes	50° ABDC
Exhaust opens	50° BBDC
Exhaust closes	16° ATDC
Valve clearances:	
Inlet	0.005 in (0.13 mm) cold, 0.008 in (0.20 mm) hot
Exhaust	0.009 in (0.23 mm) cold, 0.012 in (0.30 mm) hot

Camshaft

Maximum run-out	0.0012 in (0.03 mm)
Endfloat:	
Standard	0.0028 to 0.0055 in (0.07 to 0.14 mm)
Maximum	0.0118 in (0.3 mm)
Bearing running clearance:	
Standard	0.0010 to 0.0026 in (0.025 to 0.066 mm)
Maximum	0.004 in (0.1 mm)
Standard journal diameter (from front):	
No 1	1.7011 to 1.7018 in (43.209 to 4.3225 mm)
No 2	1.6911 to 1.6917 in (42.954 to 42.970 mm)
No 3	1.6813 to 1.6819 in (42.704 to 42.720 mm)
No 4	1.6716 to 1.6722 in (42.459 to 42.475 mm)
Bearing undersizes available	0.0049, 0.0098 in (0.125, 0.250 mm)

Cylinder block

Warpage limit	0.002 in (0.05 mm)
Standard bore diameter:	
2K series	2.8346 to 2.8366 in (72.00 to 72.05 mm)
3K series	2.9528 to 2.9547 in (75.00 to 75.05 mm)
Bore wear limit	0.008 in (0.2 mm)
Bore maximum taper	0.0008 in (0.02 mm)
Bore maximum ovality	0.0008 in (0.02 mm)
Cam follower bore diameter:	
Standard	0.7874 to 0.7882 in (20.000 to 20.021 mm)
Oversize	0.7894 to 0.7902 in (20.050 to 20.071 mm)

Pistons

Standard diameter:	
2K series	2.8331 to 2.8350 in (71.96 to 72.01 mm)
3K series	2.9512 to 2.9531 in (74.96 to 75.01 mm)
Oversizes available	+ 0.0098, 0.0197, 0.0295, 0.0394 in (0.25, 0.50, 0.75, 1.00 mm)
Piston to bore clearance	0.0012 to 0.002 in (0.03 to 0.05 mm)
Piston ring endgap:	
Top and middle (compression)	0.0039 to 0.0110 in (0.10 to 0.28 mm)
Bottom (oil control)	0.0079 to 0.0354 in (0.20 to 0.90 mm)
Ring to groove clearance:	
Top (compression)	0.0012 to 0.0028 in (0.03 to 0.07 mm)
Middle (compression)	0.0008 to 0.0024 in (0.02 to 0.06 mm)

Connecting rods

Twist limit	0.006 in (0.15 mm)

Bend limit	0.002 in (0.05 mm)
Small end bush to piston pin clearance:	
Standard	0.0002 to 0.0003 in (0.004 to 0.008 mm)
Maximum	0.002 in (0.05 mm)
Big-end endfloat:	
Standard	0.0043 to 0.0083 in (0.11 to 0.21 mm)
Maximum	0.012 in (0.3 mm)
Big-end running clearance:	
Standard	0.0006 to 0.0016 in (0.016 to 0.040 mm)
Maximum	0.0039 in (0.10 mm)

Crankshaft

Maximum run-out	0.0012 in (0.03 mm)
Endfloat:	
Standard	0.0016 to 0.0087 in (0.040 to 0.222 mm)
Maximum	0.012 in (0.3 mm)
Journal and crankpin maximum taper and ovality	0.0004 in (0.01 mm)
Journal diameter – standard	1.9676 to 1.9685 in (49.976 to 50.000 mm)
Journal undersizes	0.0098, 0.0197, 0.0295 in (0.25, 0.50, 0.75 mm)
Journal running clearance:	
Standard	0.0006 to 0.0016 in (0.016 to 0.040 mm)
Maximum	0.0039 in (0.10 mm)
Crankpin diameter – standard	1.6526 to 1.6535 in (41.976 to 42.000 mm)
Crankpin undersizes	0.0098, 0.0197, 0.0295, (0.25, 0.50, 0.75 mm)
Crankpin running clearance:	
Standard	0.0009 to 0.0019 in (0.024 to 0.048 mm)
Maximum	0.0039 in (0.1 mm)
Thrust washer thickness:	
Standard	0.0957 to 0.0976 in (2.43 to 2.48 mm)
Oversizes available	+ 0.0049, 0.0098 in (0.125, 0.250 mm)
Flywheel maximum run-out	0.008 in (0.2 mm)

Lubrication system

Oil pump type	Trochoid
Oil pump rotor tip clearance:	
Standard	0.0016 to 0.0063 in (0.04 to 0.16 mm)
Maximum	0.008 in (0.2 mm)
Oil pump rotor endfloat:	
Standard	0.0012 to 0.0035 in (0.03 to 0.09 mm)
Maximum	0.0059 in (0.15 mm)
Oil pump outer rotor to body clearance:	
Standard	0.0039 to 0.0063 in (0.10 to 0.16 mm)
Maxiumum	0.008 in (0.2 mm)
Relief valve opening pressure	51.2 to 62.6 lbf/ft^2 (3.6 to 4.4 kgf/cm^2)
Relief valve spring free length	1.85 in (47.0 mm)
Oil filter type	Disposable canister, full flow
Oil filter by-pass valve operating pressure	11.4 to 17.1 lbf/in^2 (0.8 to 1.2 kgf/cm^2)
Engine oil capacity:	
With filter	6.6 pints (3.5 litres)
Without filter	4.8 pints (2.7 litres)

Torque wrench settings

	lbf ft	kgf m
Main bearing cap bolts	45	6.2
Big-end cap nuts	35	4.8
Camshaft thrust plate bolts	6	0.8
Crankshaft pulley bolt	35	4.8
Cylinder head bolts	45	6.2
Camshaft sprocket bolt	45	6.2
Manifold bolts	20	2.8
Sump bolts	3	0.4
Flywheel bolts	45	6.2
Oil pump bolts	11	1.5
Front plate bolts	6	0.8
Timing chain tensioner and vibration damper bolts	6	0.8
Timing chain cover bolts	6	0.8
Rear oil seal retainer bolts	6	0.8
Valve rocker shaft pedestal bolts	16	2.2
Engine mounting bracket bolts	20	2.8
Oil filter bracket bolts	16	2.2
Alternator bracket bolts	11	1.5
Cylinder block drain plug	20	2.8
Rear plate bolts	6	0.8
Clutch bellhousing to engine bolts	45	6.2

1 General description

The engine fitted to the models covered by this manual are the 993 cc 2K series and the 1166 cc 3K series. Both engines are of identical construction, and are of overhead valve, four-cylinder in-line type.

The crankshaft is supported on five main bearings and endfloat is taken by thrust washers located on the centre bearing.

The camshaft is supported in four bearings and is driven by a chain from the crankshaft; chain tension is controlled by a hydraulic tensioner. The valves are operated by rockers mounted on a single shaft bolted to the cylinder head.

A positive crankcase ventilation system is incorporated to reduce the emission of blow-by gases.

Lubrication is by a rotor type pump located in the crankcase and driven by the distributor driveshaft. Engine oil is fed through an externally mounted full-flow filter to the main oil gallery, then through oilways to the crankshaft, camshaft, rocker shaft, and timing components. The oil pump incorporates a pressure relief valve. The disposable type canister oil filter is located on the right-hand side of the engine.

2 Major operations possible with engine in car

The following operations can be carried out without having to remove the engine from the car:

(a) *Removal and servicing of the cylinder head*
(b) *Renewal of the engine mountings*
(c) *Removal and refitting of the flywheel (after first removing the gearbox and clutch)*
(d) *Removal and refitting of the tappets (cam followers)*

3 Major operations only possible after removal of engine

The following operations can only be carried out after removal of the engine from the car:

(a) *Removal and refitting of the camshaft*
(b) *Removal and refitting of the crankshaft, pistons, and sump*
(c) *Renewal of the timing chain and gears*
(d) *Removal and refitting of the oil pump (after first removing the sump)*

4 Methods of engine removal

The engine can be removed complete with the gearbox, or independently leaving the gearbox in the car. Even though the gearbox may not require overhauling, it is much easier to remove the complete unit and then separate the gearbox. However, both methods of engine removal are described in the following Sections.

5 Engine – removal with gearbox

1 Open the bonnet and mark the position of the hinges with a pencil. Disconnect the windscreen washer tubing.
2 Unscrew the retaining bolts and with the help of an assistant, lift the bonnet from the car and store it in a safe place where it will not be scratched.
3 Disconnect the battery terminals, unscrew the clamp, and remove the battery and tray from the car.
4 Protect the tops of the front wings with thick cloth to prevent scratching during the removal procedure.
5 Drain the cooling system during the removal procedure.
6 Remove the sump drain plug and drain the engine oil into a suitable container. When completed, wipe the plug and refit it.

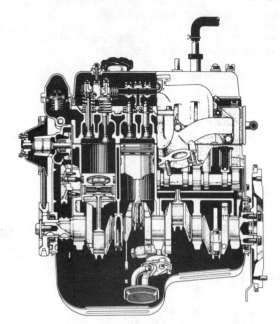
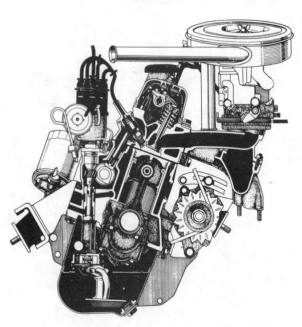

Fig. 1.1 Cutaway views of the engine (Sec 1)

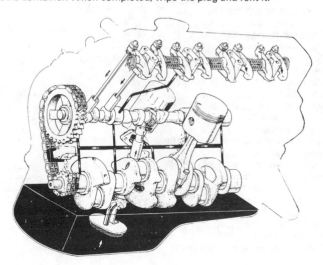

Fig. 1.2 Engine lubrication system (Sec 1)

5.9 Front grille mounting clip location

5.14 Heater hose connections to the engine

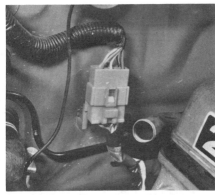

5.15A Engine wiring multiplug location

5.15B Fixed half of the engine wiring multiplug

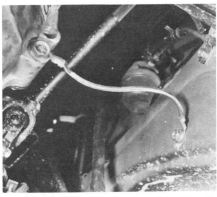

5.15C Engine right-hand rear earth lead location

5.15D Engine front earth lead location

5.18 Engine compartment front guard plate location

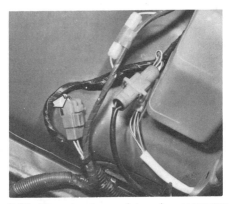

5.19 Alternator to regulator plug connector location (arrowed)

5.21 Engine right-hand side mounting

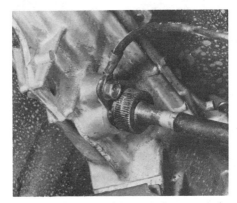

5.28 Speedometer cable to gearbox connection showing earth lead

5.33 Engine rear lifting hook location

5.34 Removing engine and gearbox assembly

7   Remove the radiator as described in Chapter 2.
8   Remove the electric cooling fan as described in Chapter 2.
9   Remove the headlight surrounds and front grille (photo).
10 Remove the air cleaner assembly as described in Chapter 3.
11 Disconnect the choke and throttle cables from the carburettor.
12 Disconnect the brake vacuum hose from the inlet manifold.
13 Remove the fuel hose from the fuel pump and plug it to prevent loss of fuel.
14 Remove the top and bottom radiator hoses from the engine and disconnect the heater hoses from the bulkhead valve (photo).
15 Separate the two halves of the engine wiring multiplug on the bulkhead. Detach the earth leads from each side of the engine (photos).
16 Disconnect the fuel cut lead connection at the rear of the engine.
17 Remove the headlight cleaner reservoir where fitted.
18 Remove the guard plate from the front frame, then dismantle the front frame and tie it to one side out of the way. There is no need to remove the bonnet lock (photo).
19 Remove the alternator as described in Chapter 10. Disconnect the regulator plug (photo).
20 Detach the HT lead from the coil.
21 Unscrew and remove the engine mounting nuts and washers noting that the larger washer is located on the left-hand side (photo).
22 Jack-up the front of the car and support it on axle stands, or alternatively locate it over an inspection pit.
23 Unscrew the retaining nuts and separate the exhaust downpipe from the manifold; remove the sealing gasket.
24 Unscrew the bolts securing the exhaust front pipe to the rear exhaust section and the front bracket to the clutch bellhousing (where fitted). Remove the exhaust front pipe and gasket from the car.
25 Remove the clutch cable from the gearbox with reference to Chapter 5.
26 Detach the battery lead from the starter solenoid.
27 Remove the drain plug and drain the gearbox oil into a suitable container. When completed wipe the plug and refit it.
28 Unscrew the bolt securing the speedometer clamp to the gearbox, remove the earth lead and unscrew the speedometer cable retaining ring (photo).
29 Temporarily remove the speedometer gear and drain any oil present in the gearbox extension housing.
30 Remove the propeller shaft as described in Chapter 7.
31 Working inside the car, remove the gearstick as described in Chapter 6.
32 Lower the car to the ground, support the gearbox with a trolley jack, and remove the rear mounting bolts.
33 Fit a chain or sling to the engine lifting hooks and connect up to a suitable hoist (photo).
34 Make a final check to ensure that all wires, cables and hoses have been disconnected, then lift the engine and gearbox from the engine compartment, simultaneously lowering the gearbox trolley jack. When the sump has cleared the steering gear, the complete unit can be drawn forward away from the car (photo).

6   Engine – separation from gearbox

1   With the engine and gearbox removed from the car, the gearbox and clutch can be removed with reference to Chapters 6 and 5 (photo).

7   Engine – removal without gearbox

1   Carry out operations 1 to 26 inclusive in Section 5.
2   Remove the starter motor with reference to Chapter 10.
3   Disconnect the wiring from the reversing light switch on the gearbox and pull it into the engine compartment.
4   Remove the remaining bolts securing the clutch bellhousing to the engine, and support the gearbox with a trolley jack.
5   Fit a chain or sling to the engine lifting hooks and connect up to a suitable hoist.
6   Check that all wires, cables, and hoses have been disconnected, then lift the engine until it clears the front mountings.
7   Adjust the trolley jack beneath the gearbox then pull the engine

forwards until the gearbox input shaft clears the clutch. The engine can now be lifted forwards from the engine compartment.

8   Engine dismantling – general

1   It is best to mount the engine on a dismantling stand but if one is not available, then stand the engine on a strong bench so as to be at a comfortable working height. Failing this, the engine can be stripped down on the floor.
2   During the dismantling process the greatest care should be taken to keep the exposed parts free from dirt. As an aid to achieving this, it is a sound scheme to thoroughly clean down the outside of the engine, removing all traces of oil and congealed dirt.
3   Use paraffin or a good water-soluble grease solvent. The latter will make the job much easier, as, after the solvent has been applied and allowed to stand for a time, a vigorous jet of water will wash off the solvent and all the grease and filth. If the dirt is thick and deeply embedded, work the solvent into it with a wire brush.
4   Finally wipe down the exterior of the engine with a rag and only then, when it is quite clean, should the dismantling process begin. As the engine is stripped, clean each part in a bath of paraffin or petrol.
5   Never immerse parts with oilways in paraffin, eg the crankshaft, but to clean, wipe down carefully with a petrol dampened rag. Oilways can be cleaned out with wire. If an air line is present all parts can be blown dry and the oilways blown through as an added precaution.
6   Re-use of old engine gaskets is false economy and can give rise to oil and water leaks, if nothing worse. To avoid the possibility of trouble after the engine has been reassembled always use new gaskets throughout.
7   Do not throw the old gaskets away as it sometimes happens that an immediate replacement cannot be found and the old gasket is then very useful as a template. Hang up the old gaskets as they are removed on a suitable hook or nail.
8   To strip the engine it is best to work from the top down. The sump provides a firm base on which the engine can be supported in an upright position. When the stage where the sump must be removed is reached, the engine can be turned on its side and all other work carried out with it in this position.
9   Wherever possible, refit nuts, bolts and washers fingertight from wherever they were removed. This helps avoid later loss and muddle. If they cannot be refitted then lay them out in such a fashion that it is clear from where they came.

6.1 Separating the gearbox from the engine

9 Ancillary components – removal

1 With the engine removed from the car and separated from the gearbox, the externally mounted ancillary components should be removed before dismantling begins. The suggested order of removal is listed below with the relevant Chapter references in brackets where necessary (photos).

(a) *Distributor and spark plugs (Chapter 4)*
(b) *Carburettor (Chapter 3)*
(c) *Inlet and exhaust manifolds (Chapter 3)*
(d) *Fuel pump (Chapter 3)*
(e) *Water pump and thermostat (Chapter 2)*
(f) *Clutch (Chapter 5)*
(g) *Oil filter, oil pressure switch, bracket and gasket*
(h) *Engine mounting brackets*
(j) *Engine wiring loom*
(k) *Alternator mounting bracket*

10 Cylinder head – removal

If the engine is still in the car, first carry out the following operations:

(a) *Drain the cooling system*
(b) *Remove the carburettor and manifolds*
(c) *Remove the water pump by-pass hose*
(d) *Disconnect the battery negative terminal*
(e) *Disconnect the radiator top hose from the thermostat outlet*
(f) *Remove the spark plugs*

1 Detach the ventilation tube from the rocker cover.
2 Remove the fuel pump to carburettor fuel pipe.
3 Remove the distributor vacuum pipe.
4 Unscrew the retaining nuts and remove the rocker cover and gasket (photo).
5 Unscrew the retaining nuts and bolts, remove the washers, and lift the rocker shaft assembly from the cylinder head.
6 Remove the valve pushrods, keeping them in order so that they can be refitted in their original positions (photo).
7 Unscrew each of the cylinder head bolts a little at a time in the reverse order to that shown in Fig. 1.25.
8 With all the bolts removed, lift the cylinder head from the block. If it is stuck, try to rock it to break the seal or use a screwdriver in the slots provided, but only prise upwards with the screwdriver; **do not** wedge the screwdriver between the surfaces of the cylinder head and block (photo).
9 Remove the cylinder head gasket.

11 Cylinder head – dismantling

1 The valves are easily removed from the cylinder head by the following method. First remove the O-rings (if fitted), then compress each spring in turn with a universal valve spring compressor until the two halves of the collets can be removed. Release the compressor and lift away the spring retainer collets, retainer, spring, seal, plate washer and finally the valve (photos).
2 If, when the valve spring compressor is screwed down, the valve spring retainer refuses to free and expose the split collets, do not continue to screw down on the compressor as there is a likelihood of damaging it.
3 Gently tap the top of the tool directly over the retainer with a light hammer. This should free the retainer. To avoid the compressor jumping off the valve retainer when it is tapped, hold the compressor firmly in position with one hand.
4 It is essential that the valves are kept in their correct sequence unless they are so badly worn that they are to be renewed. If they are going to be re-used place them in a sheet of card having eight holes numbered 1 to 8 corresponding with the relative positions the valves were in when fitted. Also keep the valve springs, retainers etc in this same correct order.
5 Numbering from the front of the engine, exhaust valves are 1-4-5-8, inlet valves are 2-3-6-7.

12 Sump – removal

1 Invert the engine and rest it on the cylinder block upper face after removing the cam followers as described in Section 14.
2 Unscrew and remove all the sump bolts.
3 Remove the sump, then lift the rubber gasket from the cylinder block (photo).

13 Timing cover, sprockets and chain – removal

1 Unscrew and remove the crankshaft pulley retaining bolt. To prevent the crankshaft from turning, use a block of wood in the crankcase to jam a crankshaft web, or an angled piece of metal to lock the flywheel ring gear teeth.
2 Prise the pulley from the crankshaft using two levers.
3 Unscrew and remove the retaining bolts, noting the location of the spring clip, then withdraw the timing cover from the cylinder block (photo).
4 Unscrew the retaining bolts and remove the timing chain tensioner and damper (photo).

9.1A Removing the oil filter bracket and gasket

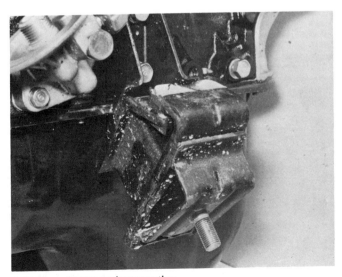

9.1B Removing an engine mounting

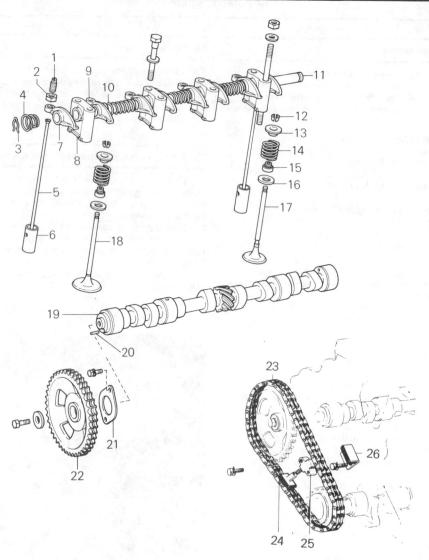

Fig. 1.3 Engine valve operating components (Sec 10)

1 Adjusting screw	10 Spring	19 Camshaft
2 Locknut	11 Rocker shaft	20 Dowel pin
3 Spring clip	12 Split collets	21 Thrust plate
4 Spring	13 Retainer	22 Camshaft sprocket
5 Pushrod	14 Valve spring	23 Timing chain
6 Cam follower	15 Seal	24 Chain tensioner pad
7 Rocker arm	16 Plate washer	25 Chain tensioner body
8 Pedestal	17 Exhaust valves	26 Chain vibration damper
9 Rocker arm	18 Inlet valve	

10.4 Removing the rocker cover

10.6 Removing a pushrod

10.8 Lifting the cylinder head from the block

11.1A Compressing a valve spring

11.1B Removing a valve spring retainer and spring

11.1C Valve stem oil seal and plate washer location

11.1D Removing an exhaust valve

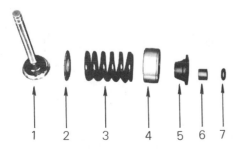

Fig. 1.4 Valve components (Sec 11)

1 Valve
2 Plate washer
3 Spring
4 Seal
5 Retainer
6 Split collet
7 O-ring (when fitted)

12.3 Withdrawing the sump

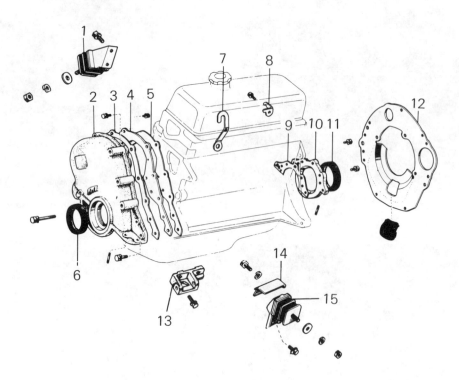

Fig. 1.5 Engine front and rear components and mountings (Sec 13)

1	Engine right-hand mounting	6	Crankshaft front oil seal	11	Crankshaft rear oil seal
2	Timing cover	7	Front lifting hook	12	Rear plate
3	Gasket	8	Rear lifting hook	13	Alternator bracket
4	Front plate	9	Gasket	14	Insulator
5	Gasket	10	Retainer	15	Engine left-hand mounting

13.3 Removing the timing cover

13.4 Timing chain vibration damper location

5   Lock the crankshaft with a block of wood as described earlier, then unscrew and remove the crankshaft sprocket retaining bolt.

6   Withdraw the camshaft sprocket and unloop the chain from the crankshaft sprocket.

7   Prise the sprocket from the front of the crankshaft using two levers, and remove the Woodruff key.

14 Camshaft and followers – removal

1   Using a finger, remove the cam followers from the top of the cylinder block and place them in their order of removal to ensure correct refitting (photo).

2   Invert the engine and unbolt the camshaft thrust plate.

3   Unbolt and withdraw the engine front plate and gasket.

4   Withdraw the camshaft from the front of the crankcase taking care not to damage the bearings with the cam lobes (photo).

15 Crankshaft front oil seal – renewal

If the engine is still in the car, first carry out the following operations:

   (a)   Drain the cooling system
   (b)   Remove the radiator and cooling fan
   (c)   Remove the front grille and dismantle the front engine compartment frame
   (d)   Remove the drivebelt and water pump pulley
   (e)   Remove the engine splash guard

1   Remove the crankshaft pulley with reference to Section 13.

2   Carefully prise the oil seal from the timing cover with a screwdriver, or preferably use an internal puller on the end of the crankshaft.

3   Refitting the oil seal is a reversal of removal, but insert the new seal using a suitable diameter tubular drift.

16 Flywheel and engine rear plate – removal

If the engine is still in the car, first carry out the following operations:

   (a)   Remove the gearbox (Chapter 6)
   (b)   Remove the clutch (Chapter 5)

1   Lock the flywheel with an angled piece of metal on the ring gear jammed against the locating dowel.

2   Unscrew and remove the retaining bolts and withdraw the flywheel.

3   Unscrew and remove the retaining bolts and withdraw the engine rear place (photo).

17 Crankshaft rear oil seal – renewal

Note: *The engine must be removed from the car for this operation.*

1   Remove the flywheel as described in Section 16.

2   Unbolt the oil seal retainer from the rear of the crankcase, then withdraw the retainer and gasket (photo).

3   Tap the new seal centrally into the retainer.

4   Refitting is a reversal of removal, but use a new gasket.

18 Oil pump – removal

1   With the sump removed, unscrew the retaining bolt and withdraw the oil pump from the crankcase (photo).

14.1 Removing a cam follower

14.4 Removing the camshaft

16.3 Engine rear plate location

17.2 Removing the crankshaft rear oil seal retainer

18.1 Oil pump location

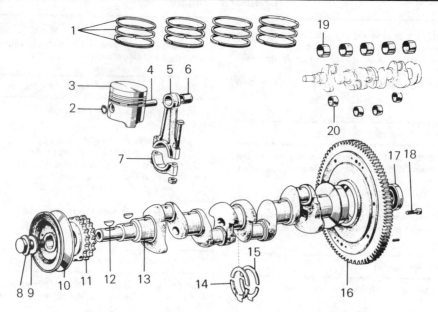

Fig. 1.6 Engine crankshaft and piston components (Sec 19)

1	Piston ring set	8	Bolt	15	Upper thrust washers
2	Circlip	9	Washer	16	Flywheel
3	Piston	10	Pulley	17	Spigot bearing
4	Gudgeon pin	11	Sprocket	18	Bolt
5	Connecting rod	12	Woodruff key	19	Main bearing shells
6	Small end bush	13	Crankshaft	20	Big-end bearing shells
7	Cap	14	Lower thrust washers		

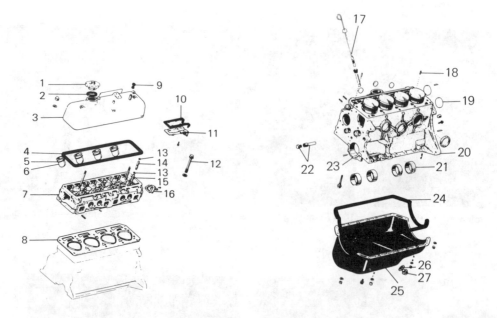

Fig. 1.7 Engine top and bottom components (Sec 19)

1	Oil filler cap	10	Gasket	19	Expansion plug
2	Gasket	11	Ventilation baffle plate	20	Cylinder block
3	Rocker cover	12	Head bolt	21	Camshaft bearing
4	Gasket	13	Circlip	22	Block drain cock
5	Gasket	14	Valve guide (inlet)	23	Main bearing cap
6	Spark plug tube	15	Valve guide (exhaust)	24	Gasket
7	Cylinder head	16	Cover	25	Sump
8	Gasket	17	Oil level dipstick	26	Gasket
9	Grommet	18	Dowel pin	27	Drain plug

19 Pistons and connecting rods – removal

1   Temporarily refit two flywheel retaining bolts and press a large screwdriver between them. Using the driver as a lever, turn the crankshaft so that No 1 crankpin is at the lowest point of its travel.
2   If the big-end caps and connecting rods are not already numbered, dot punch them on their sides nearest the camshaft and in relation to their position from the timing chain end of the engine.
3   Unscrew and remove the big-end bearing cap nuts and remove the cap complete with shell bearing (photos).
4   Using the wooden handle of a hammer, push the connecting rod and piston assembly out of the top of the cylinder block.
5   Repeat the procedure given in paragraphs 1 to 4 inclusive on the remaining piston/connecting rod assemblies. Make sure that the bearing shells are identified for their correct original locations with respect to cap or rod if they are to be renewed. Use masking tape for this, do not scratch marks on the shells.

20 Crankshaft and main bearings – removal

1   The main bearing caps are usually marked for location and an arrow indicates the front of the engine. However if these marks are not evident, dot punch the caps for location and direction.
2   Unscrew and remove the main bearing cap bolts and withdraw the caps complete with bearing shells. Note the location of the thrust washers each side of the centre main bearing (photos).
3   Lift the crankshaft carefully from the crankcase (photo).
4   Extract the bearing shells and thrust washers from the crankcase recesses. If the original shells are to be refitted, identify them for location. Similarly remove the bearing shells from the main bearing caps (photo).

21 Oil filter – renewal

1   Before removing the canister, place a cloth around the base of the filter to catch escaping oil.
2   Unscrew the canister from the filter head and discard it. If it is tight, use an oil filter wrench or drive a screwdriver through it to provide extra leverage.
3   Wipe away all old engine oil and smear the sealing surface of the new filter with clean engine oil.
4   Tighten the new filter canister into place using the hand only (photo).

19.3A Removing a big-end bearing cap

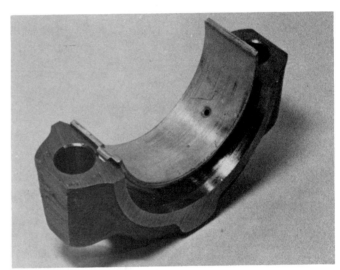

19.3B Big-end bearing cap and shell

20.2A Removing crankshaft centre main bearing cap

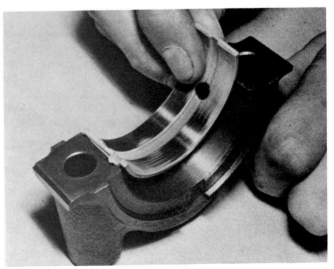

20.2B Main bearing cap and shell

I

20.3 Removing the crankshaft from the crankcase

20.4 Main bearing shell location in crankcase

21.4 Oil filter canister location

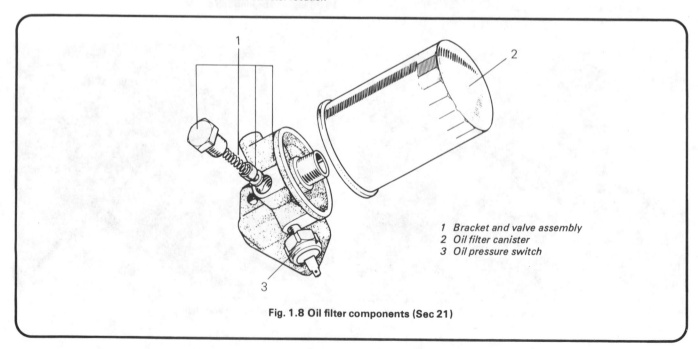

1 Bracket and valve assembly
2 Oil filter canister
3 Oil pressure switch

Fig. 1.8 Oil filter components (Sec 21)

22 Crankcase ventilation system – general

1   This comprises a hose connected between the rocker cover and the air filter and a further hose connected between the rocker cover and the inlet manifold via a ventilation valve.
2   With the engine idling, blow-by gas past the piston rings is small but inlet manifold vacuum is high. Under these conditions air passes from the air cleaner and circulates through the crankcase. The PCV (Positive Crankcase Ventilation) valve is only partially open and allows the diluted gases to be drawn into the inlet manifold.
3   With the engine accelerating or at high load, blow-by gas past the pistons is high but inlet vacuum is low. Under these conditions the PCV valve is fully open to allow maximum gases to be drawn through the inlet manifold, but if this is not sufficient excess gases can pass through the second hose to be drawn into the air cleaner.
4   Maintenance consists of periodically cleaning the hoses and PCV valve with paraffin.

23 Examination and renovation – general

With the engine now completely stripped, clean all components and examine them for wear. Each part should be checked and where necessary renewed or renovated as described in the following Section.

24 Oil pump – examination and renovation

1   Unbolt the strainer and remove it together with the gasket.
2   Unscrew the retaining bolts and remove the cover after marking it in relation to the main body.
3   Remove the inner and outer rotors together with the driveshaft, then remove the relief valve and spring.
4   Clean the components and check them for wear. If wear is not evident visually, reassemble the inner and outer rotors and use a feeler gauge to check the specified clearances as shown (Figs. 1.12 to 1.14). If the maximum clearances are exceeded, renew the complete oil pump (photo).
5   The oil pressure relief valve is non-adjustable, but it is possible after high mileages for the coil spring to weaken. Check that the specified free length is correct. If not, renew the spring (photo).
6   When reassembling the inner and outer rotors, note that the punch marks must be towards the main pump body (Fig. 1.15).

25 Crankshaft and main bearings – examination and renovation

1   Examine the bearing surfaces of the crankshaft for scratches or scoring and using a micrometer check each journal and crankpin for out of round and taper. Where the specified maximum amount is

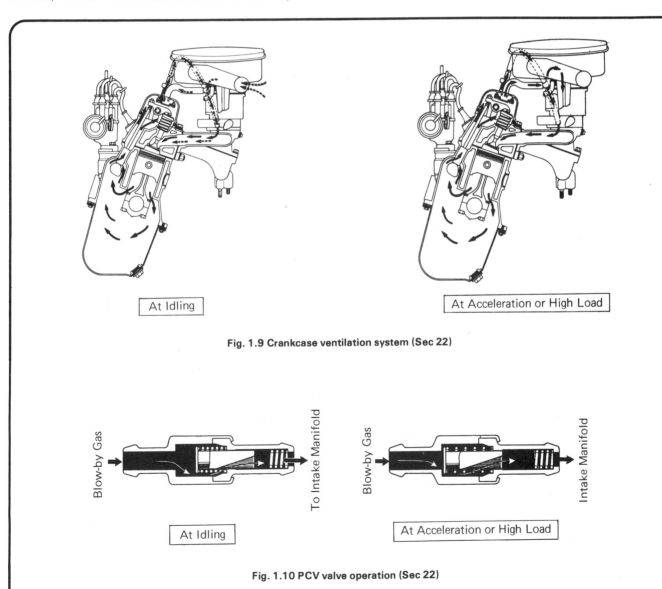

Fig. 1.9 Crankcase ventilation system (Sec 22)

Fig. 1.10 PCV valve operation (Sec 22)

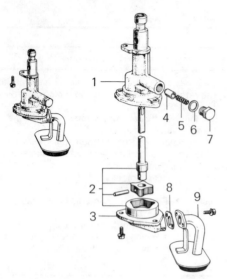

Fig. 1.11 Exploded view of the oil pump (Sec 24)

1 *Body*	4 *Relief valve*	7 *Plug*
2 *Bi-rotor assembly*	5 *Spring*	8 *Gasket*
3 *Cover*	6 *Washer*	9 *Strainer*

24.4 Checking the oil pump rotor tip clearance

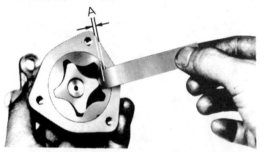

Fig. 1.12 Checking the oil pump rotor tip clearance (A) (Sec 24)

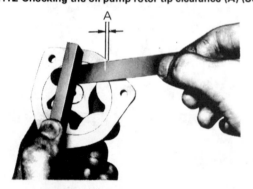

Fig. 1.13 Checking the oil pump rotor endfloat (A) (Sec 24)

24.5A Oil pressure relief valve location

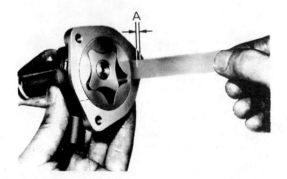

Fig. 1.14 Checking the oil pump outer rotor to body clearance (A) (Sec 24)

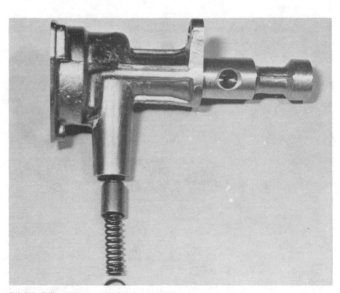

24.5B Oil pressure relief valve components

exceeded, the crankshaft must be reground and undersize bearings fitted.

2   The permitted crankshaft undersizes are listed in the Specifications but your regrinding specialist will decide how much to remove and supply the matching undersize main and big-end shell bearings.

3   When installed, the main and big-end bearings should have a running clearance within the specified tolerances. To check these clearances a proprietary product such as 'Plastigage' should be used, but if the reconditioning has been carried out by a reliable company, it can be assumed that they are correct.

4   If the gearbox input shaft pilot bearing needs renewing, extract it with an internal puller. Smear a little multipurpose grease onto the bearing before driving it into the crankshaft with a suitable diameter tubular drift. Use a liquid locking agent to retain it in the crankshaft.

26 Cylinder block and crankcase – examination and renovation

1   The cylinder bores must be examined for taper, ovality, scoring and scratches. Start by examining the top of the cylinder bores; if these are worn, a slight ridge will be found which marks the top of the piston ring travel. If the wear is excessive, the engine will have had a high oil consumption accompanied by blue smoke from the exhaust.

2   If available, use an inside dial gauge to measure the bore diameter just below the ridge and compare it with the diameter at the bottom of the bore which is not subject to wear. If the difference between the two measurements is more than the specified wear limit or if the specified maximum taper and ovality is exceeded, the cylinders must be rebored and new oversize pistons fitted.

3   If the maximum wear limits are not exceeded, special oil control rings and pistons can be fitted to restore compression and stop the engine burning oil.

4   If new pistons are being fitted to old bores, it is essential to roughen the bore walls slightly with fine glasspaper to enable the new piston rings to bed in properly.

5   Thoroughly examine the crankcase for cracks and damage and use a piece of wire to probe all oil and waterways to ensure they are unobstructed.

6   Check the cam follower bores for damage. If necessary oversize followers can be fitted, but it will first be necessary to have the bores reamed by an engineering works.

27 Pistons and connecting rods – examination and renovation

1   If new pistons are to be fitted to a rebored cylinder block, first check that the connecting rods are marked in relation to the piston crown notches. If not, mark them as necessary.

2   Remove the circlips, then heat the piston in boiling water and push out the piston pin (photo).

3   Heat the new pistons in boiling water and press the piston pin through the pistons and connecting rods, making sure that the notch in

27.2 Piston pin circlip location

Fig. 1.15 Oil pump rotor alignment punch marks (Sec 24)

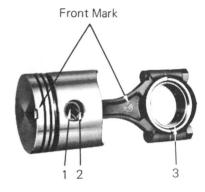

Fig. 1.16 Forward facing identification marks on the pistons and connecting rods (Sec 27)

1 Piston pin   2 Circlip
3 Big-end bearing shells

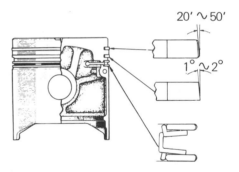

Fig. 1.17 Cross-section of the piston rings (Sec 27)

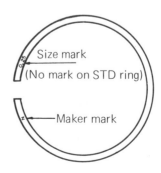

Fig. 1.18 Piston ring identification mark location (Sec 27)

the crown faces the same way as the mark on the connecting rods.

4   If new rings are to be fitted to the original pistons, expand the old rings over the top of the pistons. The use of two or three old feeler blades will be helpful in preventing the rings dropping into empty grooves. Note that the oil control ring is in three sections.

5   Before fitting the new rings to the pistons, insert them into the cylinder bore and use a feeler gauge to check that the ring endgaps are within the specified limits.

6   After fitting the new rings to the pistons, check the compression rings for groove clearances using a feeler gauge, and arrange the piston ring gaps at equidistant points so that they are not in alignment.

7   Check the connecting rods for wear and damage. If the small end bushes are worn they must be renewed using a suitable press and finally reamed to size. The connecting rods can also be checked for alignment if this is uncertain, but each of these jobs requires special tooling which is normally only available to official Toyota garages.

28 Camshaft, camshaft bearings and cam followers – examination and renovation

1   Examine the camshaft bearing surfaces, cam lobes and gearteeth for wear or scoring. Remove the shaft if evident.

2   Check the endfloat by temporarily fitting the thrust plate and gear to the front of the shaft (see Fig. 1.20).

3   Check the camshaft bearings for wear and if necessary remove them with a suitable diameter length of tubing. Note that the rear expansion plug must be removed before driving out the rear bearing.

4   Fit the new bearings with their oil holes aligned with the oilways in the cylinder block.

5   Smear jointing compound on the new expansion plug and fit it to the rear of the cylinder block.

6   The bearings are finished to size and require no reaming.

7   Examine the cam followers for wear and renew them if necessary.

Fig. 1.19 Checking the connecting rods on an alignment tool
(Sec 27)

Fig. 1.20 Checking the camshaft endfloat with a feeler gauge
(Sec 28)

29 Timing sprockets and chain – examination and renovation

1   Examine all the teeth on the camshaft and crankshaft sprockets. If these are hooked in appearance, renew the sprockets.

2   Examine the chain tensioner and vibration damper for wear and renew them as necessary. Make sure that the tensioner oilways are clear.

3   Examine the timing chain for wear. If it has been in operation for a considerable time, or if when held horizontally (rollers vertical) it takes on a deeply bowed appearance, renew it.

30 Cylinder head – decarbonising, valve grinding and renovation

1   This operation will only normally be required after the car has covered a high mileage. At this time the engine will lack performance and may show signs of overheating and pre-ignition (pinking).

2   With the cylinder head removed and dismantled, use a blunt scraper to move the carbon from the combustion chambers and ports. Scrape away all traces of gasket and jointing compound, then thoroughly clean the cylinder head with paraffin. Wipe it dry with a cloth.

3   Use a straight edge and feeler gauge to check that the cylinder head surface is within the specified warpage limit. If not, it must be resurfaced by a suitably equipped engineering works.

4   *If the engine is in the car*, clean the piston crowns and cylinder bore upper edges, but make sure that no carbon drops between the pistons and bores. To do this, clean each piston at the top of its bore and mask off all the surrounding oilways and waterways. Stuff rags into the bores of the pistons which are at the bottom of their stroke. A little grease pressed around the piston crown will collect any carbon dust and when the piston is lowered this can be wiped away.

5   Examine the heads of the valves for pitting and burning and similarly check the valve seatings in the cylinder head. If the pitting is slight, it can be removed by grinding the seats and valves together with coarse and then fine grinding paste. If the pitting is only excessive on the valve head, renew the valve only, but if it is excessive on the seat, the seat must be recut or renewed by a suitably equipped engineering works.

6   Valve grinding is carried out as follows:
Smear a trace of coarse carborundum paste on the seat face and apply a suction grinder tool to the valve head. With a semi-rotary motion, grind the valve head to its seat, lifting the valve occasionally to redistribute the grinding paste. When a full matt even surface finish is produced on both the valve seat and the valve, wipe off the paste and repeat the process with fine carborundum paste, lifting and turning the valve to redistribute the paste as before. A light spring placed under the valve head will greatly ease this operation. When a smooth unbroken ring of light grey matt finish is produced, on both valve and valve seat faces, the grinding operation is completed.

7   Scrape away all carbon from the valve head and the valve stem. Carefully clean away every trace of grinding compound, taking care to leave none in the ports or in the valve guides. Clean the valves and valve seats with a paraffin soaked rag, with a clean rag and finally, if an air line is available blow the valves, valve guides and valve ports clean.

8   If the valve guides are worn, indicated by a side-to-side motion of the valve, new guides must be fitted. As this work involves heating the cylinder head up to 264°F (130°C) it is best entrusted to a suitably equipped engineering works. However, if an oven is available, removal is straightforward after extracting the circlip. Drive the guide out through the combustion chamber and install the new guide (with circlip fitted) from the top of the head. If the new guide is a loose fit in the head (only likely after several insertions) oversize guides are available, but the holes in the head must be reamed to fit. Note also that inlet and exhaust guides are different.

9   Examine the pushrods and rocker shaft assembly for wear and renew them as necessary. Dismantling and reassembly of the rocker components is straightforward if reference is made to Figs. 1.21 and 1.22.

10   Check the valve springs for damage and loss of tension. If the free length is not as specified on any of the valve springs, renew the complete set.

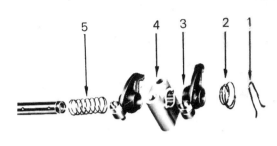

Fig. 1.21 Rocker shaft components (Sec 30)

1 *Spring clip*   4 *Pedestal*
2 *Spring*   5 *Spring*
3 *Rocker arm*

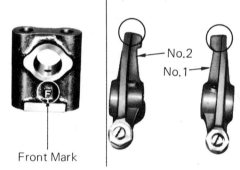

No.2
No.1

Front Mark

Fig. 1.22 Rocker shaft pedestal location mark and rocker arm identification (Sec 30)

31 Flywheel – examination and renovation

1   Examine the clutch driven plate mating surface of the flywheel; if this is excessively scored, it must be either resurfaced or a new flywheel obtained (photo).
2   Check the starter ring gear teeth. If they are chipped or worn, the ring must be renewed. To do this, partially drill the ring gear from the side, then carefully split it with a cold chisel and remove it.
3   Heat the new ring to 392°F (200°C) in an electric oven, then quickly fit it to the flywheel. Allow the ring to cool naturally without quenching.

32 Engine reassembly – general

1   To ensure maximum trouble-free life from the engine it must be rebuilt with each component cleaned of all dirt and foreign material. Make sure that the work area is spotlessly clean and check that the following items are at hand:

   (a) *Complete set of new gaskets*
   (b) *Supply of clean rags*
   (c) *Oil can full of clean engine oil*
   (d) *Torque wrench*
   (e) *New spare parts as necessary*

2   Before starting work, check the threads of all bolts and nuts and obtain new ones where necessary.

33 Crankshaft and main bearings – refitting

1   Clean the backs of the main bearing shells and the bearing recesses in both the crankcase and the caps.
2   Press the main bearing upper shells into the crankcase and locate the upper halves of the thrust washers on each side of the centre bearing, retaining them with a little grease and making sure that the oil grooves are facing away from the bearing (photos).

3   Press the main bearing lower shells into the main bearing caps and locate the lower halves of the thrust washers each side of the centre cap with the oil grooves facing outwards.
4   Oil the bearings liberally, then lower the crankshaft into position and refit the caps in their correct location and direction (photo).
5   Tighten the main bearing cap bolts evenly in two or three stages to the specified torque (photo). Turn the crankshaft and check that it rotates smoothly.
6   Using a feeler gauge between the thrust washer and crankshaft web, check that the endfloat is within the specified limits (photo).

34 Pistons and connecting rods – refitting

1   Clean the backs of the big-end bearing shells and the recesses in the connecting rods and caps.
2   Press the bearing shells into No 1 connecting rod and cap, then apply engine oil liberally to the cylinder bores, bearing shells, and piston rings (photo).
3   Fit a piston ring compressor to No 1 piston, then insert the connecting rod into No 1 cylinder bore with the notch on the piston facing the front of the engine (photo).
4   Insert the piston skirt into the bore and turn the crankpin to its lowest point. Tap the piston crown through the compressor and into the cylinder using the wooden handle of a hammer (photo).
5   Continue to tap the piston into the cylinder and at the same time guide the connecting rod onto the crankpin. Make sure that the big-end bearing shell has not become displaced.
6   Refit the big-end bearing cap with the previously made marks aligned, then tighten the nuts to the specified torque (photo).
7   Repeat the procedure given in paragraphs 2 to 6 inclusive on the remaining piston/connecting rod assemblies, using two flywheel retaining bolts and a lever between them to turn the engine.

35 Oil pump and crankshaft rear oil seal – refitting

1   Insert the oil pump into the crankcase and tighten the retaining bolt to the specified torque.
2   With the new crankshaft rear oil seal fitted to the retainer as described in Section 17, smear the seal lip with engine oil then locate the retainer onto the crankcase together with a new gasket (photos).
3   Tighten the retaining bolts evenly to the specified torque.

36 Flywheel and engine rear plate – refitting

1   Locate the rear plate to the engine cylinder block and tighten the bolts to the specified torque.
2   Locate the flywheel to the rear of the crankshaft, and tighten the retaining bolts to the specified torque while locking the starter ring gear with an angled piece of metal (photo).
3   *If the engine is in the car,* reverse the procedures listed in Section 16.

37 Camshaft – refitting

1   Fit the front plate to the front of the engine over a new gasket. Insert and tighten the two retaining bolts (photos).
2   Oil the camshaft bearings and carefully insert the camshaft from the front of the cylinder block.
3   Fit the thrust plate with the dot facing outwards, then tighten the retaining bolts to the specified torque (photo).

38 Timing cover, sprockets and chain – refitting

1   Locate the Woodruff key in the slot on the front of the crankshaft.
2   Press the crankshaft timing sprocket onto the crankshaft with the timing dot facing outwards.
3   Turn the crankshaft until No 1 piston is at TDC (top dead centre).
4   Turn the camshaft until the locating dowel is aligned with the dot on the thrust plate.
5   Locate the timing chain on the camshaft sprocket with the bright

31.1 Flywheel retaining bolts and clutch friction surface

33.2A Fitting crankshaft centre main bearing shell

33.2B Fitting crankshaft centre main bearing thrust washers

33.4 Main bearing cap location marks

33.5 Tightening the main bearing cap bolts

33.6 Checking the crankshaft endfloat

34.2 Big-end bearing components

34.3 Piston crown, showing the front facing notch

34.4 Installing a piston to the cylinder block

34.6 Tightening the big-end bearing cap nuts

35.2A Crankshaft rear oil seal location in retainer

35.2B Rear oil seal and retainer located over crankshaft

36.2 Tightening the flywheel retaining bolts

37.1A Fitting the engine front plate gasket

37.1B Engine front plate located over the dowel pins

37.3 Correct location of the camshaft thrust plate

38.5A Camshaft sprocket timing mark and chain bright link alignment

38.5B Crankshaft sprocket timing mark and chain bright link alignment

38.6 Timing chain and sprockets fitted to the engine

38.7A Assembling the timing chain tensioner

38.7B Timing chain tensioner and vibration damper correctly installed

38.9 Timing cover oil seal correct location

38.10 Fitting the crankshaft front pulley

39.2 Locating the sump gasket over the rear oil seal retainer

link aligned with the timing dot, then loop the timing chain over the crankshaft sprocket with the remaining bright link aligned with the second timing dot (photos).

6   Fit the camshaft sprocket onto the end of the camshaft and tighten the retaining bolt while locking the crankshaft with a block of wood (photo).

7   Assemble the chain tensioner, and install it to the front of the cylinder block while pressing the pad into the main body. Tighten the bolts to the specified torque (photos).

8   Fit the timing chain vibration damper and tighten the retaining bolts.

9   Fit the timing cover together with a new oil seal and a new gasket to the front of the cylinder block (photo). Insert the retaining bolts and tighten them evenly to the specified torque. Remember to locate the spring clip over one of the bolts.

10 Slide the pulley over the Woodruff key onto the front of the crankshaft (photo). Tighten the retaining bolt to the specified torque while locking the crankshaft with a block of wood.

39 Sump – refitting

1   Smear jointing compound on the sump gasket in the areas indicated in Fig. 1.23.

2   With the engine inverted, locate the gasket onto the crankcase, front timing cover, and rear oil seal retainer (photo).

3   Lower the sump over the gasket, insert the retaining bolts, and tighten them in diagonal sequence to the specified torque.

4   Turn the engine the correct way up and rest it in the sump.

5   Lubricate the cam followers with engine oil and insert them into the cylinder block in their original bores as previously noted.

40 Cylinder head – reassembly and refitting

1   Insert the valves into the valve guides in their original sequence or, if new valves have been purchased, to the seats to which they have been ground. Lightly lubricate the valve stems with engine oil.

2   Locate the plate washer, seal, spring and retainer over the first valve stem. Compress the valve spring with the compressor and locate the split collets in the valve stem cut-out. Release the compressor and tap the end of the valve stem with a block of wood to settle the collets. Refit the rubber O-ring (if fitted).

3   Repeat the procedure described in paragraph 2 on the remaining valves.

4   Make sure that the faces of the cylinder head and block are perfectly clean, then place the gasket on the cylinder block with the top side uppermost (see Fig. 1.24). Make sure that all oil and waterways are unobstructed by the gasket (photos).

5   Lower the cylinder head into position, insert the head bolts and tighten them in two or three stages to the specified torque in the sequence shown in Fig. 1.25.

6   Locate the valve pushrods in the cam followers in their original positions.

7   Lower the rocker shaft assembly over the two studs. Turn the shaft if necessary to align the grooves with the bolt holes, then insert the bolts together with the nuts and washers.

8   Locate the rocker arms in the pushrods and tighten the nuts and bolts evenly to the specified torque (photo).

9   Adjust the valve clearances as described in Section 41. This will have to be done again once the engine has been run to normal operating temperature.

10 Fit the rocker cover and gasket and tighten the retaining nuts.

11 Install the distributor vacuum pipe and the fuel pump to carburettor fuel pipe.

12 Install the ventilation tube to the rocker cover.

13 If the engine is in the car, reverse the procedures listed in Section 10.

41 Valve clearances – adjustment

If the engine is in the car, first carry out the following operations:

(a)   Run the engine until it reaches normal operating temperature

(b)   Remove the complete air cleaner assembly

(c)   Remove the rocker cover

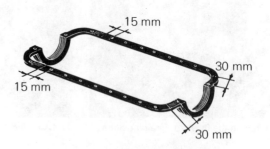

Fig. 1.23 Sump gasket areas for jointing compound (Sec 39)

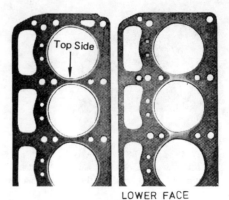

Fig. 1.24 Cylinder head gasket top side identification (Sec 40)

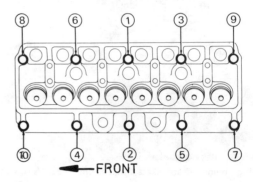

Fig. 1.25 Cylinder head bolt tightening sequence (Sec 40)

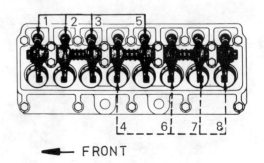

Fig. 1.26 Valve clearance adjustment stages (arrow indicates front of engine) (Sec 41)

40.4A Cylinder head gasket located onto the block

40.4B The upper face of the cylinder head gasket

40.8 Fitting the rocker shaft

41.2 Adjusting the valve clearances

1   Turn the engine with a ring spanner on the crankshaft pulley bolt until No 1 piston is at TDC (top dead centre) with the TDC mark on the timing cover aligned with the mark on the pulley. In this position the exhaust valve on No 4 cylinder will be closing and the inlet valve opening.

2   Numbering the valves from the front of the engine, valves 1 (Ex), 2 (In), 3 (In) and 5 (Ex) can now be adjusted. To do this, insert a feeler blade of the specified thickness (note hot and cold clearances) between the end of the valve stem and the rocker; the feeler blade should be a firm sliding fit. If necessary, loosen the hexagon locknut with a ring spanner and rotate the ballpin with a screwdriver to correct the clearance. Always check the final adjustment after tightening the locknut (photo).

3   Turn the crankshaft one complete turn and adjust valves 4 (Ex), 6 (In), 7 (In) and 8 (Ex).

4   *If the engine is in the car,* refit the rocker cover and air cleaner assembly.

42 Ancillary components – refitting

Refer to Section 9 and refit the components listed in reverse order, where necessary making reference to the relevant Chapters of this manual.

43 Engine – refitting without gearbox

1   This is a reversal of the removal procedure described in Section 7. Provided the clutch driven plate has been centralised as described in Chapter 5, the gearbox input shaft should locate without any trouble. However, if necessary, select top gear to hold the input shaft stationary and turn the engine crankshaft to assist entry of the input shaft.

2   Refill the cooling system as described in Chapter 2.

3   Refill the engine with oil.

4   Top-up the gearbox oil level as necessary.

44 Engine – refitting with gearbox

1   Refit the clutch and gearbox to the engine with reference to Chapter 5 and 6. The remaining operations are a reversal of the removal procedures described in Section 5.

2   Refill the cooling system as described in Chapter 2.

3   Refill the engine with oil.

4   Refill or top-up the gearbox oil level as necessary.

45 Engine – adjustment after major overhaul

1   With the engine refitted to the car, make a final check that all connections have been made and that no tools etc have been left in the
engine compartment. Double-check the oil and water levels.
2   Turn the carburettor slow running (throttle stop) adjustment screw
in half a turn (see Chapter 3) to compensate for the stiffness of new
engine components.
3   Pull the choke fully out and start the engine. If the carburettor or
fuel pump have been dismantled this may take a little longer than
usual as fuel must first be drawn up into the pump and carburettor
float bowl.
4   As soon as the engine starts, push in the choke until the engine
runs at a fast tickover. Check the engine for oil, fuel and water leaks.
5   When the normal engine temperature has been reached, adjust
the idling speed with reference to Chapter 3.
6   Road test the car for performance and acceleration, but do not
race the engine if new components have been fitted.
7   After 500 miles (800 km), change the engine oil if new components have been fitted, check the head bolts for tightness, and
adjust the valve clearances.

46 Fault diagnosis – engine

Symptom	Reason/s
Engine fails to start	Discharged battery Loose battery connections Disconnected or broken ignition leads Moisture on spark plugs, distributor or HT leads Incorrect contact points gap, cracked distributor cap or rotor Incorrect spark plug gap Dirt or water in carburettor jets Empty fuel tank Faulty fuel pump Faulty starter motor Faulty carburettor choke mechanism
Engine idles erratically	Air leak in intake manifold Leaking cylinder head gasket Worn timing sprockets Worm camshaft lobes Overheating Faulty fuel pump
Engine misses at idling speed	Incorrect spark plug gap Uneven compression between cylinders Faulty coil or condenser Faulty contact points Poor connections or condition of ignition leads Dirt in carburettor jets Incorrectly adjusted carburettor Worn distributor cam Air leak at carburettor flange gasket Faulty ignition advance mechanism Sticking valves Incorrect valve clearance Low cylinder compression
Engine misses throughout speed range	Dirt or water in carburettor or fuel lines Incorrect ignition timing Contact points incorrectly gapped Worn distributor Faulty coil, condenser or HT leads Spark plug gaps incorrect Weak valve spring Overheating
Engine stalls	Incorrectly adjusted carburettor Dirt or water in fuel Ignition system incorrectly adjusted Sticking choke mechanism Faulty spark plugs or incorrectly gapped Faulty coil or condenser Incorrect contact points gap Exhaust system clogged Distributor advance inoperative Air leak at intake manifold Air leak at carburettor mounting flange Incorrect valve clearance Sticking valve Overheating Low compression Poor electrical connections in ignition system

Symptom	Reason/s
Engine lacks power	Incorrect ignition timing
	Faulty coil or condenser
	Worn distributor
	Dirt in carburettor
	Spark plugs incorrectly gapped
	Incorrectly adjusted carburettor
	Faulty fuel pump
	Weak valve springs
	Sticking valve
	Incorrect valve timing
	Incorrect valve adjustment
	Blown cylinder head gasket
	Low compression
	Brakes dragging
	Clutch slipping
	Overheating

Chapter 2 Cooling system

For modifications, and information applicable to later models, see Supplement at end of manual

Contents

Specifications

System type .... Thermo-syphon, pump-assisted, pressurised, with thermostatically controlled electric cooling fan

Radiator cap pressure .... 12.8 lbf/in² (0.9 kgf/cm²)

Thermostat
Type .... Wax pellet
Starts to open .... 177° to 182°F (80.5° to 83.5°C)
Fully open .... 203°F (95°C)
Minimum lift .... 0.31 in (8 mm)

Thermostatic fan
Starts .... 208°F (98°C)
Stops .... 196°F (91°C)

Water pump
Type .... Centrifugal impeller
Impeller to body clearance .... 0.012 to 0.024 in (0.3 to 0.6 mm)

Coolant capacity .... 9.2 pints (5.2 litres)

Torque wrench settings

	lbf ft	kgf m
Water outlet elbow	11	1.5
Water pump retaining bolts	11	1.5
Water pump pulley	7	1.0
Alternator bolts	15	2.1

1 General description

1   The cooling system is of pressurised type and includes a front mounted radiator, a belt-driven water pump, and a thermostatically controlled electric fan.
2   The wax type thermostat is located in an outlet housing on the front of the cylinder head.
3   The water temperature monitor switch is located on the right-hand side of the cylinder head water outlet elbow. It operates the thermostatically controlled electric cooling fan motor through a relay.
4   Drain cocks are provided on the bottom of the radiator and on the front of the cylinder block below the water pump pulley.
5   The system functions as follows. With the engine running, cold water from the bottom of the radiator is drawn through the bottom radiator hose to the water pump. The water pump then forces the water through the cylinder block and water jackets to the cylinder head.
6   When the engine is cold and the thermostat is closed, the water passes through the by-pass hose and is drawn into the water pump again; the water circulation is thus confined to the cylinder block and head.
7   When the temperature of the coolant reaches the predetermined level, the thermostat opens and the water is forced through the top radiator hose to the radiator. The water is air cooled as it passes down through the radiator matrix and the cycle is then repeated.
8   Water temperature is measured by a thermo-electric capsule located below the thermostat housing, and the reading is shown on a gauge mounted on the car instrument panel (photo).

1.8 Water temperature sender unit location (arrowed)

2.1 Removing the radiator cap

2.3A Radiator drain tap location

2.3B Radiator drain tap extension tube

2 Cooling system – draining

With the car on level ground drain the system as follows:
1   If the engine is cold, remove the filler cap from the radiator by turning it anticlockwise. If the engine is hot, then turn the filler cap very slightly until the pressure in the system has had time to disperse. Use a rag over the cap to protect your hand from escaping steam. If, with the engine very hot, the cap is released suddenly, the drop in pressure can cause the water to boil. With the pressure released the cap can be removed (photo).
2   If the recommended coolant solution is in the cooling system drain it into a clean bowl for re-use. A wide bowl will be necessary to catch all the coolant.
3   Open the radiator and cylinder block drain plugs/taps. When the coolant has finished running probe the plug holes or taps with a piece of short wire to dislodge any particles of rust or sediment which may be causing a blockage and preventing all the coolant draining out (photos).

3 Cooling system – flushing

1   With time the cooling system will gradually lose its efficiency as the radiator becomes choked with rust scale, deposits from the water

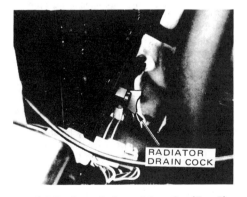

Fig. 2.1 Radiator drain cock location (Sec 1)

and other sediment. To clean the system out, first drain it – leaving the drains open. Then remove the radiator cap and leave a hose running in the radiator cap orifice for ten to fifteen minutes.

2   In very bad cases the radiator should be reverse flushed. This can be done with the radiator in position. A hose must be arranged to feed water into the lower radiator outlet pipe. Water, under pressure, is then forced up through the radiator and out of the header tank filler orifice.

3   The hose is then removed and placed in the filler orifice and the radiator washed out in the usual manner.

Note: The use of the recommended coolant solution will considerably reduce the necessity for flushing.

Fig. 2.2 Cylinder block drain cock location (Sec 1)

4   Cooling system – filling

1   Tighten the radiator and cylinder block drain taps and move the heater control to the hot position; this will minimise the formation of air locks.

2   Fill the system with an antifreeze/rust inhibitor coolant mixture to the top of the radiator filler orifice, and refit the radiator cap. Turn it fully clockwise to lock it in position.

3   Fill the reservoir to the 'FULL' line with the same mixture (photo).

4   Run the engine for approximately half a minute at a fast idle speed, then stop it and top-up the reservoir as necessary.

5   Radiator – removal, inspection, cleaning and refitting

1   Drain the cooling system as described in Section 2.

2   Loosen the retaining clips and disconnect the top and bottom hoses from the radiator (photo).

3   Unscrew and remove the two lower radiator retaining bolts, then support the radiator and unscrew and remove the two upper bolts. The radiator can now be lifted from the engine compartment (photo).

4   Flush the radiator as described in Section 3.

5   Clean the exterior of the radiator by hosing down with a strong jet of water, making sure that any leaves and dead flies are removed from the matrix fins.

6   If it is thought that the radiator is partially blocked, a good proprietary chemical product should be used to clean it.

7   With the radiator away from the car it can be soldered or repaired if necessary with a filler paste.

8   Inspect the radiator hoses for cracks, internal or external perishing and damage caused by the securing clips. Renew the hoses as necessary. Examine the radiator hose securing clips and renew them if they are rusted or distorted.

9   Refitting the radiator is the reverse sequence to removal. Fill the system as described in Section 4.

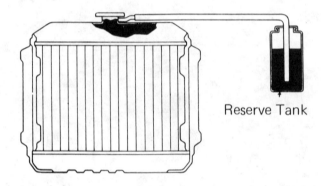

Fig. 2.3 Coolant reserve tank connection to radiator (Sec 4)

6   Radiator pressure cap – testing

1   If the level of coolant in the reservoir is much higher than the 'FULL' mark when the engine is hot, and if the engine tends to over-heat, the radiator pressure cap may be faulty.

2   The cap can be tested at most garages using a pressure pump, and if found faulty it must be renewed.

3   Clean the sealing surfaces of the cap and radiator filler neck before refitting it.

7   Electrical cooling fan – testing, removal and refitting

1   Should the electric cooling fan fail to operate at the correct temperature, first check that current is reaching the supply wire connection, with the temperature monitor wire earthed to the engine and the ignition switched on. If not, the relay located beneath the facia panel may be faulty and should be checked, or the fuse may be blown (see Chapter 10). If current is reaching the fan motor, it should be removed for further investigation. Use a 12 volt test lamp and leads to test for current.

2   Disconnect the battery negative terminal.

3   Remove the radiator as described in Section 5.

4   Disconnect the cooling fan motor supply wire from the wiring harness.

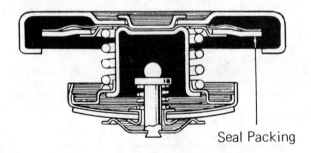

Fig. 2.4 Cross-section of the radiator pressure cap (Sec 6)

4.3 Coolant reservoir location

5.2 Radiator top hose location

5.3 Removing the radiator

7.5 Electric cooling fan location

5   Unscrew the fan cowl mounting bolts and lift the assembly from the engine compartment (photo).
6   If necessary, the fan and motor can be detached from the cowl after removing the retaining screws.
7   Refitting is a reversal of removal.

8   Thermostat – removal, testing and refitting

1   Refer to Section 2 and drain the cooling system of approximately 4 pints (2·3 litres).
2   Disconnect the wire from the electric fan monitor switch (photo).
3   Unscrew the retaining bolts from the water outlet elbow located at the front of the engine, and withdraw the elbow from the thermostat housing (photo).
4   Remove the thermostat after peeling off the housing gasket. If necessary, unbolt the thermostat housing from the cylinder head (photo).
5   If the thermostat is stuck open, it must be discarded and a new unit obtained. To test the thermostat, proceed as follows.
6   Suspend the thermostat by a piece of string together with a thermometer in a saucepan of cold water. Neither the thermostat nor the thermometer should touch the sides or bottom of the saucepan or a false reading could be obtained.

7   Heat the water, stirring it gently with the thermometer to ensure temperature uniformity, and note when the thermostat begins to open. Note the temperature: this should be comparable with the figure given in the Specifications Section at the beginning of this Chapter.
8   Continue heating the water until the thermostat is fully open. Now let it cool down naturally and check that it closes fully. If the thermostat does not fully open or close a new one must be fitted.
9   Refitting is a reversal of removal, but always use a new gasket and clean the mating surfaces of the housing and outlet elbow. Make sure that the thermostat is located centrally in the housing (photo). Top-up the coolant level as described in Section 4.

9   Water pump – removal and refitting

1   Refer to Section 5 and remove the radiator.
2   Refer to Section 12 and remove the engine front drivebelt.
3   Loosen the retaining clip and remove the bottom hose from the water pump.
4   Loosen the two retaining clips and remove the by-pass hose from the water pump and thermostat housing.
5   Unscrew the four retaining bolts and remove the drivebelt pulley from the water pump flange.
6   Unscrew the retaining bolts and lift the water pump from the cylinder block (photo). Note the drivebelt adjusting bar location.

8.2 Electric cooling fan monitor switch location

8.3 Removing the thermostat water outlet elbow

8.4 Removing the thermostat housing from the cylinder head

8.9 Correct location of the thermostat

7　Scrape away all traces of gasket from the mating surfaces.
8　Refitting is a reversal of removal, but the following additional points should be observed:-

　　(a) *Thoroughly clean the mating surfaces and always use a new gasket*
　　(b) *Adjust the tension of the drivebelt as described in Section 12*

10　Water pump – overhaul

1　Before dismantling the water pump check the economics of overhaul compared with the cost of a guaranteed new unit. Then make quite sure all the spare parts and tools required are to hand.
2　Using a universal puller carefully draw the flange from the end of the spindle.
3　Remove the pump plate securing screws and lift off the plate and gasket.
4　Using a universal puller carefully draw the impeller from the end of the spindle.
5　Remove the seal set from the seal cover.

6　Immerse the water pump body in hot water for about ten minutes and using a large bench vice or press carefully remove the bearing assembly from the front of the pump. It is possible to use a suitable size soft metal drift if a large vice or press is not available.
7　Remove the seat and gasket from the water pump body.
8　With all parts clean, inspect the bearing assembly for wear.
9　Examine the seal seat on the impeller for signs of pitting or score marks. Obtain a new impeller if either are evident.
10　Generally inspect the impeller and water pump body for signs of damage or wear. Obtain new parts as necessary.
11　Immerse the water pump body in hot water for about ten minutes and press the bearing assembly into the body until the outer track is flush with the water pump body.
12　Press the pulley flange onto the end of the spindle as shown in Fig. 2.12.
13　Insert the gasket and seat cover into the body.
14　Fit the new seal set and press the impeller onto the spindle until it is flush with the spindle end. The impeller to body clearance should be as specified and can be checked using a feeler gauge.
15　Fit the pump plate with a new gasket and tighten the retaining screws.

9.6 Removing the water pump

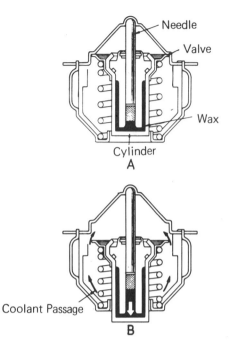

Fig. 2.5 Cross-section of the thermostat (Sec 8)

A Closed   B Open

11 Antifreeze solution

1   The coolant should be renewed every two years not only to maintain the antifreeze properties, but also to prevent corrosion in the system which would otherwise occur as the inhibitors in the coolant became progressively less effective.
2   Before adding the antifreeze mixture to the system, check all hose connections and check the tightness of the cylinder head bolts as such solutions are searching. The cooling system should be drained and partly refilled with clean water, before adding antifreeze mixture.
3   The quantity of antifreeze which should be used for various levels of protection is given in the table below, expressed as a percentage of the system capacity.

Antifreeze volume	Protection to	Safe pump circulation
25%	−25°C (−15°F)	−12°C (10°F)
30%	−33°C (−28°F)	−16°C (3°F)
35%	−39°C (−38°F)	−20°C (−4°F)

4   Where the cooling system contains an antifreeze solution any topping-up should be done with a solution made up in similar proportions to the original in order to avoid dilution.

12 Engine front drivebelt – renewal and adjustment

1   Reach down the left-hand side of the engine and loosen the alternator pivot and adjustment bolts.
2   Push the alternator in towards the engine, then slip the belt from the alternator, water pump and crankshaft pulleys.
3   Refitting is a reversal of removal, but it will be necessary to adjust the tension using the following procedure. Note that it is advisable to remove and examine the drive belt every 12 000 miles (20 000 km) and to renew it every 24 000 miles (40 000 km).
4   With the alternator pivot and adjustment bolts partly tightened, pull the alternator away from the engine until the deflection of the belt midway between the water pump and alternator pulleys under firm thumb pressure is between 0·3 and 0·5 in (8 and 12 mm). A lever may be used at the pulley end of the alternator if necessary to retain the alternator while checking the tension.
5   Tighten the adjustment bolt followed by the mounting bolt, then recheck the adjustment.
6   Finally check the tightness of the adjusting bar mounting bolt on the engine.

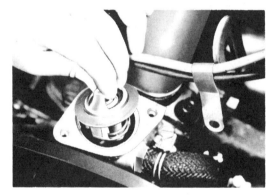

Fig. 2.6 Removing the thermostat (Sec 8)

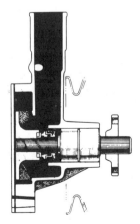

Fig. 2.7 Cross-section of the water pump (Sec 10)

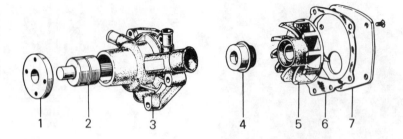

Fig. 2.8 Exploded view of the water pump (Sec 10)

1	Pulley flange	5	Impeller
2	Bearing assembly	6	Gasket
3	Body	7	Plate
4	Seal		

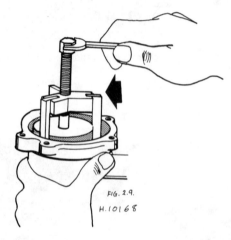

Fig. 2.9 Removing the impeller with a puller (arrowed) (Sec 10)

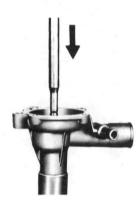

Fig. 2.10 Removing the water pump bearing using a press and tubular support (arrowed) (Sec 10)

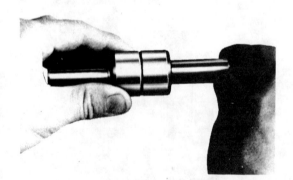

Fig. 2.11 Checking the bearing assembly for wear (Sec 10)

Fig. 2.12 Assembling the water pump pulley flange using a press (Sec 10)

Fig. 2.13 Assembling the water pump impeller using a press (Sec 10)

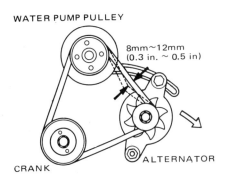

Fig. 2.14 Diagram showing drivebelt tension adjustment (Sec 12)

13 Fault diagnosis – cooling system

Symptom	Reason/s
Overheating	Low coolant level Faulty radiator pressure cap Thermostat stuck shut Drivebelt slipping or incorrectly tensioned Clogged radiator matrix Incorrect engine timing Corroded system Faulty electric cooling fan
Cool running	Incorrect type, faulty or missing thermostat Faulty electric cooling fan
Slow warm up	Incorrect type thermostat Faulty or missing thermostat
Coolant loss	Worn water pump bearing and seal Faulty radiator pressure cap Split hose Leaking water pump gasket Blown cylinder head gasket Cracked cylinder head or block

Chapter 3 Carburation, fuel and exhaust systems

For modifications, and information applicable to later models, see Supplement at end of manual

Contents

Specifications

Fuel pump
Type	Mechanical, driven from eccentric on camshaft
Delivery capacity	900 cc/min (54.9 cu in/min) at 2900 camshaft rpm
Delivery pressure	2.8 to 4.3 lbf/in² (0.2 to 0.3 kgf/cm²)

Carburettor
Type	Aisin, downdraught, twin choke, two-stage progressive
Primary main jet diameters:	
2K engine	0.0362 in (0.92 mm)
3K-H engine	0.0413 in (1.05 mm)
Secondary main jet diameters:	
2K engine	0.064 in (1.62 mm)
3K-H engine	0.056 in (1.41 mm)
Accelerator pump stroke:	
2K engine	0.24 in (6.0 mm)
3K-H engine	0.128 in (3.25 mm)
Float level (raised)	0.24 in (6.0 mm)
Float level (lowered)	0.035 in (0.9 mm)
Primary throttle valve fast idle setting	0.0512 in (1.30 mm)
Idle mixture screw initial setting:	
2K engine	2½ turns from lock
3K-H engine	3 turns from lock

Idling speed
2K engine	650 rpm
3K-H engine	600 rpm

Fuel tank capacity . . . .   8.8 gallons (40.0 litres)

Fuel grade . . . .   89 octane

Torque wrench settings
	lbf ft	kgf m
Inlet and exhaust manifold bolts	20	2.8
Fuel pump nuts	11	1.5

1   General description

The fuel system comprises a rear mounted fuel tank located beneath the underbody, a camshaft-operated fuel pump, and a twin choke downdraft carburettor.

The air cleaner incorporates a disposable paper element.

The exhaust system is in two sections and incorporates compression type joints. Rubber O-ring mountings support the rear of the system, and the front downpipe is supported by a bracket attached to the clutch bellhousing on models fitted with the 2K engine.

2   Air cleaner and element – removal and refitting

1   Unscrew the wing nut located on the top of the air cleaner and withdraw the cover (photo).
2   Remove the cover seal, then lift out the element together with the two gaskets (photo).
3   If necessary, remove the air cleaner body after dismantling the hose and loosening the support bracket bolt (photo). Recover the gasket.
4   Clean the air cleaner body and shake any accumulated dust from the element. The element should be renewed at 24 000 miles (40 000 km) intervals and cleaned at 12 000 mile (20 000 km) intervals under normal conditions, but earlier renewal will be necessary if the car is operated in very dusty conditions.
5   Refitting is a reversal of removal but make sure that the gaskets and seal are seated correctly, and align the arrow on the air cleaner cover with that on the body.
6   With ambient temperature above 15°C (60°F), move the lever on the side of the body to the summer position. When the ambient temperature falls below this level, move the lever to the winter position.

3   Fuel pump – general description

The mechanically operated fuel pump is actuated through a spring loaded rocker arm. One end of the split rocker arm bears against an eccentric on the camshaft and the other end operates the diaphragm pullrod.

As the engine camshaft rotates, the eccentric moves the pivoted rocker arm outwards which in turn pulls the diaphragm pullrod and diaphragm drum against the pressure of the diaphragm spring.

This creates sufficient vacuum in the pump chamber to draw in fuel from the tank through the sediment chamber and non-return inlet valve.

The rocker arm is held in constant contact with the eccentric by an anti-rattle spring, and as the engine camshaft continues to rotate, the eccentric allows the rocker arm to move inwards. The diaphragm spring is thus free to push the diaphragm upwards, forcing the fuel in the pump chamber out to the carburettor through the non-return outlet valve.

When the float chamber in the carburettor is full the float chamber needle valve will close, so preventing further flow from the fuel pump.

The pressure in the delivery line will hold the diaphragm downwards against the pressure of the diaphragm spring, and it will remain in this position until the needle in the float chamber opens to admit more petrol.

4   Fuel pump – testing and cleaning

1   If the operation of the fuel pump is suspect, disconnect the fuel pipe from the carburettor and remove the distributor cap as a means of preventing the engine firing.
2   Spin the engine on the starter and check that well-defined spurts of fuel are ejected from the open end of the pipe. If not, the pump is faulty, provided fuel from the tank is reaching the inlet union of the pump.
3   To clean the fuel pump, unscrew the crosshead screws and remove the cover and gasket. Carefully clean away any dirt and sediment with a small brush and clean fuel.
4   Refit the gasket and cover and tighten the screws evenly.

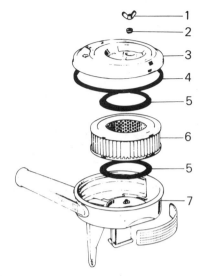

Fig. 3.1 Exploded view of the air cleaner (Sec 2)

1 Wing nut	5 Gaskets
2 Washer	6 Element
3 Cover	7 Body
4 Seal	

Fig. 3.2 Season adjustment on the air cleaner body (Sec 2)

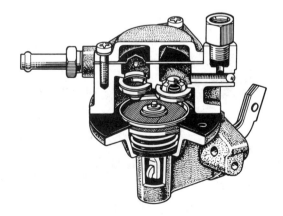

Fig. 3.3 Cutaway view of the fuel pump (Sec 3)

2.1 Removing the air cleaner cover

2.2 Removing the air cleaner element

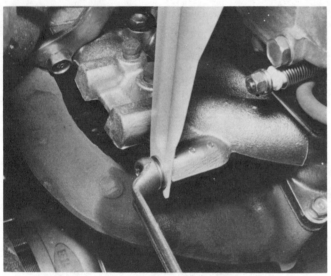

2.3 Loosening the air cleaner support bracket bolt

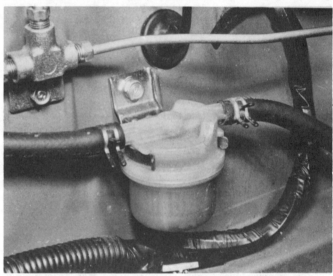

4.5 In-line fuel filter location

5.3A Removing the fuel pump

5.3B Fuel pump insulator and gaskets

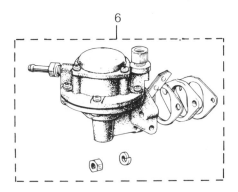
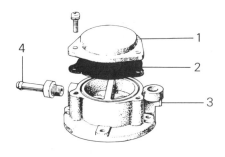
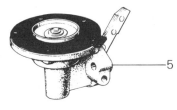

Fig. 3.4 The fuel pump components (Sec 6)

1 Cover
2 Gasket
3 Upper body
4 Union
5 Lower body
.6 Complete assembly with gaskets

5   After closing the fuel pump it is recommended that the in-line filter located on the right hand side of the engine compartment is examined for accumulation of sediment. The filter cannot be dismantled and must be renewed at 24 000 (40 000 km) intervals (photo).

5 Fuel pump – removal and refitting

1   Disconnect the fuel inlet pipe and plug it to prevent loss of fuel.
2   Disconnect the fuel outlet pipe from the pump.
3   Unscrew the retaining nuts and withdraw the pump from the crankcase. Recover the spring washers, insulator, and gaskets (photos).
4   Refitting is a reversal of removal but first clean the mating surfaces of the pump and crankcase, and fit new gaskets. Tighten the nuts to the specified torque.

6 Fuel pump – dismantling, inspection and reassembly

1   Clean the exterior of the fuel pump with paraffin and wipe dry.
2   Unscrew and remove the crosshead screws, washers, cover and gasket.
3   Mark the upper and lower pump bodies in relation to each other.
4   Unscrew the crosshead screws and remove the upper body. Take care not to damage the diaphragm and if necessary, ease it from the upper body with a knife.
5   Wash the components in clean fuel and brush away any sediment or dirt. Using a footpump, blow through the upper body internal channels and valves. Examine the bodies for wear and deterioration, and the diaphragm for splits. Check the operation of the valves in the upper body by sucking and blowing through the inlet and outlet ports, after refitting the cover and gasket. Renew any faulty components.
6   Reassembly is a reversal of dismantling, but tighten the crosshead screws evenly and lubricate the rocker arm and pullrod with engine oil. Make sure that the rocker arm moves freely.

7 Fuel tank transmitter unit – removal and refitting

1   Disconnect the battery negative terminal.
2   Pull back the rear floor carpet.
3   Unscrew the retaining screws and withdraw the inspection cover (photo).

Fig. 3.5 Fuel tank transmitter unit location (Sec 7)

2 Cover   3 Connector   4 Transmitter unit

7.3 Removing the fuel tank transmitter unit inspection cover

4   Disconnect the supply wires, unscrew the crosshead screws, and lift the transmitter unit from the fuel tank. Remove the gasket.
5   Refitting is a reversal of removal, but always use a new gasket with jointing compound smeared on both sides. Apply a little jointing compound to the threads of the retaining screws.

8   Fuel tank – removal, servicing and refitting

Note: *Before removing the fuel tank, allow the fuel level to fall as far as possible by normal use.*
1   Jack-up the rear of the car and support it on axle stands. Disconnect the battery negative terminal.
2   Unscrew the drain plug and drain all the fuel into a suitable container (photo). Check that the gasket is serviceable, then retighten the drain plug into the fuel tank.
3   Pull back the rear floor carpet and remove the inspection cover. Disconnect the wires from the transmitter unit.
4   Open the fuel filler door and remove the cap.
5   Prise out the spring ring and pull the rubber grommet from the filler pipe.
6   Unscrew the securing screws and remove the retainer from the filler pipe.
7   Working inside the car, unscrew the retaining screws and remove the filler pipe protector.
8   Working beneath the car, disconnect the main outlet hose and

breather hose from the hose connections on the underbody. Note the location of each hose.
9   Unscrew the retaining strap bolts, and lower the fuel tank from the underbody.
10   Disconnect the vent hose from the filler pipe and tank.
11   Loosen the clips and remove the filler pipe and hose.
12   Unscrew the retaining screws and remove the lower filler pipe and gasket from the fuel tank.
13   Unscrew the retaining screws and remove the outlet pipe, gasket, and filter from the fuel tank.
14   Unscrew the retaining screws and remove the transmitter unit and gasket from the fuel tank.
15   If the fuel tank is contaminated with sediment or water, swill it out using several changes of fuel. If the tank has a leak, *do not attempt to solder or weld it as this is extremely dangerous.* Repairs should always be carried out by specialists.
16   Refitting is a reversal of removal, but smear jointing compound to both sides of the gaskets before installing them.

9   Carburettor – general description

1   The carburettor is of twin choke, two-stage, downdraught type and incorporates a single float chamber.
2   The manually-operated choke valve operates in the primary barrel only. The float chamber is internally vented to both air horns to

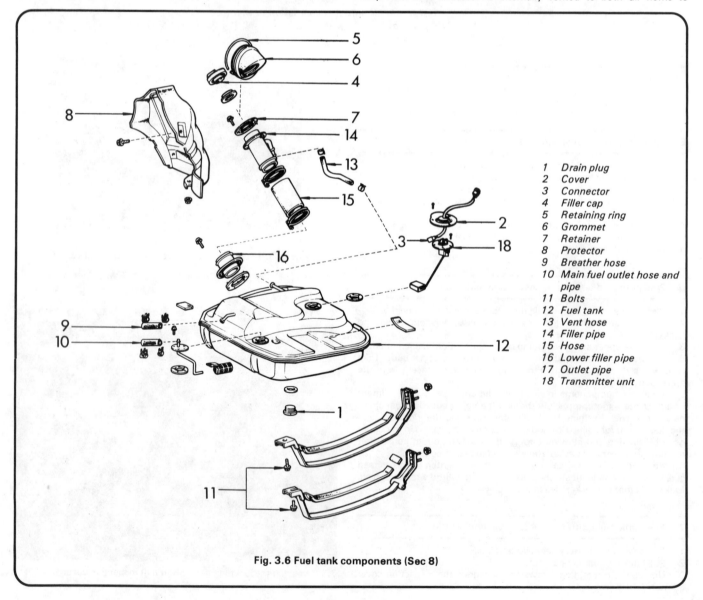

1   Drain plug
2   Cover
3   Connector
4   Filler cap
5   Retaining ring
6   Grommet
7   Retainer
8   Protector
9   Breather hose
10   Main fuel outlet hose and pipe
11   Bolts
12   Fuel tank
13   Vent hose
14   Filler pipe
15   Hose
16   Lower filler pipe
17   Outlet pipe
18   Transmitter unit

Fig. 3.6 Fuel tank components (Sec 8)

eliminate the effects of a blocked air cleaner and to ensure that the air horns are balanced.

3 Both primary and secondary emulsion tube wells are vented to atmosphere to reduce the accumulation of vapour within the carburettor and air cleaner.

4 The secondary throttle valve starts to open when the primary throttle valve is approximately two thirds open, but a weight restrained high speed valve located above the secondary throttle valve allows the secondary barrel to function only when the engine speed reaches a predetermined level and the inlet manifold depression is sufficient to open the valve (photo).

5 The primary circuit incorporates a power valve which supplements the fuel supplied by the main jet when the throttle valve is opened quickly. The carburettor also incorporates an accelerator pump of the plunger type which discharges fuel into the primary barrel.

6 The hot idle compensator incorporates a bi-metallic valve which supplies an air bleed direct to the carburettor flange when the carburettor body reaches a pre-determined temperature, dependent upon the temperature of the surrounding air in the engine compartment. The compensator weakens the fuel/air mixture supplied to the engine and compensates for the rich mixture caused by increased fuel temperature. Although on the early version of the carburettor the compensator was an integral part of the main body, it is now mounted on a bracket attached to the carburettor cover.

7 The fuel-cut solenoid is operated by the ignition circuit. With the ignition on, the solenoid is energised and the valve opens the idling circuit. When the ignition is switched off, the valve shuts and prevents the engine from running-on.

10 Choke cable – adjustment

1 Loosen the screw securing the inner cable to the choke lever (photo).

2 Push the choke knob fully into the facia panel.

3 Relieve any slack in the inner cable at the carburettor end, then tighten the inner cable screw. Lightly oil the inner cable and check that it moves freely.

4 Pull the choke knob fully out and check that the choke flap on the carburettor is closed. With the knob fully in, the flap must be open.

11 Carburettor – idling speed adjustment

1 Turn the idle mixture screw fully in, then unscrew it the specified number of turns to achieve the initial setting.

2 Connect a vacuum gauge and tachometer to the engine.

3 Run the engine until normal operating temperature is reached.

4 Turn the throttle stop and idle mixture screws to give the maximum vacuum gauge reading (approximately 16.9 in Hg - 430 mm HG) at the specified idling speed.

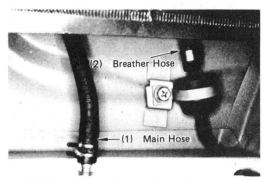

Fig. 3.7 Fuel tank main outlet hose (1) and breather hose (2) location (Sec 8)

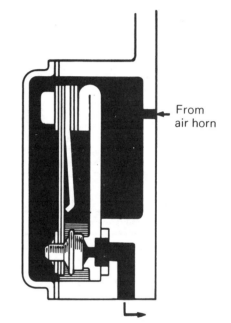

To carbureter flange

Fig. 3.8 Carburettor hot idle compensator (thermostatic valve) – typical integral type (Sec 9)

8.2 Fuel tank drain plug location

9.4 The carburettor control levers

5   Turn the idle mixture screw clockwise to the point just before the idling speed and vacuum start to fall.

6   Stop the engine and remove the vacuum gauge and tachometer.

7   On later models, in order to comply with current anti-pollution regulations, the idle mixture screw is fitted with a limiter cap or is sealed. Unless the carburettor has been the subject of major overhaul, the setting of the mixture screw should be restricted to the movement provided by the limiter cap, or if sealed, it should not be disturbed as the screw is factory adjusted during production.

8   If major overhaul has been carried out, then the mixture screw can be removed by breaking off the limiter cap or prising out the sealing cap. Adjust the mixture as described in earlier paragraphs, or use an exhaust gas analyser, and fit a new cap or plug on completion.

12 Carburettor – removal and refitting

1   Remove the air cleaner as described in Section 2.

2   Disconnect the fuel inlet pipe from the carburettor.

3   Pull the distributor vacuum pipe from the carburettor.

4   Disconnect the accelerator and choke cables from the carburettor (photos).

5   Unscrew and remove the four retaining nuts, and withdraw the carburettor from the inlet manifold. The accelerator return spring bracket and cable support will also be released at the same time and their locations should be noted (photos).

6   If necessary, remove the heat insulator plate from the manifold after disconnecting the crankcase ventilation hose.

7   Refitting is a reversal of removal, but always use new gaskets and adjust the accelerator and choke cables. The accelerator cable can be adjusted by loosening and repositioning the two locknuts at the carburettor end of the outer cable so that a small amount of slack exists in the inner cable with the accelerator pedal released.

13 Carburettor – dismantling and reassembly

1   Clean the exterior of the carburettor and wipe it dry with a lint-free cloth.

2   The carburettor will normally require dismantling for cleaning and adjustment; removal of the throttle and choke valves is not recommended since if these items are worn, a new or reconditioned carburettor should be obtained.

3   To ensure that correct reassembly, each component should be placed in order in a clean area.

4   Unscrew the accelerator pump lever pivot bolt, disconnect the link from the throttle arm, and withdraw the arm assembly.

5   Extract the split-pin, disengage and withdraw the choke control link.

6   Unscrew the retaining screws and lift the air horn and cover assembly from the carburettor body together with the gasket. At the same time, remove the choke cable support bracket and hot idle compensator after disconnecting the hoses (photo).

7   Remove the accelerator pump plunger and spring (photo).

8   Invert the carburettor body and collect the accelerator pump discharge weight and steel ball (Fig. 3.13).

9   Unscrew and remove the fuel cut solenoid valve and O-ring.

10   Unscrew the flange retaining screws and remove the flange and gasket from the main body; note that the screw with the hole is located on the float chamber side (Fig. 3.16).

11   Working on the air horn assembly, extract the pivot pin and remove the float and needle.

12   Unscrew and remove the needle valve seat and gasket.

13   Remove the power piston retainer and withdraw the piston and spring.

14   Remove the accelerator pump rubber boot.

15   Working on the main body, unscrew the retaining screws and remove the primary and secondary auxiliary venturis and gaskets. Identify each venturi for correct reassembly.

16   Extract the retainer from the bottom of the accelerator pump bore.

17   Invert the carburettor and recover the steel non-return valve ball from the bottom of the accelerator pump bore.

18   Unscrew and remove the slow-running jet.

19   Unscrew the plug on the float chamber exterior, insert a screwdriver, and remove the primary main jet and gasket.

10.1 Choke cable attachment to the carburettor

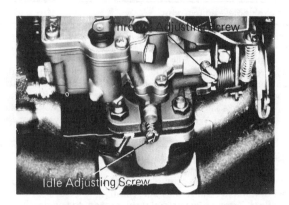

Fig. 3.9 Carburettor idling adjustment screw locations (Sec 11)

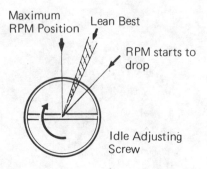

Fig. 3.10 Carburettor idle mixture screw adjustment (Sec 11)

12.4A Accelerator cable connection to the carburettor

12.4B Accelerator cable connection to the accelerator pedal

12.4C Accelerator pedal return spring location

12.5A Throttle lever return spring and bracket. Arrow shows the sealed type mixture screw

12.5B View of the carburettor showing the accelerator cable support bracket and fuel cut valve lead connector

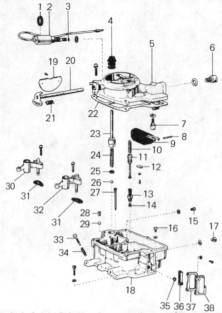

Fig. 3.11 Exploded view of the carburettor internal components (Sec 13)

1	Retainer	12	Retainer	23	Accelerator pump plunger	32	Secondary auxiliary
2	Fuel cut solenoid valve	13	Power valve	24	Spring		venturi
3	O-ring	14	Power jet	25	Retainer	33	Throttle stop adjusting
4	Boot	15	Primary main jet	26	Ball		screw
5	Air horn cover	16	Secondary main jet	27	Slow running jet	34	Spring
6	Union	17	Plug	28	Accelerator pump	35*	O-ring
7	Needle valve	18	Main body		discharge weight	36*	Thermostatic valve
8	Pivot pin	19	Choke valve	29	Ball	37*	Gasket
9	Float	20	Choke shaft	30	Primary auxiliary venturi	38*	Cover
10	Spring	21	Return spring	31	Gasket	*	Early models
11	Power piston	22	Gasket				

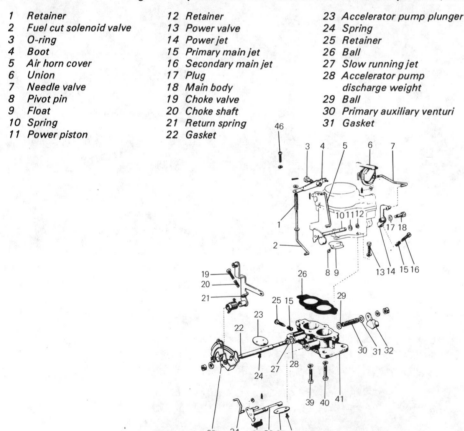

Fig. 3.12 Exploded view of the carburettor external components (Sec 13)

1	Spring	12	C-clip	23	Primary throttle valve	33	Throttle arm
2	Link	13	Retaining screw	24	Screw	34	Link
3	Pivot bolt	14*	Stop lever	25	Idle mixture screw	35	Spring
4	Accelerator pump lever	15*	Spring	26	Gasket	36	Secondary throttle shaft
5	Choke link	16*	Adjusting screw	27	Collar	37	Secondary throttle valve
6*	Throttle return damper	17*	Washer	28	Shim	38	Screw
7*	Link rod	18*	Screw	29	Shim	39	Retaining screw
8	Screw	19	Fast idle adjusting screw	30	Spring	40	Retaining screw
9	High speed valve	20	Spring	31	Shim	41	Flange
10	Shaft	21	Choke lever	32	Lever	*	Not fitted to UK models
11	Shim	22	Primary throttle shaft				

13.6A Hot idle compensator (thermostatic valve) location on the carburettor (later models)

13.6B View of the carburettor with cover removed

13.7 Accelerator pump plunger location in the carburettor cover

13.21 Carburettor power valve location

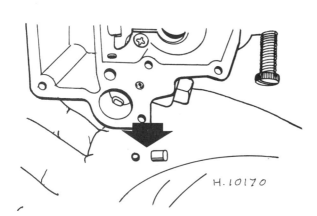

H.10170

Fig. 3.13 Removing the accelerator pump discharge weight and ball (Sec 13)

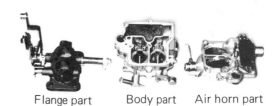

Flange part   Body part   Air horn part

Fig. 3.14 The carburettor dismantled into the three main assemblies (Sec 13)

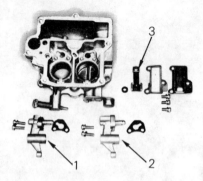

Fig. 3.15 Carburettor primary venturi (1), secondary venturi (2), and thermostatic valve (early models) (3)

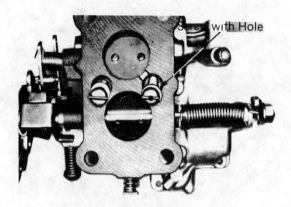

Fig. 3.16 Flange retaining screw locations

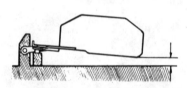

Fig. 3.17 Carburettor float raised dimension

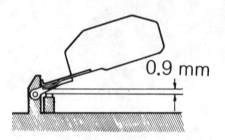

0.9 mm

Fig. 3.18 Carburettor float lowered dimension

A (Adjust the raised position)

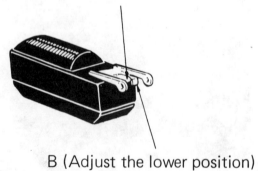

B (Adjust the lower position)

Fig. 3.19 Carburettor float level adjustment tabs A and B

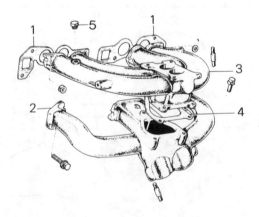

Fig. 3.20 Views of the inlet and exhaust manifolds

1 Gasket
2 Exhaust manifold
3 Inlet manifold
4 Intermediate gasket
5 Plug

20 Remove the secondary main jet from the bottom of the float chamber together with the gasket.

21 Using a box spanner remove the power valve, then unscrew the power jet from the valve (photo).

22 Working on the flange assembly, unscrew and remove the idle adjusting screw and spring.

23 Wash all components with clean fuel and clear internal passageways with compressed air from a tyre foot-pump. **Do not** probe the jets or passageways with wire. Wipe the components dry with a lint-free cloth.

24 Examine each component for wear and damage, and renew them if defective. Obtain a set of new gaskets and seals. If the high speed valve endfloat is excessive, the shaft can be removed and additional shims located on each end of the shaft.

25 Reassembly is a reversal of dismantling, but lubricate all moving surfaces with a little engine oil. Before refitting the air horn, the float level must be adjusted in the following manner. Invert the air horn so that the float and arm are resting on the needle valve needle. Using vernier calipers check that the clearance between the end of the float and the air horn surface (see Fig. 3.17) is the same as the specified raised dimension. If not, bend the tap A (Fig. 3.19) on the arm as necessary. Lift the float until the angled tab contacts the pivot post, then using a feeler gauge, check that the specified lowered dimension exists between the needle and the flat tab (see Fig. 3.18). If not, bend the angled tab B (Fig. 3.19) as necessary.

26 With the carburettor reassembled, turn the idle mixture screw to its specified initial setting, and make the following checks.

27 Fully open the primary throttle valve and check that the secondary throttle valve is also fully open. If not, bend the intermediate link as necessary.

28 Using a feeler gauge, check that the clearance between the inner periphery of the high speed valve (when closed) and the barrel wall is between 0.008 and 0.016 in (0.2 and 0.4 mm). If not, loosen the retaining screws and reposition the valve.

29 Operate the choke lever so that the choke flap is shut. Using a feeler gauge, check that the clearance between the inner periphery of the primary throttle valve and the barrel wall is on the specified fast idle setting. If not, turn the adjusting screw as necessary.

30 Make sure that the flange retaining screw with the hole is located on the float chamber side; if it is located on the opposite side, the power valve will remain open and fuel consumption will be excessive.

14 Manifolds and exhaust system

1 The aluminium alloy inlet manifold and cast iron exhaust manifold are bolted together below the carburettor mounting flange where heat from the exhaust ensures fuel evaporization in the inlet manifold.

14.5 Removing the inlet and exhaust manifolds from the cylinder head

2 The exhaust front downpipe is attached to the manifold by a three stud flange and a compression gasket.

3 To remove the manifolds, first remove the carburettor and insulation plate as described in Section 12.

4 Disconnect the exhaust downpipe and pull the brake vacuum hose from the inlet manifold. Unbolt the heater pipe.

5 Unscrew the retaining nuts and bolts and withdraw the manifolds from the cylinder head (photo).

6 Remove the gaskets and scrape the mating surfaces clean (photo).

7 Refitting the manifolds is a reversal of removal, but use new gaskets.

8 Examination of the exhaust pipe and silencers at regular intervals is worthwhile as small defects may be repairable when, if left, they will almost certainly require renewal of one of the sections of the system. Also, any leaks, apart from the noise factor, may cause poisonous exhaust gases to get inside the car which can be unpleasant, to say the least, even in mild concentrations. Prolonged inhalation could cause sickness and giddiness.

9 Renewal of the exhaust system is straightforward, but the compression type flange gaskets should always be renewed. If necessary, renew the rubber O-ring mountings (photos).

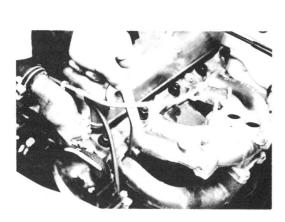

Fig. 3.21 Engine lifting hook location on the manifolds

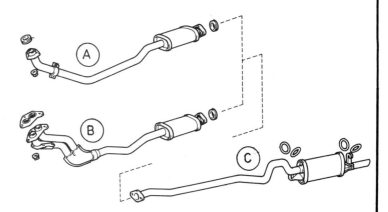

Fig. 3.22 Exhaust system components

A With 2K engine   B With 3K–H engine
C Rear section both engine types

14.6 Manifold port locations in the cylinder head

14.9A Exhaust downpipe to manifold clamp location (2K engine)

14.9B Exhaust manifold flange gasket location (2K engine)

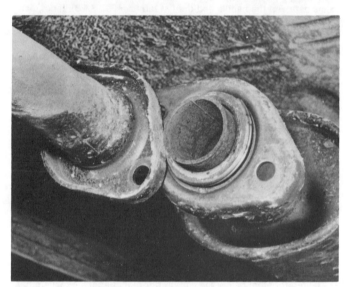

14.9C Exhaust system central flange components

14.9D Exhaust system forward mounting

14.9E Exhaust system rear mounting

15 Fault diagnosis – fuel and exhaust systems

Symptom	Reason/s
Excessive fuel consumption	Choked air filter element Leaks in fuel tank, carburettor, or fuel lines incorrect float level setting Incorrect carburettor adjustment Incorrect valve clearances Binding brakes Tyres underinflated Incorrect carburettor assembly Worn needle valve
Insufficient fuel delivery or weak mixture	Excessive sediment in fuel Sticking needle valve Faulty fuel pump Leaking inlet manifold gasket or carburettor flange gasket Incorrect carburettor adjustment

Chapter 4 Ignition system

For modifications, and information applicable to later models, see Supplement at end of manual

Contents

Specifications

System type .... 12 volt, contact breaker and coil

Firing order .... 1 – 3 – 4 – 2

Distributor
Direction of rotation .... Clockwise
Contact breaker gap .... 0.016 to 0.020 in (0.4 to 0.5 mm)
Dwell angle .... 50° to 54°
Static ignition timing .... 8° BTDC
Centrifugal advance (vacuum hose disconnect):
    Starts .... 1000 engine rpm
    Intermediate .... 24° @ 3500 rpm
    Maximum .... 28° @ 6000 rpm
Vacuum advance:
    Starts .... 4.33 in (110 mm) Hg
    Intermediate .... 12° @ 7.87 in (200 mm) Hg
    Maximum .... 18° @ 10.24 in (260 mm) Hg
Mainshaft endfloats .... 0.0059 to 0.0197 in (0.15 to 0.50 mm)

Spark plugs
Standard type .... Nippon Denso W16 EP or W16 EX-U, or NGK BP5ES-L or BP5EA-L
Resistive type .... Nippon Denso W16 EPR or W16 EXR-U, or NGK BPR5ES or BPR5EA-L

Gap .... 0.031 in (0.8 mm)

Torque wrench setting

	lbf ft	kgf m
Spark plugs	15	2.1

1 General description

1 The ignition system is conventional and comprises a 12-volt battery, coil, distributor and spark plugs. The distributor is driven by a skew gear on the camshaft in tandem with the oil pump.

2 In order that the engine can run correctly it is necessary for an electrical spark to ignite the fuel/air mixture in the combustion chamber at exactly the right moment in relation to engine speed and load. The ignition system is based on feeding low tension (LT) voltage from the battery to the coil where it is converted to high tension (HT) voltage. The high tension voltage is powerful enough to jump the spark plug gap in the cylinders many times a second under high compression

pressures, providing that the system is in good condition and that all adjustments are correct.

3 The ignition system is divided into two circuits: the low tension circuit and the high tension circuit.

4 The low tension (sometimes known as the primary) circuit consists of the battery, lead to the ignition switch, lead from the ignition switch to the low tension or primary coil windings (terminal +), and the lead from the low tension coil windings (coil terminal –) to the contact breaker points and condenser in the distributor.

5 The high tension circuit consists of the high tension or secondary coil windings, the heavy ignition lead from the centre of the coil to the center of the distributor cap, the rotor arm, and the spark plug leads and spark plugs.

6   The system functions in the following manner. Low tension voltage is changed in the coil into high tension voltage by the opening and closing of the contact breaker points in the low tension circuit. High tension voltage is then fed via the carbon brush in the centre of the distributor cap to the rotor arm of the distributor cap, and each time the rotor arm comes in line with one of the four metal segments in the cap, which are connected to the spark plug leads, the opening and closing of the contact breaker points causes the high tension voltage to build up, jump the gap from the rotor arm to the appropriate metal segment and so via the spark plug lead to the spark plug, where it finally jumps the spark plug gap before going to earth.

7   The ignition advance is controlled both mechanically and by a vacuum operated system. The mechanical governor mechanism com-prises two weights, which move out from the distributor shaft as the engine speed rises due to centrifugal force. As they move outwards they rotate the cam relative to the distributor shaft, and so advance the spark. The weights are held in position by two light springs and it is the tension of the springs which is largely responsible for correct spark advancement.

8   The vacuum control consists of a diaphragm, one side of which is connected via a small bore tube to the carburettor, and the other side to the contact breaker plate. Depression in the inlet manifold and car-burettor, which varies with engine speed and throttle opening, causes the diaphragm to move, so moving the contact breaker plate, and advancing or retarding the spark. A fine degree of control is achieved by a spring in the vacuum assembly.

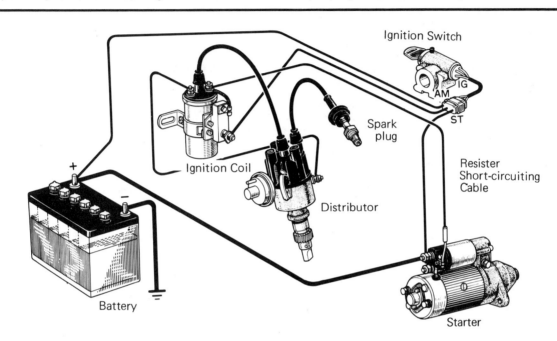

Fig. 4.1 Ignition circuit diagram (Sec 1)

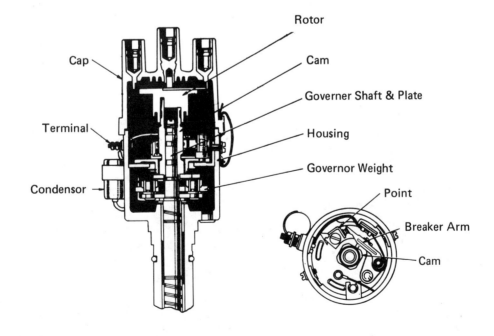

Fig. 4.2 Cutaway and plan views of the distributor (Sec 1)

2   Contact breaker points – adjustment and lubrication

1   To adjust the contact breaker points to the correct gap first release the two clips securing the distributor cap to the distributor body, and lift away the cap. Clean the cap inside, and out, with a dry cloth. It is unlikely that the four segments will be badly burned or scored, but if they are the cap will have to be renewed.

2   Inspect the contact located in the centre of the cap and make sure it is serviceable.

3   Lift off the rotor arm and dust proof cover. Gently prise the contact breaker points open and examine the condition of their faces. If they are rough, pitted or dirty it will be necessary to remove them for refacing or for a new set to be fitted (photo).

4   Presuming that the points are satisfactory, or that they have been cleaned and refitted, measure the gap between the points by turning the engine over until the heel of the breaker arm is on the highest point of the cam.

5   A feeler gauge of the specified thickness should now just fit between the points (photo). Take care not to contaminate the points with oil from the feeler gauge.

6   If the gap varies from the specified amount, slacken the lockscrew and adjust the contact gap by resetting the moving contact position. When the gap is correct, tighten the securing screw and check the gap again.

7   For lubrication purposes apply a spot of petroleum jelly onto the distributor cam and a drop of oil on the contact breaker arm spindle. To lubricate the automatic timing contol and cam spindle, allow a few drops of light oil to pass through the centre of the contact breaker baseplate.

8   Always be sparing with the lubricant to avoid contamination of the contact breaker points.

9   Refit the dust cover, the rotor and the distributor cap. Clip the spring blade retainers into position.

3   Dwell angle – description and adjustment

1   On modern engines, setting the distributor contact breaker gap as described in the preceding Section must be regarded as a basic adjustment. For optimum engine performance, the dwell angle must be checked.

2   The dwell angle is the number of degrees through which the distributor cam turns during the period between the instants of closure and opening of the contact breaker points. It can be checked with a dwell meter connected in accordance with the maker's instructions.

3   Not only does the dwell angle provide a more accurate setting of the contact breaker gap, but the method also evens out any variation in gap caused by wear in the distributor shaft or bushes or differences

Fig. 4.3 Removing the contact breaker points (Sec 4)

in any of the four cam peak heights.

4   The correct dwell angle is given in the Specifications.

5   If the angle is too large, increase the points gap; if it is too small, reduce the points gap.

4   Contact breaker points – removal and refitting

1   If the contact breaker points are burned, pitted or badly worn they must be removed and renewed.

2   With the distributor cap removed, lift off the rotor arm by pulling it straight up from the spindle. Also remove the dust cover.

3   Detach the contact breaker point wire from the condenser and coil terminal by slackening the through bolt nut and drawing the terminal connection upwards.

4   Undo and remove the two contact breaker points assembly securing screws and washers and withdraw the assembly. Note that on some later versions it is only necessary to loosen the securing screws, then slide the assembly out.

5   Reassembly is the revese sequence to removal. The gap must be reset as described in Section 2. **Note**: Should the contact points be badly worn a new assembly must be fitted. As an emergency measure clean the faces with fine emery paper folded over a thin steel rule. It is necessary to remove completely the built up deposits, but not necessary to rub the pitted point right down to the stage where all the pitting has disappeared. When the surfaces are flat a feeler gauge can be used to reset the gap.

2.3 Contact breaker points location in the distributor

2.5 Checking the contact breaker points gap with a feeler blade

5 Condenser – testing, removal and refitting

1 The purpose of the condenser, (sometimes known as a capacitor) is to ensure that when the contact breaker points open there is no sparking across them, which would waste voltage and cause wear.

2 The condenser is fitted in parallel with the contact breaker points. If it develops a short circuit, it will cause ignition failure, as the points will be prevented from interrupting the low tension circuit.

3 If the engine becomes very difficult to start or begins to misfire after several miles running and the contact breaker points show signs of excessive burning, then the condition of the condenser must be suspect. A further test can be made by separating the points by hand with the ignition switched on. If this is accompanied by a strong blue flash it is indicative that the condenser has failed.

4 Without special test equipment the only sure way to diagnose condenser trouble is to replace a suspected unit with a new one and note if there is any improvement.

5 To remove a condenser from the distributor take off the distributor cap to give better access (photo).

6 Detach the condenser lead from the terminal block.

7 Undo and remove the screw and washer securing the condenser to the distributor body. Lift away the condenser and lead.

8 Refitting the condenser is the reverse sequence to removal.

6 Distributor – removal and refitting

1 Mark the HT leads and detach from the spark plugs and ignition coil.

2 Detach the vacuum line from the vacuum advance diaphragm, and disconnect the LT lead.

3 To make refitting simpler rotate the crankshaft until the timing notch on the crankshaft pulley lines up with the scale on the front of the timing cover. The exact setting will depend on the ignition timing as found in the Specifications Section at the beginning of this Chapter. Ascertain that the number 1 piston is on the compression stroke by removing the spark plug and feeling the compression with a thumb as the piston rises in the cylinder. The distributor rotor arm should now point to number 1 cylinder HT lead segment in the cap.

4 Undo and remove the distributor securing bolt spring and plain washer and withdraw the distributor and clamp (photo).

5 Before refitting the distributor turn the engine until No 1 piston is on the compression stroke and the timing mark on the crankshaft pulley is lined up with the 8° mark on the timing cover.

6 Position the distributor rotor arm as shown in Fig. 4.4 (cap removed).

7 Check that the slot at the top of the oil pump shaft is aligned with the tongue on the bottom of the distributor shaft with respect to the large and small segments. If necessary, use a screwdriver to reposition the slot in the oil pump shaft (photo).

8 Lubricate the distributor spiral gear with engine oil and lower the distributor into its recess, at the same time keeping the vacuum unit pointing towards the front of the engine and parallel with the engine centre line. As the gears mesh, the rotor arm will turn; when the distributor is fully fitted, the arm will point towards number 2 spark plug (photos).

9 A certain amount of trial and error may be necessary in positioning the rotor arm initially to achieve the correct final setting.

10 With the distributor in position, fit the clamp and the retaining bolt.

11 Reconnect the LT lead, the vacuum pipe and the cap to the distributor.

12 Reconnect the HT leads to the spark plugs and the coil.

13 Adjust the ignition timing as described in Section 8.

7 Distributor – dismantling and reassembly

Providing the distributor is lubricated at the prescribed intervals it will last a considerable time without causing problems.

However, if wear does eventually occur the best policy is to exchange the complete assembly for a new or factory reconditioned unit.

To enable the owner to check the centrifugal advance mechanism for any faults and the shaft and drivegear for wear, the following procedure is given.

5.5 Condenser location on the distributor (arrowed)

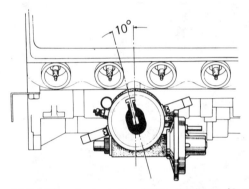

Fig. 4.4 Position of rotor before fitting distributor (Sec 6)

1 Remove the cap, dust cover and rotor arm.

2 Refer to Section 4 and remove the contact breaker points.

3 Unscrew the terminal post through bolt securing nut and disconnect the condenser lead.

4 Undo and remove the screw securing the condenser to the distributor body. Lift the condenser and lead away from the distributor body.

5 Unscrew the vacuum unit adjusting screw and recover the gasket. Disconnect the lead from the distributor baseplate.

6 Unscrew the retaining screw and withdraw the vacuum unit.

7 Undo and remove the two screws securing the distributor cap spring clips to the distributor body. Lift away the two clips.

8 The contact breaker plate assembly may now be lifted from the distributor body. To assist refitting note which way round it is fitted.

9 Undo and remove the screw located at the top of the cam spindle and lift away the cam. Mark it in relation to the spindle.

10 Using a suitable diameter parallel pin punch carefully tap out the pin securing the spiral gear to the spindle. It may be found that the pin ends are peened over. If so it will be necessary to file flat before attempting to drift out the pin. The gear may now be removed from the spindle.

11 The shaft may now be drawn upwards from the distributor body. Take care to recover the washer(s) fitted between the centrifugal weight plate and distributor body.

12 Check the action of the centrifugal weights; when moved from the centre and released they should snap back into position quite sharply. If the mechanism appears sloppy and the weight pivots worn it is advisable to renew the complete assembly.

13 Examine the fit of the drive spindle in the distributor body. If there is excessive side play it is recommended that a new distributor is obtained.

14 Reassembly is a reversal of dismantling, but check that the mainshaft endfloat is within the specified limits using a feeler gauge. If necessary, vary the thickness of the shaft shims to obtain the correct endfloat, making sure that an 0·08 in (2·10 mm) shim is always

6.4 Distributor clamp location

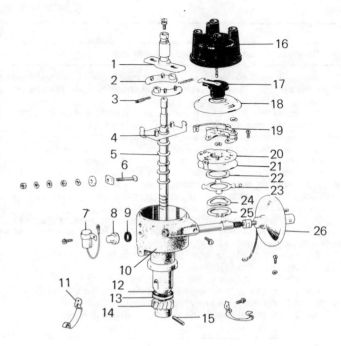

Fig. 4.5 Exploded view of the distributor (Sec 7)

1	Cam	14	Gear
2	Centrifugal weight	15	Pin
3	Spring	16	Cap
4	Shaft assembly	17	Rotor
5	Shim	18	Dust cover
6	Terminal bolt	19	Contact points assembly
7	Condenser	20	Breaker plate
8	Advance/retard fine adjuster	21	Fixed baseplate
	screw	22	Washer
9	Gasket	23	Spring
10	Body	24	Wave washer
11	Spring clip	25	Circlip
12	O-ring	26	Vacuum advance unit
13	Washer		

6.7 Oil pump shaft slot inside the distributor location hole

6.8A Fitting the distributor

6.8B Position of rotor arm with distributor fully inserted

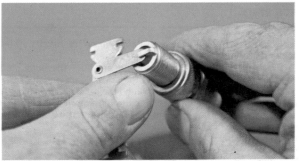

Measuring plug gap. A feeler gauge of the correct size (see ignition system specifications) should have a slight 'drag' when slid between the electrodes. Adjust gap if necessary

Adjusting plug gap. The plug gap is adjusted by bending the earth electrode inwards, or outwards, as necessary until the correct clearance is obtained. Note the use of the correct tool

Normal. Grey-brown deposits, lightly coated core nose. Gap increasing by around 0.001 in (0.025 mm) per 1000 miles (1600 km). Plugs ideally suited to engine, and engine in good condition

Carbon fouling. Dry, black, sooty deposits. Will cause weak spark and eventually misfire. Fault: over-rich fuel mixture. Check: carburettor mixture settings, float level and jet sizes; choke operation and cleanliness of air filter. Plugs can be re-used after cleaning

Oil fouling. Wet, oily deposits. Will cause weak spark and eventually misfire. Fault: worn bores/piston rings or valve guides; sometimes occurs (temporarily) during running-in period. Plugs can be re-used after thorough cleaning

Overheating. Electrodes have glazed appearance, core nose very white – few deposits. Fault: plug overheating. Check: plug value, ignition timing, fuel octane rating (too low) and fuel mixture (too weak). Discard plugs and cure fault immediately

Electrode damage. Electrodes burned away; core nose has burned, glazed appearance. Fault: pre-ignition. Check: as for 'Overheating' but may be more severe. Discard plugs and remedy fault before piston or valve damage occurs

Split core nose (may appear initially as a crack). Damage is self-evident, but cracks will only show after cleaning. Fault: pre-ignition or wrong gap-setting technique. Check: ignition timing, cooling system, fuel octane rating (too low) and fuel mixture (too weak). Discard plugs, rectify fault immediately

located next to the centrifugal weight baseplate.

15 Adjust and lubricate the contact breaker points as described in Section 2.

16 Set the vacuum unit adjustment to its standard central position.

8 Ignition timing – adjustment

One of two methods may be used to time the ignition, the use of a stroboscope being the more accurate.

Test bulb

1 Remove the distributor cap and then connect a 12 volt test bulb between a good earth and the LT Terminal on the distributor.

2 Rotate the crankshaft by applying a spanner to the crankshaft pulley bolt until, with No 1 piston on its compression stroke (ascertained by removing No 1 spark plug and feeling the compression being generated with the finger, the crankshaft pulley pointer is opposite the 8° BTDC mark on the timing cover (Fig. 4.10).

3 Check that the advance/retard adjuster on the distributor is in the standard position, then switch on the ignition.

4 Release the distributor clamp bolt and turn the body clockwise until the lamp goes out, then turn the body slowly anticlockwise until the lamp just comes on. At this position the points have just opened.

5 Tighten the clamp and recheck the ignition timing by turning the engine two complete turns and making sure that the lamp comes on when the timing marks are aligned.

6 Fine adjustment can be made by rotating the vacuum unit adjustment knob in the desired direction (photo).

7 Switch off the ignition, remove the test lamp and refit the distributor cap.

Stroboscope (timing lamp)

8 Disconnect the vacuum pipe which runs between the distributor and the carburettor. Disconnect the pipe at the distributor end, and plug the pipe.

9 Apply white paint to the crankshaft pulley pointer and the 8° BTDC mark on the timing cover (on some models the position is

Fig. 4.6 Removing the vacuum unit (Sec 7)

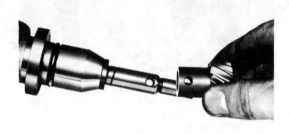

Fig. 4.7 Removing the spiral gear (Sec 7)

Fig. 4.8 Removing the distributor shaft (Sec 7)

Fig. 4.9 Distributor shaft assembly (Sec 7)

1 Shaft
2 Shims with central bakelite spacer
3 Body
4 Spiral gear
5 Pin

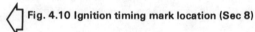

Fig. 4.10 Ignition timing mark location (Sec 8)

8.6 Distributor vacuum unit vernier adjuster

9.1 Ignition coil location. Arrow shows ballast resistor

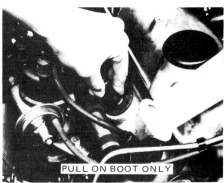

PULL ON BOOT ONLY

Fig. 4.11 Removing a spark plug cover (Sec 10)

indicated by a small hole).

10 Connect the stroboscope in accordance with the manufacturer's instructions (usually interposed between the end of No 1 spark plug HT lead and No 1 spark plug terminal).

11 Start the engine and reduce its idling speed to a minimum to ensure that the centrifugal advance mechanism does not operate.

12 Point the stroboscope at the timing marks and they will appear to be stationary. If they are in alignment, then the ignition timing is correct. If not, rotate the vernier adjuster on the distributor in the required direction until the marks are in line.

13 A check on the operation of the mechanical advance mechanism can also be carried out with the aid of the stroboscope. With the engine still running and the stroboscope pointing at the timing marks, speed up the engine momentarily by moving the throttle lever. The pulley pointer should appear to move away in an anticlockwise direction from the mark on the timing cover.

14 Check on the operation of the vacuum advance unit by switching off the engine and removing the distributor cap. Unplug the vacuum pipe and attach one end to the distributor vacuum unit. Suck the other end and observe whether the movable baseplate in the distributor rotates. If it does, then it can be assumed that the unit is serviceable.

15 Remove the stroboscope, remake the spark plug and vacuum pipe connections.

16 Readjust the engine idling speed.

9 Coil – description and polarity

1 The coil and resistor are located on the engine compartment bulkhead (photo).

2 To ensure the correct high tension current at the spark plugs, check that the LT connections are correctly made.

3 The LT wire from the distributor must connect with the negative (–) terminal on the coil.

4 The coil positive (+) terminal is connected to the ignition starter solenoid switch and to the resistor on the coil.

5 An incorrect connection can cause as much as 60% loss of spark efficiency and can cause rough idling and misfiring at speed.

6 The resistor is attached to the ignition coil and is in circuit all the time that the engine is running. When the starter is actuated however, the resistor is bypassed to provide increased voltage at the spark plugs.

7 Testing the coil needs special equipment and the simplest way is by substitution of a new unit.

10 Spark plugs and HT leads – general

1 Correct functioning of the spark plugs is vital for the highest performance and engine efficiency. The spark plugs installed as standard equipment cannot be improved upon.

2 At intervals of 6000 miles (10 000 km) remove the spark plugs and clean and regap them to the specified gap. Cleaning can be carried

out using a wire brush but taking the plugs to a service station to be sand blasted is to be preferred. Note that the plug covers must be removed without pulling on the HT leads as this action could break the carbon core inside the leads. The insulation tubes may also be removed from the cylinder head and the sealing jackets checked for deterioration; if faulty, oil leakage may occur.

3 The spark plug gap is of considerable importance, as, if it is too large or too small, the size of the spark and its efficiency will be seriously impaired. To set it, measure the gap with a feeler gauge, and then bend open, or close, the outer plug electrode until the correct gap is achieved. The centre electrode should never be bent as this may crack the insulation and cause plug failure, if nothing worse.

4 The condition and appearance of the spark plugs will tell much about the condition and tune of the engine.

5 If the insulator nose of the spark plug is clean and white, with no deposits, this is indicative of a weak mixture, or too hot a plug (a hot plug transfers heat away from the electrode slowly – a cold plug transfers it away quickly).

6 If the tip and insulator nose is covered with hard black-looking deposits, then this is indicative that the mixture is too rich. Should be plug be black and oily, then it is likely that the engine is fairly worn, as well as the mixture being too rich.

7 If the insulator nose is covered with light tan to greyish brown deposits, then the mixture is correct and it is likely that the engine is in good condition.

8 If there are any traces of long brown tapering stains on the outside of the white portion of the plug, then the plug will have to be renewed, as this shows that there is a faulty joint between the plug body and the insulator, and compression is being allowed to leak away.

9 Every 12 000 miles (20 000 km) renew the spark plugs.

10 Always tighten a spark plug to the specified torque – no tighter.

11 Wipe the spark plug leads occasionally with a rag and always connect them in the correct order. At the same time check the carbon brush in the distributor cap as shown in Fig. 4.13. Note that the rotor segment edge is covered with a special coating which must not be mistaken for arcing build-up; no attempt must be made to remove the coating.

11 Fault diagnosis – ignition system

By far the majority of breakdown and running troubles are caused by faults in the ignition system either in the low tension or high tension circuits.

There are two main symptoms indicating ignition faults. Either the engine will not start or fire, or the engine is difficult to start and misfires. If it is a regular misfire, ie the engine is running on only two or three cylinders, the fault is almost sure to be in the secondary or high tension circuit. If the misfiring is intermittent, the fault could be in either the high or low tension circuits. If the car stops suddenly, and will not start at all, it is likely that the fault is the low tension circuit. Loss of power and overheating, apart from faulty combustion settings, are normally due to faults in the distributor or to incorrect ignition timing.

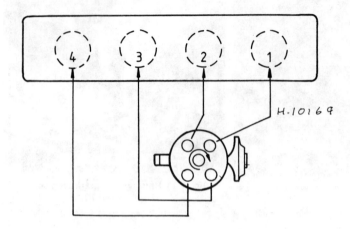

Fig. 4.12 Spark plug lead connecting diagram (Sec 10)

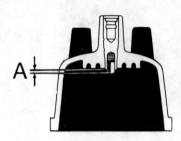

Fig. 4.13 Distributor cap carbon brush minimum projection (Sec 10)

A = 0.28 in (7.0 mm)

Engine fails to to start

1   If the engine fails to start and the car was running normally when it was last used, first check there is fuel in the petrol tank. If the engine turns over normally on the starter motor and the battery is evidently well charged, then the fault may be in either the high or low tension ignition circuits. First check the HT circuit. **Note:** If the battery is known to be fully charged, the ignition light comes on, and the starter motor fails to turn the engine, **check the tightness of the leads on the battery terminals** and also the securing of the earth lead at its connection to the body. It is quite common for the leads to have worked loose, even if they look and feel secure. If one of the battery terminal posts gets very hot when trying to work the starter motor this is a sure indication of a faulty connection to the terminal.

2   One of the commonest reasons for bad starting is wet or damp spark plug leads and/or distributor. Remove the distributor cap and if condensation is visible internally dry the cap with a rag and also wipe over the leads. Refit the cap.

3   If the engine still fails to start, check that current is reaching the plugs, by disconnecting each plug lead in turn at the spark plug end, and holding the end of the cable about $\frac{3}{16}$ inch (5 mm) away from the cylinder block. Spin the engine on the starter motor.

4   Sparking between the end of the cable and the block should be fairly strong with a strong regular blue spark. (Hold the lead with rubber to avoid electric shocks.) If current is reaching the plugs, then remove them, and clean and regap them. The engine should now start.

5   If there is no spark at the plug leads take off the HT lead from the centre of the distributor cap and hold it to the block as before. Spin the engine on the starter once more. A rapid succession of blue sparks between the end of the lead and the block indicates that the coil is in order and that either the distributor cap is cracked, the rotor arm faulty, or the brush in the top of the distributor cap is not making good contact with the rotor arm.

6   If there are no sparks from the end of the lead from the coil check the connections at the coil end of the lead. If it is in order start checking the low tension circuit. Possibly the points are in poor condition. Clean and re-gap them as described in Section 2, and make quite sure that there is no oil or dirt on the contact faces. If the engine still fails to start, proceed with the checks below.

7   Use a 12v voltmeter or 12v bulb and two lengths of wire. With the ignition switched on and the points open, test between the low tension terminal or the coil (marked '+') and earth. No reading indicates a break in the supply from the ignition switch. Check the connections at the switch to see if any are loose. Refit them and the engine should run.

8   Connect the test leads between the moving contact breaker point and earth. With the ignition on and the points closed there should be no reading: a reading indicates dirt or oil in the contact faces, or incomplete closing of the points. With the points open and the ignition on, no reading shows a faulty coil or condenser, or broken lead between the coil and the distributor.

9   Take the condenser wire off the points assembly terminal and with the points open test between the moving point and earth. If there now

is a reading then the fault is in the condenser. Fit a new one and the fault is cleared.

10   With no reading from the moving point to earth, take a reading between earth and the negative (−) terminal of the coil. A reading here shows a broken wire which will need to be replaced between the coil and distributor. No reading confirms that the coil has failed and must be renewed, after which the engine will run once more. Remember to refit the condenser wire to the points assembly terminal. For this test it is sufficient to separate the points with a piece of thin, dry, card while testing with the points open.

Engine misfires

11   If the engine misfires regularly run it at a fast idle speed. Pull off each of the plug caps in turn and listen to the note of the engine. Hold the plug cap in a dry cloth or with a rubber glove as additional protection against a shock from the HT supply.

12   No difference in engine running will be noticed when the lead from the defective circuit is removed. Removing the lead from one of the good cylinders will accentuate the misfire.

13   Remove the plug lead from the end of the defective plug and hold it about $\frac{3}{16}$ inch (5 mm) away from the block. Re-start the engine. If the sparking is fairly strong and regular the fault must lie in the spark plug.

14   The plug may be loose, the insulation may be cracked, or the points may have burnt away giving too wide a gap for the spark to jump. Worse still, one of the points may have broken off. Either renew the plug, or clean it, reset the gap and then test it.

15   If there is no spark at the end of the plug lead, or if it is weak and intermittent, check the ignition lead from the distributor to the plug. If the insulation is damaged renew the lead. Check the connections at the distributor cap.

16   If there is still no spark, examine the distributor cap carefully for tracking. This can be recognised by a very thin black line running between two, or more, electrodes; or between an electrode and some other part of the distributor cap. These lines are paths which now conduct electricity across the cap thus letting it run to earth. The only answer is a new distributor cap.

17   Apart from the ignition timing being incorrect, other causes of misfiring have already been dealt with under the section dealing with the failure of the engine to start. To recap, these are:

   (a) The coil may be faulty giving an intermittent misfire
   (b) There may be a damaged wire or loose connection in the low tension circuit
   (c) The condenser may be short circuiting
   (d) There may be a mechanical fault in the distributor (broken driving spindle or contact breaker spring)

18   If the ignition timing is too far retarded, it should be noted that the engine will tend to overheat, and there will be quite a noticeable drop in power. If the engine is overheating and the power is down, and the ignition timing is correct, then the carburettor should be checked, as it is likely that this is where the fault lies.

Chapter 5 Clutch

Contents

Specifications

Clutch type . . . . Single dry plate, diaphragm spring, cable actuated

Driven plate
Number of torsion springs 4
Maximum run-out . . . . 0.02 in (0.5 mm)
Minimum lining surface to rivet clearance . . . . 0.01 in (0.3 mm)

Diaphragm spring
Maximum finger height difference . . . . 0.02 in (0.5 mm)

Pedal adjustment
Height from floor pan waterproof covering . . . . 6.9 in (176 mm)
Free play . . . . 0.8 to 1.4 in (20 to 35 mm)

Torque wrench settings

	lbf ft	kgf m
Pressure plate to flywheel	15	2.1
Clutch housing to engine	45	6.2
Pedal shaft nut	35	4.8

1 General description

1   The clutch is of single dry plate type with a diaphragm spring. Actuation is by means of a cable through a pendant mounted pedal. The unit comprises a pressed steel cover which is dowelled to the rear face of the flywheel and bolted to it and which incorporates the pressure plate, diaphragm spring and fulcrum rings.

2   The clutch driven plate is free to slide along the splined first motion shaft and is held in position between the flywheel and the pressure plate by the pressure of the diaphragm spring. Friction lining material is riveted to the clutch driven plate and it has a spring cushioned hub to absorb transmission shocks and to help ensure a smooth take-off.

3   The circular diaphragm spring is mounted on shouldered pins held in place in the cover by two fulcrum rings. The spring is also held to the pressure plate by three spring steel clips which are riveted in position.

4   When the clutch pedal is depressed, the cable moves the release arm to which is attached the release bearing and so moves the centre of the diaphragm inwards. The spring is sandwiched between two annular rings which act as fulcrum points. As the centre of the spring is pushed in, the outside of the spring is pushed out, so moving the pressure plate backwards and disengaging the pressure plate from the clutch driven plate.

5   When the clutch pedal is released the diaphragm spring forces the pressure plate into contact with the friction linings on the clutch driven plate and at the same time pushes the clutch driven plate a fraction of an inch forwards on its splines, so engaging the clutch driven plate with the flywheel. The clutch driven plate is now firmly sandwiched between the pressure plate and the flywheel so the drive is taken up.

6   As the friction linings wear, the pressure plate friction surface will move closer to the flywheel and the clutch release arm free movement will increase. Periodic adjustment must therefore be carried out as described in Section 2.

2 Clutch – adjustment

1   There are two points of adjustment on the clutch; these are pedal height and pedal free play.

2   To check the pedal height, lift the clutch pedal to ensure that it is in contact with the stop bolt, then measure the distance from the top of the rubber foot pad to the floor waterproof covering below the carpet. If necessary adjust the height by loosening the locknut on the stop bolt and turning the remaining nut as required. Tighten the locknut when the adjustment is correct.

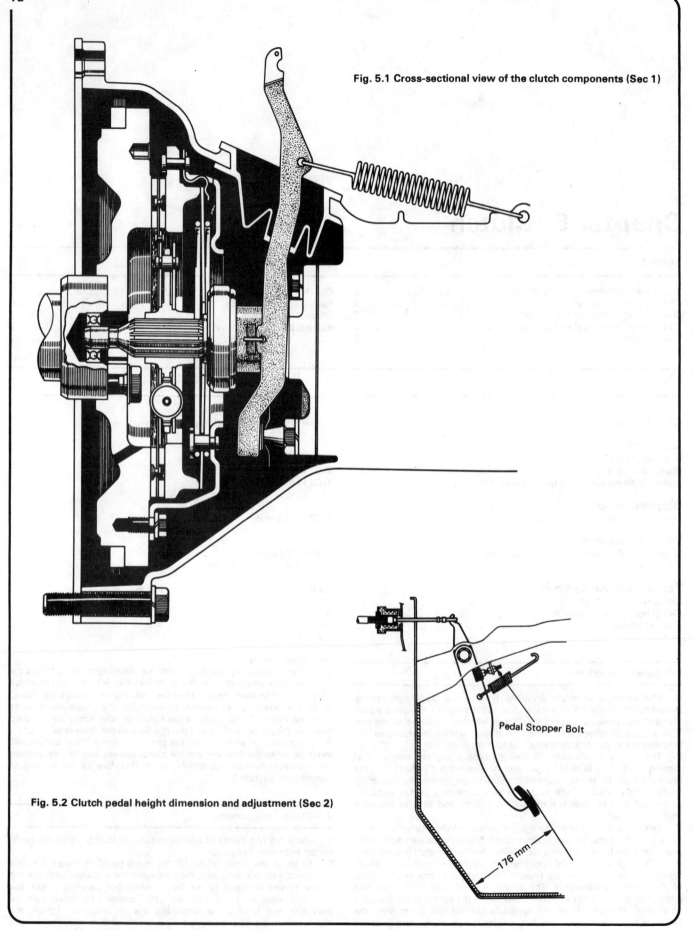

Fig. 5.1 Cross-sectional view of the clutch components (Sec 1)

Pedal Stopper Bolt

176 mm

Fig. 5.2 Clutch pedal height dimension and adjustment (Sec 2)

3 To check the clutch pedal free play, depress the pedal by hand until firm resistance is felt, indicating that the clutch release bearing is in contact with the diaphragm. Measure the distance from the top of the rubber foot pedal to the floor waterproof covering and deduct the amount from the distance obtained in paragraph 2. The difference should be within the specified clutch pedal free play limits. If not, proceed as follows.

4 Locate the clutch cable on the bulkhead inside the engine compartment, and pull it out until firm resistance is felt. There should be 5 or 6 grooves on the metal ferrule between the E clip and the bulkhead (photo). Prise the clip out and reposition it as necessary, then recheck the free play as described in paragraph 3. Note that the pedal should be fully depressed and release several times in order to settle the cable before checking the free play.

3 Clutch cable – renewal

1 Prise the E clip from the cable ferrule on the bulkhead inside the engine compartment.
2 Working inside the car, unhook the inner cable from the clutch pedal.
3 From the release fork end of the cable, remove the crosshead screw and lift the two halves of the counterweight from the cable (photo).
4 Remove the split-pin and detach the cable from the release fork (photo).
5 Withdraw the clutch cable from within the engine compartment (photo).
6 Examine the cable hooks, ferrule and rubber boot for damage and deterioration. Check the outer cable for damage and the inner cable for freedom of movement. Renew the complete cable if necessary.
7 Refitting is a reversal of removal, but lubricate the moving parts and cable ends with a little multi-purpose grease, and adjust the clutch pedal height and free play as described in Section 2.

4 Clutch pedal – removal and refitting

RHD models

1 Unhook the return springs from the clutch and brake pedals.
2 Extract the spring clip and remove the clevis pin retaining the brake pedal to the servo unit pushrod.
3 Unscrew the clutch pedal stop bolt and unhook the inner cable. Disconnect the stoplight wire connector.
4 Unscrew and remove the pedal shaft pivot bolt and lower both

2.4 Clutch cable adjustment ferrule location

3.3 Clutch cable counterweight

3.4 Clutch cable disconnected from release fork

3.5 Removing the clutch cable

pedals from the bulkhead.

5   Note the location of the spacer and bushes, then remove the pedals from the sleeve.

LHD models

6   Unhook the clutch pedal return spring.

7   Unscrew the clutch pedal stop bolt and unhook the inner cable.

8   Unscrew the pedal shaft pivot bolt and withdraw the clutch pedal.

9   Remove the bushes and sleeve from the clutch pedal.

All models

10   Examine all components for damage and wear and renew them as necessary.

11   Refitting is a reversal of removal, but the following points should be observed:

   (a)   *Lubricate all moving surfaces with grease*
   (b)   *Tighten the pedal shaft bolt to the specified torque*
   (c)   *Make sure that the shorter return spring is fitted to the clutch pedal*
   (d)   *Adjust the clutch pedal height and free play as described in Section 2.*

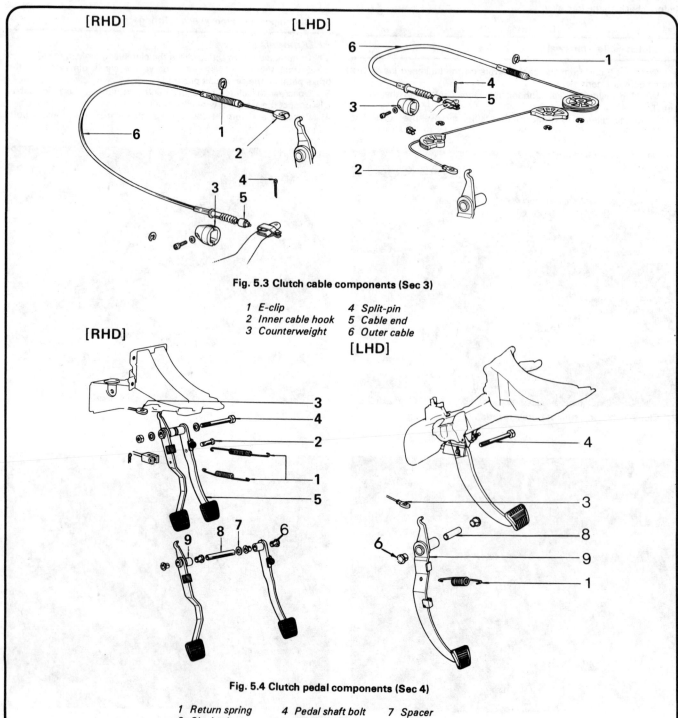

Fig. 5.3 Clutch cable components (Sec 3)

1 *E-clip*	4 *Split-pin*
2 *Inner cable hook*	5 *Cable end*
3 *Counterweight*	6 *Outer cable*

Fig. 5.4 Clutch pedal components (Sec 4)

1 *Return spring*	4 *Pedal shaft bolt*	7 *Spacer*
2 *Clevis pin*	5 *Brake pedal*	8 *Sleeve*
3 *Clutch cable*	6 *Bush*	9 *Clutch pedal*

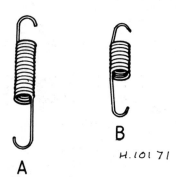

Fig. 5.5 Brake pedal return spring (A) and clutch pedal return spring (B) (Sec 4)

5 Clutch – removal

1   Access to the clutch may be obtained on one of two ways. Either remove the engine (Chapter 1) or remove the gearbox (Chapter 6). Unless the engine requires major overhaul, removal of the gearbox is much the easier and quicker method.

2   Mark the relationship of the clutch cover to the flywheel and unscrew the bolts which secure the clutch pressure plate cover to the flywheel. Unscrew the bolts only a turn at a time, until the pressure of the diaphragm spring is relieved, before completely withdrawing them.

3   Lift away the pressure plate/diaphragm spring assembly and the driven plate (friction disc) from the face of the flywheel (photo).

4   Make careful note of which side of the friction disc faces outwards. The torsion blocks should be towards the gearbox.

6 Clutch – inspection and renovation

1   The clutch will normally need renewal when the free movement adjustment on the cable has been taken up or when the clutch can be felt to be slipping under conditions of hard acceleration or when climb-ing a hill. Sometimes squealing noises are evident when the clutch is engaged. This may be due to the friction linings having worn down to the rivets and/or a badly worn release bearing. A clutch will wear according to the way in which it is used. Much intentional slipping of the clutch while driving – rather than the correct selection of gears – will accelerate wear.

2   Examine the surfaces of the pressure plate and flywheel for signs of scoring. If this is only light it may be left, but if very deep, the pressure plate unit will have to be renewed. If the flywheel is deeply scored it should be taken off and advice sought from an engineering firm.

7 Release bearing – removal and refitting

1   The release bearing is of ball bearing, grease sealed type and although designed for long life it is worth renewing at the same time as the other clutch components are being renewed or serviced (photos).

2   Deterioration of the bearing should be suspected when there are signs of grease leakage or the unit is noisy when spun with the fingers.

3   Unhook the return spring on the gearbox casing from the release fork (photo).

4   Prise the spring clips from the release fork and release bearing, and slide the bearing and hub from its locating sleeve.

5   Pull the release fork out of the clutch housing sufficiently to release the spring clip from the fulcrum pin.

6   Withdraw the release fork from within the clutch housing.

7   Prise the rubber insert from the clutch housing.

8   If the release bearing is worn, use suitable tubing to drive the hub from the bearing. The new bearing can be pressed in using a vice and packing but note that the curved side of the bearing must face away from the hub flange.

9   Examine all components for wear and damage, including the sleeve on the gearbox front bearing retainer, and renew them as necessary.

10   Refitting is a reversal of removal, but apply grease sparingly to the release fork fulcrum pin. The release bearing hub and gearbox front bearing retainer sleeve should **not** be greased, but should be wiped clean before assembly.

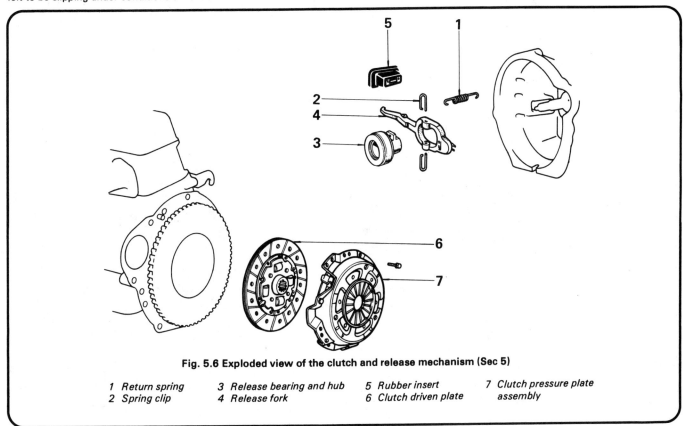

Fig. 5.6 Exploded view of the clutch and release mechanism (Sec 5)

1 Return spring	3 Release bearing and hub	5 Rubber insert	7 Clutch pressure plate
2 Spring clip	4 Release fork	6 Clutch driven plate	assembly

5.3 Removing the clutch pressure plate and driven plate

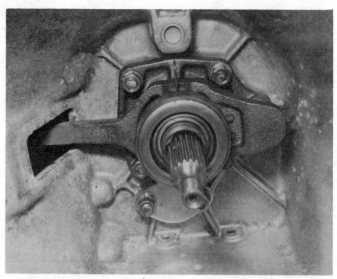

7.1A Clutch release bearing location on the gearbox front bearing retainer

7.1B Clutch release fork and bearing

7.1C Clutch release bearing spring clip locations

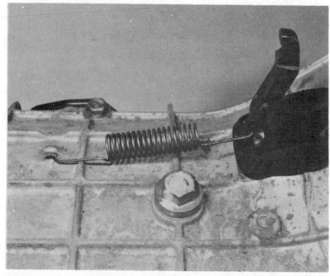

7.3 Clutch release fork return spring location

8.5 Using an input shaft to centralise the clutch driven plate

8 Clutch – refitting

1 To refit the clutch plate, place the clutch disc against the flywheel with the greater projection of the hub away from the flywheel. On no account should the clutch disc be refitted the wrong way round as it will be found impossible to operate the clutch.

2 Refit the clutch cover assembly loosely on the dowels. Refit the six bolts and tighten them finger-tight so that the clutch disc is gripped but can still be moved.

3 The clutch disc must now be centralised to ensure that the gearbox input shaft splines engage with the splines in the disc.

4 Centralisation can be carried out quite easily by inserting a round bar or wooden dowel of suitable size through the hole in the centre of the clutch, so that the end of the bar rests in the small hole in the crankshaft containing the input shaft bearing bush. Moving the bar sideways or up and down will move the clutch disc in whichever direction is necessary to achieve centralisation.

5 Centralisation is easily judged by removing the bar and viewing the disc hub in relation to the hole in the centre of the diaphragm spring. When the hub is exactly in the centre of the release bearing hole, all is correct. Alternatively, if an old input shaft can be borrowed this will eliminate all the guesswork as it will fit the bearing and centre of the clutch hub exactly, obviating the need of the visual alignment (photo).

6 Tighten the clutch bolts firmly in a diagonal sequence to ensure that the cover plate is pulled evenly and without distortion of the flange. Tighten the bolts to the specified torque wrench setting.

7 Refit the gearbox or engine as described in Chapters 6 or 1 respectively. If difficulty is experienced in engaging the clutch splines, select top gear and turn either the gearbox output shaft or engine crankshaft pulley bolt.

8 When refitting is completed, adjust the clutch as described in Section 2.

9 Fault diagnosis – clutch

Symptom	Reason/s
Judder when taking up drive	Loose engine or gearbox mountings Badly worn friction surfaces or contaminated with oil Worn splines on gearbox input shaft or driven plate hub Worn input shaft spigot bush in flywheel
Clutch drag (failure to disengage) so that gears cannot be meshed	Incorrectly adjusted clutch cable Driven plate sticking on input shaft splines due to rust. May occur after vehicle standing idle for long period Damaged or misaligned pressure plate assembly
Clutch slip (increase in engine speed does not result in increase in vehicle road speed – particularly on gradients)	Incorrectly adjusted clutch cable Friction surface worn out or oil contaminated
Noise evident on depressing clutch pedal	Dry, worn or damaged release bearing Insufficient pedal free travel Weak or broken pedal return spring Weak or broken clutch release lever return spring Excessive play between driven plate hub splines and input shaft splines
Noise evident as clutch pedal released	Distorted driven plate Broken or weak driven plate cushion coil springs Insufficient pedal free play Weak or broken release lever return spring Distorted or worn input shaft

Chapter 6 Gearbox

For modifications, and information applicable to later models, see Supplement at end of manual

Contents

Specifications

Type
K40 .... 4 forward speeds and reverse, synchromesh on all forward gears
K50 .... 5 forward speeds and reverse, synchromesh on all forward gears

Ratios
1st 3.789:1
2nd 2.220:1
3rd 1.435:1
4th 1.000:1
5th (K50 only) 0.865:1
Reverse 4.316:1

Oil capacity
K40 .... 3.0 Imp pints (1.7 litres)
K50 .... 4.2 Imp pints (2.45 litres)

Dimensions and clearances
Mainshaft journal minimum diameter .... 1.25 in (31.8 mm)
Mainshaft flange minimum width .... 0.14 in (3.5 mm)
Mainshaft maximum run-out .... 0.002 in (0.06 mm)
1st gear sleeve flange minimum width .... 0.132 in (3.35 mm)
1st and 2nd gear maximum endfloat .... 0.012 in (0.30 mm)
3rd gear endfloat:
    K40 .... 0.002 to 0.006 in (0.05 to 0.15 mm)
    K50 .... 0.002 to 0.008 in (0.05 to 0.20 mm)
5th gear endfloat (K50 only) .... 0.008 to 0.012 in (0.20 to 0.30 mm)
Countergear endfloat:
    K40 .... 0.002 to 0.010 in (0.05 to 0.25 mm)
    50 .... 0.003 to 0.016 in (0.08 to 0.40 mm)
Gear teeth maximum backlash .... 0.008 in (0.020 mm)
Selector fork to synchro hub maximum clearance .... 0.03 in (0.8 mm)

Circlip, spacer and thrust washer thickness available
Input shaft circlip .... 2, from 0.093 to 0.098 in (2.35 to 2.50 mm)
3rd/4th synchro hub spacer .... 3, from 0.169 to 0.175 in (4.30 to 4.45 mm)
Rear bearing circlip:
    K40 .... 8, from 0.081 to 0.096 in (2.05 to 2.45 mm)
    K50 .... 10, from 0.081 to 0.100 in (2.05 to 2.55 mm)
3rd/4th synchro hub circlip (K50) .... 8, from 0.081 to 0.096 in (2.05 to 2.45 mm)
5th synchro hub circlip (K50) .... 15, from 0.081 to 0.100 in (2.05 to 2.80 mm)

Countergear thrust washer:		
K40	....	4, from 0.051 to 0.065 in (1.30 to 1.65 mm)
K50	....	3, from 0.067 to 0.081 in (1.71 to 2.05 mm)

Torque wrench settings

		lbf ft	kgf m
Front bearing retainer:			
K40	....	11	1.5
K50	....	15	2.1
Rear bearing locknut (K40)	....	70	9.7
Reverse shaft bolt	....	13	1.8
Extension housing bolts	....	30	4.1
Bottom cover bolts	....	5	0.7
Gearbox to engine bolts	....	45	6.2

1 General description

1 The four or five-speed gearbox has synchromesh engagement on all forward gears. Gear selection is by a centrally mounted gearshift lever.

2 The gearbox casing is integral with the clutch bellhousing. Dismantling of the gearbox is made possible by a detachable bottom cover, rear extension housing and front bearing retainer.

3 The combined filler/level plug is located on the right-hand side of the gearbox casing. The drain plug is located in the bottom cover.

2 Gearbox – removal and refitting

1 If the engine is to be removed at the same time as the gearbox, refer to Chapter 1. For the removal and refitting of the gearbox leaving the engine in place, proceed as follows.

2 Jack-up the rear of the car and support it on axle stands, making sure that there is enough clearance to remove the gearbox from under the car. Alternatively position the car over an inspection pit or on ramps.

3 Disconnect the battery negative lead.

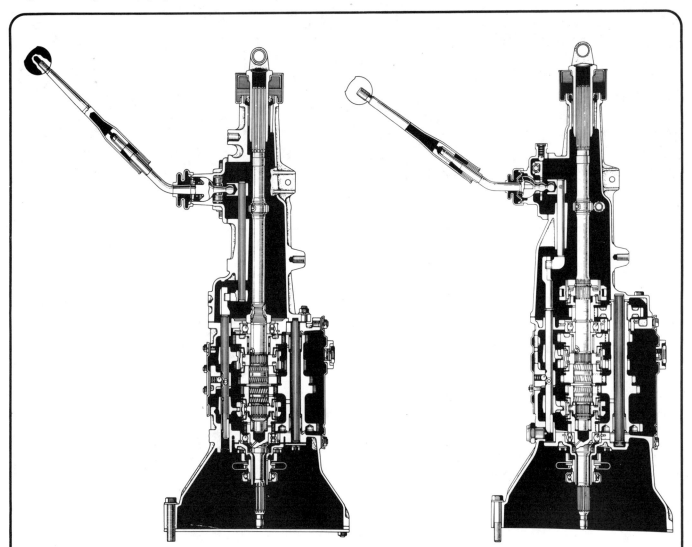

Fig. 6.1 Cutaway view of the K40 gearbox (Sec 1)   Fig. 6.2 Cutaway view of the K50 gearbox (Sec 1)

4   Working inside the car, pull aside the gearstick rubber gaiter and remove the retaining screws, then pull the gaiter up the gearstick (photo).
5   Pull the small rubber boot from the gearbox.
6   *On K40 types,* use circlip pliers to extract the circlip. Lift the gearstick from the gearbox (photos).
7   *On K50 types,* release the retaining spring by inserting a small screwdriver through the special hole. Prise the spring from the groove and lift the gearstick from the gearbox.
8   If necessary, unscrew the knob and remove the gaiter and boot from the gearstick.
9   Drain the cooling system as described in Chapter 2.
10 Disconnect the top radiator hose from the thermostat outlet.
11 Separate the two halves of the wiring multiplug located below the ignition coil on the bulkhead.
12 Detach the two mounting rings from the rear of the exhaust system.
13 Disconnect the clutch release cable from the release arm and bellhousing (see Chapter 5).
14 Remove the drain plug and drain the gearbox oil into a suitable container. Refit and tighten the plug when the oil is completely drained.
15 Unscrew the knurled nut and disconnect the speedometer cable from the gearbox (photo).
16 Unscrew the speedometer driven gear clamp retaining screw and

remove the earth lead. The driven gear can be temporarily removed from the gearbox in order to drain the small amount of oil in the extension housing; this will prevent unnecessary oil leakage when tilting the gearbox to remove it (photo).
17 Remove the propeller shaft as described in Chapter 7.
18 Remove the starter motor as described in Chapter 10.
19 Support the weight of the gearbox with a trolley jack.
20 Unscrew and remove the two mounting bolts from the crossmember (photo).
21 Remove the exhaust pipe support bracket (where fitted) after loosening the clamp bolt and unscrewing the two nuts on the bellhousing (photo).
22 Detach the earth lead from the rear of the engine.
23 Disconnect the leads from the reversing lamp switch (photo).
24 Place a piece of plywood or similar material between the rear of the cylinder head and the bulkhead, then lower the gearbox until the engine is resting on the wood.
25 Unscrew and remove the gearbox retaining nuts and bolts and withdraw the gearbox from the engine. Make sure that the weight of the gearbox is not allowed to hang on the input shaft with the latter still engaged with the clutch driven plate splines.
26 Refitting the gearbox is a reversal of removal, but if the clutch has been dismantled, the driven plate must be centralised as described in Chapter 5. Refill the gearbox with the specified grade and quantity of oil (photo).

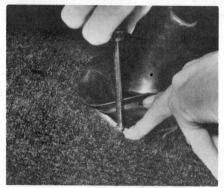
2.4 Removing the gearstick gaiter

2.6A Extracting the gearstick circlip (type K40)

2.6B Removing the gearstick (type K40)

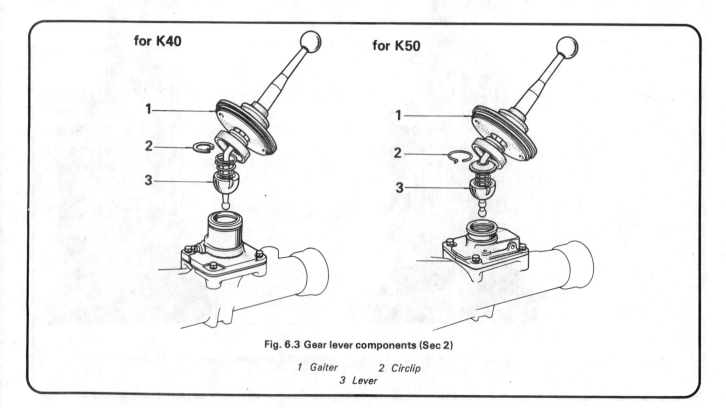

for K40   for K50

Fig. 6.3 Gear lever components (Sec 2)

1 Gaiter   2 Circlip
3 Lever

2.15 Disconnecting the speedometer cable (type K40)

2.16 Removing the speedometer driven gear (type K40)

2.20 The gearbox mounting crossmember (type K40)

2.21 Exhaust front pipe support bracket (models with 2K engine)

2.23 Reversing lamp switch location (type K40)

2.26 Filling the gearbox with oil (type K40)

3 Gearbox (type K40) – dismantling into major assemblies

1   Clean the exterior of the gearbox with paraffin and wipe dry with a cloth.

2   Refer to Chapter 5 and remove the clutch release fork and bearing.

3   Unscrew the bolts which secure the front bearing retainer to the inside of the clutch bellhousing. Slide the retainer from the input shaft (photo).

4   Remove the nuts and withdraw the cover and gasket from the top of the gearcase. Carefully recover the three detent balls and their springs. Unscrew and remove the reversing lamp switch, plungers and spring (photos).

5   Unbolt and remove the bottom cover and its gasket from the gear casing.

6   Unbolt and remove the speedometer driven gear from the extension housing, then remove the nuts which secure the rear extension housing to the main gear casing.

7   Withdraw the extension housing and peel away its joint gasket.

8   Remove the locking bolt and its washer which secures the reverse idler gear shaft to the main gearcase (photo).

9   Withdraw the reverse idler shaft and lift off the idler gear.

10   Remove the countershaft by first unscrewing the two nuts which secure the retaining plate to the front face of the gearcase (photo).

11   Hold the countergear assembly steady and drive the countershaft rearwards with a soft metal drift.

12   Lift the countergear assembly from the gearbox and recover the thrust washers.

13   Remove the input shaft by tapping its bearing track towards the front of the gearcase (photo).

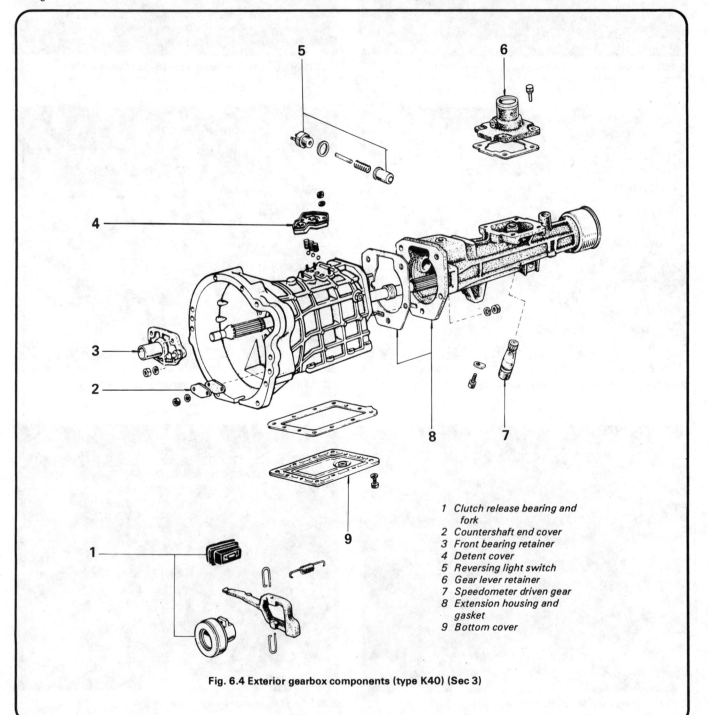

1   Clutch release bearing and fork
2   Countershaft end cover
3   Front bearing retainer
4   Detent cover
5   Reversing light switch
6   Gear lever retainer
7   Speedometer driven gear
8   Extension housing and gasket
9   Bottom cover

Fig. 6.4 Exterior gearbox components (type K40) (Sec 3)

14 The shift forks are secured to the selector shafts by roll (tension) pins which are accessible through the top cover aperture.

15 Drive out the roll pins using a suitable drift.

16 Move all three selector shafts to the neutral position then remove them one at a time while holding the relevant shift fork steady (photo).

17 Remove the interlock plug from the gearbox casing and recover the interlock plungers; recover one plunger from the 3rd/4th selector shaft. Put the three plungers in a safe place until needed for reassembly.

18 Extract the reverse shift fork from the gearbox (photo).

19 Move the 1st/2nd synchro sleeve to 2nd gear position, then extract the 1st/2nd shift fork from the gearbox.

20 Extract the 3rd/4th shift fork from the gearbox.

21 Withdraw the mainshaft assembly from the rear of the gear casing. If necessary, tap it with a plastic-faced mallet to free it (photo).

22 The reverse selector arm can be removed if it is worn or damaged, but this is not normally necessary (photo). To remove it, unscrew the pivot locknut after having noted its position.

4 Gearbox components (type K40) – inspection

1 It is assumed that the gearbox has been dismantled for reasons of excessive noise, lack of synchromesh action on certain gears or for failure to stay in gear. If serious faults have occurred (total failure, seizure or main casing cracked) it may be better to obtain a secondhand or exchange unit.

2 Check that the main casing to extension casing oil transfer tube is secured firmly to the casing (photo).

3 Examine all gears for excessively worn, chipped or damaged teeth. Any such gears should be renewed.

4 Check all synchromesh rings for wear on the bearing surfaces which normally have clear machined oil reservoir lines in them. If these are smooth or obviously uneven, renewal is essential. Also when the rings are fitted to their gears – as they would be in operation– there should be no rock. This would signify ovality or lack of concentricity. One of the most satisfactory ways of checking is by comparing the fit of a new ring with an old one on the gearwheel cone. The teeth and cut-outs in the synchro rings also wear and for this reason also, it is unwise not to fit new ones when the gearbox is dismantled.

5 All ball race bearings should be checked for chatter and roughness after they have been washed out. It is advisable to renew these anyway even though they may not appear too badly worn.

6 Circlips, which are all-important in locating bearings, gears and hubs, should be checked to ensure that they are undamaged and not distorted. In any case a selection of new circlips of varying thicknesses

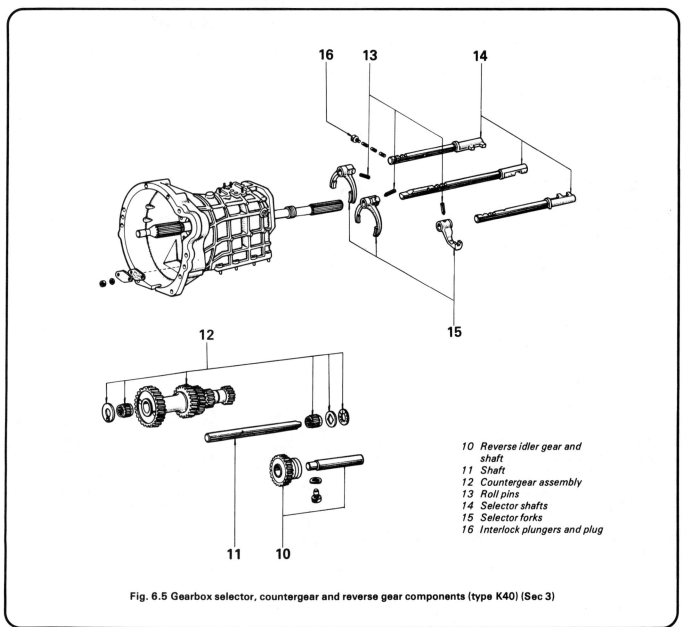

10 Reverse idler gear and shaft
11 Shaft
12 Countergear assembly
13 Roll pins
14 Selector shafts
15 Selector forks
16 Interlock plungers and plug

Fig. 6.5 Gearbox selector, countergear and reverse gear components (type K40) (Sec 3)

3.3 Removing the front bearing retainer (type K40)

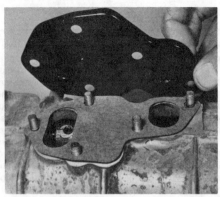

3.4A Removing the gearbox top cover (type K40)

3.4B Removing the detent springs (type K40)

3.4C Removing the reversing lamp switch (type K40)

3.4D Removing the reversing lamp switch plungers and spring (type K40)

3.8 Reverse idler gear shaft locking bolt location (type K40)

3.10 Removing the countershaft front plate (type K40)

3.13 Removing the input shaft (type K40)

3.16 Selector shafts in neutral position (type K40)

3.18 Reverse shift fork location (type K40)

3.21 Removing the mainshaft assembly (type K40)

3.22 Reverse selector arm location (type K40)

should be obtained to compensate for variations in new components fitted, and wear in old ones. The Specifications indicate what is available.

7 The thrust washers at the end of the countergear should be renewed as they will most certainly have worn if the gearbox is of any age.

8 Needle roller bearings between the input shaft and mainshaft are usually found to be in good order, but if in any doubt renew them.

5 Extension housing (type K40) – servicing

1 It is rarely necessary to dismantle the extension housing but if, due to wear or damage, this is essential, remove the gearshift lever retainer and then drive out the roll pin to release the selector control rod from the gearshift lever housing (photos).

2 The oil seal in the end of the housing can be renewed by levering out the old one and tapping in a new one using a piece of tubing as a drift. For better access, use a plastic mallet to tap the cover from the rear of the extension housing (photo).

3 The extension housing oil seal can also be renewed with the gearbox fitted to the car. To do this, drain the gearbox oil, remove the propeller shaft, and tap the cover from the extension housing; the seal can then be levered out.

4 If the bush at the rear end of the extension housing requires renewal, the oil seal must first be removed and then the extension housing must be heated in boiling water. Extract the bush and press in the new one keeping the extension housing at the same temperature. Make sure that the oil hole of the bush is uppermost (when the extension housing is in its normal 'in vehicle' attitude).

6 Input shaft (type K40) – servicing

1 The shaft and bearing are located in the front of the main casing by a large circlip in the outer track of the bearing (photo).

2 To renew the bearing first remove the circlip from the front end of

the bearing.

3 Place the outer track of the race on the top of a firm bench vice and drive the input shaft through the bearing. Note that the bearing is fitted with the circlip groove towards the forward end of the input shaft. Lift away the bearing.

4 The spigot bearing needle rollers may be slid out of the inner end of the input shaft.

5 Using a suitable diameter tubular drift carefully drive the ball race into position. The circlip in the outer track must be towards the front of the input shaft.

6 Retain the bearing in position with a circlip. This is a selective circlip which is available in two thicknesses to provide the closest fit.

7 Smear some grease into the needle bearing bore and insert the rollers into the end of the input shaft (photo).

7 Mainshaft (type K40) – servicing

1 Remove the circlip from the rearmost end of the mainshaft.

2 Slide off the speedometer drive gear and recover the ball (photos).

3 Remove the second circlip from the rear end of the mainshaft.

4 Hold the mainshaft firmly in the vice, straighten the staking locking the large nut and then remove the nut (36 mm).

5 Slide the washer from the end of the mainshaft if fitted.

6 Remove the rear bearing retainer from the end of the mainshaft (photo).

7 Slide off the first speed gear, needle roller cage and bush, then remove the synchro ring (photos).

8 Separate the bush and needle roller assembly from the first speed gear (photo).

9 The first speed gear bush is retained by a ball bearing that should be lifted out from the mainshaft.

10 The reverse gear and synchroniser assembly may next be removed from the mainshaft. Then remove the synchroniser ring (photos).

11 Slide off the second speed gear (photo).

12 Turning to the front end of the mainshaft, remove the shaft circlip located at the end of the splines.

4.2 Oil transfer tube location in the main casing (type K40)

5.1A Removing the gearshift lever retainer cover (type K40)

5.1B Gate spring location in the gearshift lever retainer (type K40)

5.2 Extension housing oil seal location (type K40)

6.1 Input shaft bearing retainer circlips (type K40)

6.7 Input shaft needle roller location (type K40)

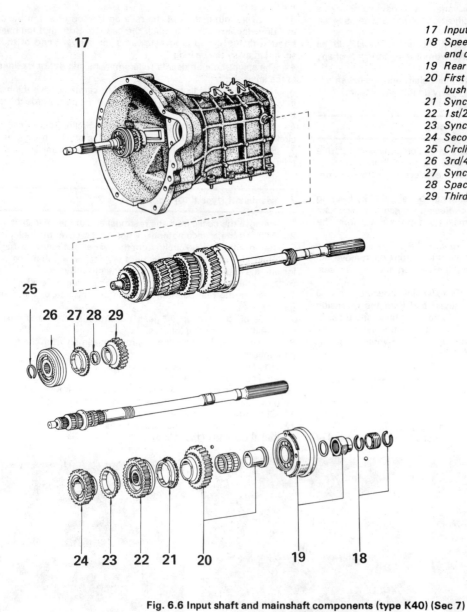

17 Input shaft
18 Speedometer drivegear
   and circlips
19 Rear bearing and locknut
20 First gear, bearing and
   bush
21 Synchro ring
22 1st/2nd synchro unit
23 Synchro ring
24 Second gear
25 Circlip
26 3rd/4th synchro unit
27 Synchro ring
28 Spacer
29 Third gear

Fig. 6.6 Input shaft and mainshaft components (type K40) (Sec 7)

7.2A Removing the speedometer drivegear
(type K40)

7.2B Speedometer drivegear locking ball
(type K40)

7.6 Removing the rear bearing retainer
(type K40)

7.7A Removing first speed gear (type K40)

7.7B Removing first speed synchro ring (type K40)

7.8 First speed gear, needle rollers and bush (type K40)

7.10A Removing reverse gear and synchroniser (type K40)

7.10B Removing second speed synchro ring (type K40)

7.11 Removing second speed gear (type K40)

7.13 Removing third/top speed synchroniser (type K40)

7.14A Removing third speed gear splined thrust washer (type K40)

7.14B Removing third speed gear (type K40)

7.15A Mainshaft rear bearing retainer and bearing (type K40)

7.15B Removing rear bearing from retainer (type K40)

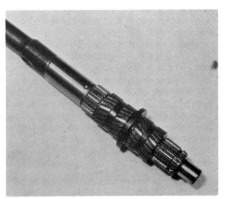

7.15C Gearbox mainshaft completely stripped (type K40)

13 Slide off the top/third synchromesh unit, noting which way round
it is fitted (photo). Remove the synchroniser ring.
14 Finally slide off the third speed gear and splined thrust washer
(photos).
15 If necessary, remove the bearing from the rear bearing retainer
using circlip pliers (photos). Dismantling of the mainshaft is now complete.
16 The synchro hubs are only too easy to dismantle – just push the
centre out and the whole assembly flies apart. The point is to prevent
this happening, before you are ready. Do not dismantle the hub
without reason and do not mix up parts of the hubs.
17 It is most important to check backlash in the splines between the
outer sleeve and inner hub. If any is noticeable the whole assembly
must be renewed.
18 Mark the hub and sleeve so that you may reassemble them on the
same splines. With the hub and sleeve separated, the teeth at the end
of the splines which engage with corresponding teeth of the
gearwheels, must be checked for damage or wear.
19 Do not confuse the keystone shape at the ends of the teeth. This
shape matches the gear teeth shape and it is a design characteristic to
minimise jump-out tendencies.
20 If the synchronising cones are being renewed it is sensible also to
renew the sliding keys and springs which hold them in position.
21 The hub assemblies are not interchangeable so they must be
reassembled with their original or identical new parts.
22 The pips on the keys are symmetrical so may be refitted either way
round into the hub.
23 Assemble the hubs and springs to the sleeves as shown in Figs.
6.7 and 6.8 (photo).
24 Make sure that the sleeve taper and hub boss of the 3rd/4th
synchro unit are facing in the same direction.
25 Temporarily assemble the selector forks to the synchro sleeves
and check that the clearance does not exceed the specified amount.
26 Commence reassembly of the mainshaft by sliding 3rd speed gear
and the splined thrust washer onto the front end of the mainshaft.
27 Fit the third speed gear synchroniser ring onto the synchromesh
unit and slide the synchromesh unit onto the end of the mainshaft.
Ensure that the ring grooves are aligned with the keys.
28 Refit the shaft located at the end of the mainshaft splines (photo).
Measure the thrust clearance between the circlip and synchromesh
unit hub. This should be zero. A range of 8 circlips is available to obtain
the correct setting (see Specifications Section).
29 Slide the second speed gear onto the rear end of the mainshaft.
30 Fit the second speed gear synchroniser ring onto the second speed
synchromesh unit and slide the reverse gear and synchromesh unit
onto the mainshaft. Ensure the ring grooves are aligned with the keys.
31 Fit the first speed gear synchroniser ring onto the synchromesh
unit ensuring the ring grooves are aligned with the keys. Note that the
first speed gear synchro ring has annular grooves facing the first speed
gear to distinguish it from the second speed gear synchro ring.
32 Insert the locking ball onto the mainshaft and assemble the first
speed gear bush, needle roller bearing and first speed gear onto the
mainshaft (photo).
33 Refit the rear bearing retainer onto the end of the mainshaft and
follow this with the washer previously removed (if fitted).
34 Hold the mainshaft firmly in the vice and refit the large nut. Do not
stake over yet. Tighten the nut to the specified torque (photo).
35 Using feeler gauges, check that the first and second gear endfloat
does not exceed the specified amount. If it does, wear is indicated in
the synchro rings, gear cones, or first speed gear bush. Check the
clearances against the mainshaft and first speed gear bush flanges.
36 Using feeler gauges, check that the third speed gear endfloat is
within the specified limits. If it is not, remove the 3rd/4th synchro unit
and select suitable thicknesses of hub spacer and circlip.
37 When all thrust clearances are correct ensure the mainshaft nut is
tight and stake the nut into the slot in the mainshaft (photo).
38 Fit the speedometer drivegear circlip to the mainshaft.
39 Replace the ball and slide the speedometer drivegear onto the
mainshaft. Fit the retaining circlip.
40 The mainshaft is now assemblied and ready for refitting to the
gearbox.

8 Countergear (type K40) – servicing

1   Extract the needle roller cages from each end of the countergear
(photo).

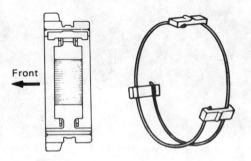
Fig. 6.7 Cross-section of 1st/2nd synchro unit (type K20) (Sec 7)

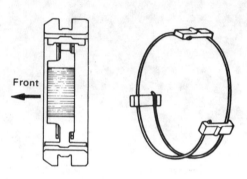
Fig. 6.8 Cross-section of 3rd/4th synchro unit (type K40) (Sec 7)

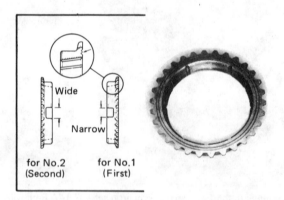
Fig. 6.9 Synchro ring identification (type K40) (Sec 7)

Fig. 6.10 Checking 2nd gear endfloat with a feeler blade (type K40)
(Sec 7)

7.23 Synchroniser spring and key location (type K40)

7.28 Third/top speed synchroniser assembled to mainshaft (type K40)

7.32A First speed bush locking ball location (type K40)

7.32B First speed bush location slot – arrowed (type K40)

7.34 Mainshaft rear locknut (type K40)

7.37 Method of locking mainshaft rear locknut (type K40)

2   Examine the countershaft and needle rollers for wear and damage; similarly check the countergear teeth. Renew the components as necessary.

3   Dip the needle rollers in gearbox oil and insert them into the countergear bores.

9   Gearbox (type K40) – reassembly

1   With all components clean, the gearbox is ready for reassembly.

2   Insert the input shaft through the front of the gearbox casing and drive the outer bearing track into position using suitable tubing.

3   Check the height of the bearing outer race in relation to the gearbox casing (Fig. 6.12). If the race protrudes *above* the casing, obtain a 0.02 in (0.5 mm) thick gasket for the bearing retainer. If the race is *below* the casing surface, obtain a 0.012 in (0.3 mm) thick gasket. Use a steel rule and feeler gauge to check the height.

4   Prise out and renew the oil seal in the front bearing retainer using suitable tubing to drive in the new seal (photo). Lubricate the seal lip with grease.

5   Fit the gasket and install the bearing retainer with the oil channel towards the bottom of the gearbox.

6   Tighten the retainer securing nuts to the specified torque in diagonal sequence.

7   Check that the needle rollers are correctly inserted in the input shaft bore, and then fit the 4th speed synchro ring to the gear cone.

8   Insert the mainshaft assembly into the gearbox casing and engage it with the input shaft, making sure that the 3rd/4th synchro shift keys are in alignment with the synchro ring slots. At the same time make sure that the rear bearing retainer peg locates in the casing cut-out.

9   Place a large washer and nut onto one of the extension housing retaining studs to hold the mainshaft in position during subsequent operations.

10   Move the 1st/2nd synchro unit to the 2nd speed position, engage the 1st/2nd selector fork in the groove, and rotate it around to its normal position (photo).

11   Engage the 3rd/4th selector fork in the 3rd/4th synchro sleeve groove and rotate it around to its normal position. Make sure that both selector forks are fitted with the roll pin bosses towards the rear of the gearbox (photo).

12   Lower the reverse selector fork into position and hook it onto the selector lever.

13   Insert the reverse selector shaft through the casing and reverse selector fork, and position it with the first detent groove visible through the detent hole in the casing.

14   Insert the 3rd/4th selector shaft through the casing and 3rd/4th selector fork, and position it with the central detent groove visible through the detent hole in the casing.

15   Insert the 1st/2nd selector shaft through the casing and 1st/2nd selector fork, and position it with the dummy hole in alignment with the interlock hole in the casing (Fig. 6.14).

16   Lubricate the interlock plungers with grease and insert all three of them through the casing and selector shafts (photo).

17   Using a screwdriver, make sure that the plungers are abutting each other, then move the 1st/2nd selector shaft to the neutral position with the central detent groove visible through the detent hole in the casing.

18   Check that the interlock plungers are correctly fitted by moving the central 3rd/4th selector shaft to the 3rd speed position; the remaining shafts should now be locked in position. Return the shaft to neutral after the check.

19   Tighten the interlock plug into the gearbox casing (photo).

20   Align the selector fork holes with the shaft holes and tap the roll pins in until flush with the forks (photos).

21   Insert the three detent balls and springs (photos) and fit the cover

Fig. 6.11 The countergear (type K40) (Sec 8)

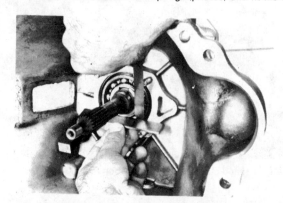

Fig. 6.12 Checking front bearing height (type K40) (Sec 9)

8.1 Removing countergear needle roller cages (type K40)

9.4 Front bearing retainer oil seal location (type K40)

9.10 Fitting 1st/2nd selector fork (type K40)

9.11 Fitting 3rd/4th selector fork (type K40)

9.16 Inserting interlock plungers (type K40)

9.19 Interlock plug location (type K40)

9.20A Inserting the selector shaft roll pins (type K40)

9.20B Driving the selector shaft roll pins home (type K40)

9.21 Inserting a detent ball (type K40)

9.22 Fitting countergear thrust washers (type K40)

9.23A Inserting the countershaft (type K40)

9.23B Countershaft end protrusion (type K40)

9.25 Inserting reverse idler gear shaft (type K40)

9.26 Checking the reverse idler gear to counter-gear clearance with a feeler gauge (type K40)

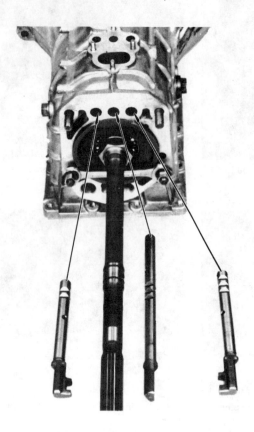

Fig. 6.13 Selector shafts and location (Sec 9)

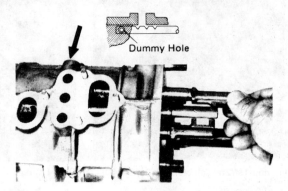

Fig. 6.14 1st/2nd selector shaft dummy hole location (type K40)
(Sec 9)

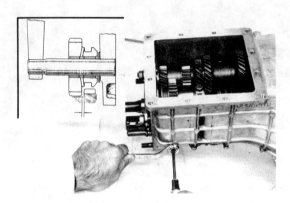

Fig. 6.15 Adjusting the reverse idle gear clearance (type K40)
(Sec 9)

with a new gasket. Tighten the retaining nuts evenly.

22 Smear some grease on the countergear thrust washers and position them on the inside faces of the main casing. Note that the plain washer at the rear must contact the countergear (photo).

23 Insert the countershaft sufficiently to retain the rear washers. Lower the countergear into position and drive the shaft through until the end recess is level with the casing, with the rectangular end projection horizontal (photos).

24 Using a feeler gauge, check that the countergear endfloat is within the specified limits. If not, new thrust washers of suitable thickness must be fitted.

25 Hold the reverse idler gear in position with the groove towards the rear of the gearbox and insert the shaft. Make sure that the selector arm is engaged in the groove (photo).

26 Push the reverse idler gear against the casing and check the clearance indicated in Fig. 6.15 (photo). If this is less than 0.02 in (0.5 mm), a special spacer must be fitted on the reverse gear shaft to increase the clearance.

27 Loosen the selector arm pivot locknut and turn the adjusting screw until the clearance described in paragraph 26 is between 0.04 and 0.08 in (1.0 and 2.0 mm). Tighten the locknut.

28 With the dowel bolt holes in alignment, tighten the reverse gear shaft retaining bolt to the specified torque.

29 Fit the countergear retaining plate to the front face of the gearcase with a new gasket. Tighten the two securing nuts and washers.

30 Remove the mainshaft retaining washer and locate a new gasket to the rear face of the gearcase.

31 With the gearbox on end, lower the extension housing into position, ensuring that the gear selector lever shaft engages with the selector fork shafts.

32 Fit and tighten the extension housing retaining nuts in diagonal sequence to the specified torque.

33 Fit a new gasket to the bottom cover and secure it with the nuts and washers, tightening them in diagonal sequence to the specified torque.

34 Insert the speedometer driven gear to the extension housing and

secure it with the clamp and bolt.

35 Refit the clutch release fork and bearing with reference to Chapter 5.

36 Insert and tighten the reversing lamp switch, plungers and spring.

37 Temporarily fit the gearstick and check that all gears are obtained with smooth operation.

10 Gearbox (type K50) – dismantling into major assemblies

1   Clean the exterior of the gearbox with paraffin and wipe dry with a cloth.

2   Refer to Chapter 5 and remove the clutch release fork and bearing.

3   Unbolt the mounting crossmember from the extension housing.

4   Unscrew and remove the reversing lamp switch.

5   Unscrew the clamp and bolt and withdraw the speedometer drive gear from the extension housing.

6   Unbolt and remove the bottom cover and its gasket from the gearbox casing.

7   Unscrew the securing bolts and remove the gearstick retainer and gasket.

8   Unscrew the extension housing retaining bolts and withdraw the housing from the gearbox casing together with the gasket.

9   Remove the thrust washer from the rear of the countergear shaft.

10 Remove the circlip from the rear end of the mainshaft and withdraw the speedometer drivegear. Recover the locating ball from the mainshaft and remove the remaining circlip.

11 Unscrew the two crosshead screws and remove the 5th gear shift arm bracket assembly from the rear of the gearbox casing and the selector grooves. These screws are tight and it will be necessary to use a lever or the screwdriver.

12 Extract the circlip from the mainshaft and prise off the retainer ring and 5th gear synchro hub assembly, noting which way round this is fitted.

13 Remove the 5th gear synchro ring and slide the 5th gear and

needle roller cage from the mainshaft. Keep the synchro ring and 5th gear together to ensure correct reassembly.

14 Extract the circlip from the end of the countergear shaft and prise off the counter 5th gear with two wide blade screwdrivers. Be careful not to damage the gearbox casing.

15 Expand the countergear rear bearing retainer circlip, and use a screwdriver to prise out the outer track and needle roller bearing.

16 Remove the lock bolt and withdraw the reverse idle gear and shaft.

17 Move the countergear and shaft towards the rear, then lift the assembly from the gearbox together with the front thrust washer.

18 Unscrew the nuts and withdraw the small cover from the top of the gearbox. Extract the four springs and detent balls from the casing; a small magnet is useful to remove the balls.

19 Using a suitable drift through the apertures in the casing, drive out the roll pins from the selector shafts.

20 Move the selector shafts to the neutral position, then remove them one at a time while holding the relevant shift fork steady.

21 Remove the interlock plug from the gearbox casing and recover the interlock plungers; one plunger will have been removed with the 3rd/4th selector shaft. Place the three plungers in a safe place until needed for reassembly.

22 Using a screwdriver, prise the short reverse selector shaft from the rear of the casing.

23 Extract the reverse shift fork from the gearbox and recover the interlock ball.

24 Move the 4th/2nd synchro sleeve to the 2nd gear position, then extract the 1st/2nd shift fork from the gearbox.

25 Extract the 3rd/4th shift fork from the gearbox.

26 Unbolt the front bearing retainer from the front of the gearbox and remove it together with the gasket, 4th speed synchro ring and input shaft. Keep the synchro ring with the input shaft, and check that all the

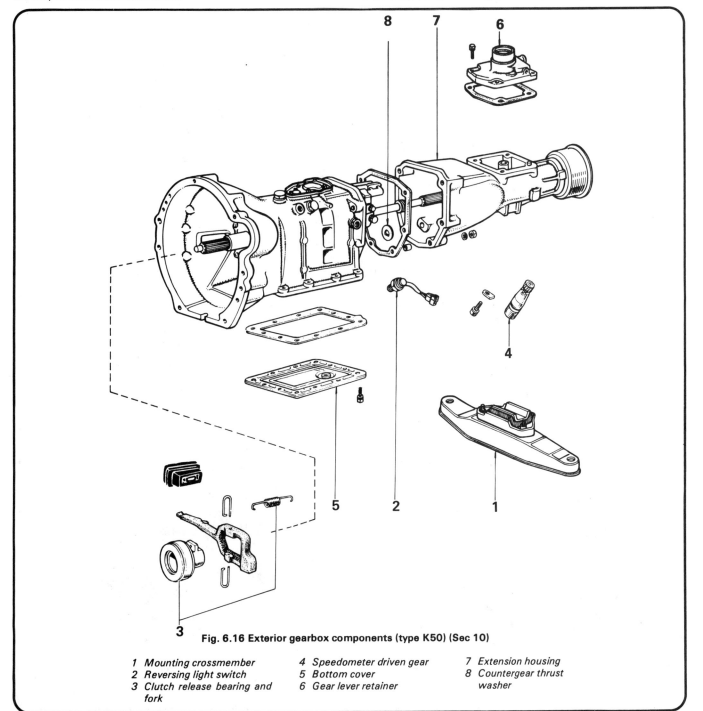

Fig. 6.16 Exterior gearbox components (type K50) (Sec 10)

1 Mounting crossmember
2 Reversing light switch
3 Clutch release bearing and fork

4 Speedometer driven gear
5 Bottom cover
6 Gear lever retainer

7 Extension housing
8 Countergear thrust washer

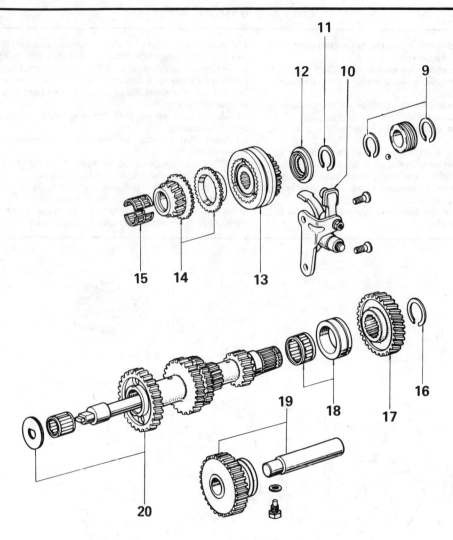

Fig. 6.18 Gearbox countergear, reverse, and 5th gear components (type K50) (Sec 10)

9 Speedometer drivegear and circlips	12 Sliding key retainer	17 Counter 5th gear
10 5th gear selector arm and bracket	13 5th gear synchro unit	18 Countergear rear bearing
11 Circlip	14 5th gear and synchro ring	19 Reverse idle gear and shaft
	15 Needle roller bearing	20 Countergear assembly
	16 Circlip	

Fig. 6.17 Removing the countergear rear thrust washer (type K50) (Sec 10)

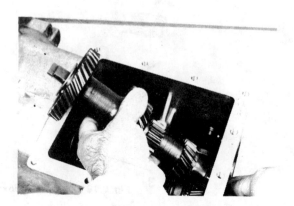

Fig. 6.19 Removing the countergear assembly (type K50) (Sec 10)

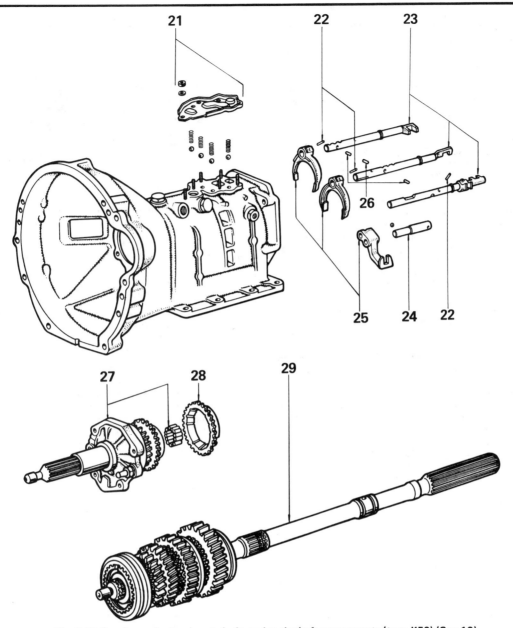

Fig. 6.20 Gearbox selector, input shaft, and mainshaft components (type K50) (Sec 10)

21 Detent cover	24 Reverse selector shaft	27 Input shaft assembly
22 Roll pins	25 Selector forks	28 Synchro ring
23 Selector shafts	26 Interlock plungers	29 Mainshaft assembly

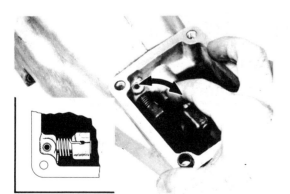

Fig. 6.21 5th gear tension pin and spring location (type K50) (Sec 12)

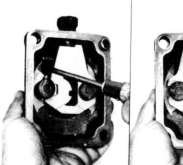

Fig. 6.22 Checking gear lever gate movement (type K50) (Sec 12)

needle rollers are positioned in the shaft bore.

27 Using circlip pliers, expand the mainshaft rear bearing retaining circlip and withdraw the complete mainshaft assembly through the front of the gearbox.

28 The reverse selector arm can be removed if it is worn or damaged, but this is not normally necessary. To remove it, unscrew the pivot locknut after having noted the position of the pivot.

11 Gearbox components (type K50) – inspection

Refer to Section 4 of this Chapter.

12 Extension housing (type K50) – servicing

Refer to Section 5 of this Chapter, but in addition check the tension pin and spring located beneath the gear lever retainer for wear and damage (Fig. 6.21). Also check that the gate in the gear lever retainer slides freely from side to side and assumes a central position when released under the tension of the two springs (Fig. 6.22).

13 Input shaft (type K50) – servicing

1 The shaft and bearing are located in the front bearing retainer by a large circlip. To remove the shaft and bearing, expand the circlip and press the assembly from the retainer while supporting the retainer in a vice.

2 To renew the bearing, extract the circlip from the front end of the bearing, support the outer track of the bearing in a vice, and drive out the input shaft. Note that the groove in the bearing outer track faces the rear of the input shaft (ie towards the gear teeth).

3 Slide the spigot bearing needle rollers out of the input shaft bore.

Fig. 6.23 Front bearing retainer housing and oil seal (type K50) (Sec 13)

4 Prise the oil seal from the bearing retainer housing and drive the new seal into position using suitable tubing. Smear a little grease onto the oil seal lip.

5 Using a tubular drift, drive the gearing fully onto the input shaft, the outer track groove side towards the gear teeth. Select and fit a retaining circlip which will eliminate any endfloat.

6 Refit the input shaft and bearing assembly to the bearing retainer while expanding the circlip; make sure that the circlip is fully entered in the groove.

7 Smear some grease into the input shaft bore and insert the rollers.

14 Mainshaft (type K50) – servicing

1 To dismantle the mainshaft, extract the circlip from the front end of the shaft, withdraw the 3rd/4th synchro assembly, the synchro hub spacer, the synchro ring and 3rd gear. Note carefully the location of

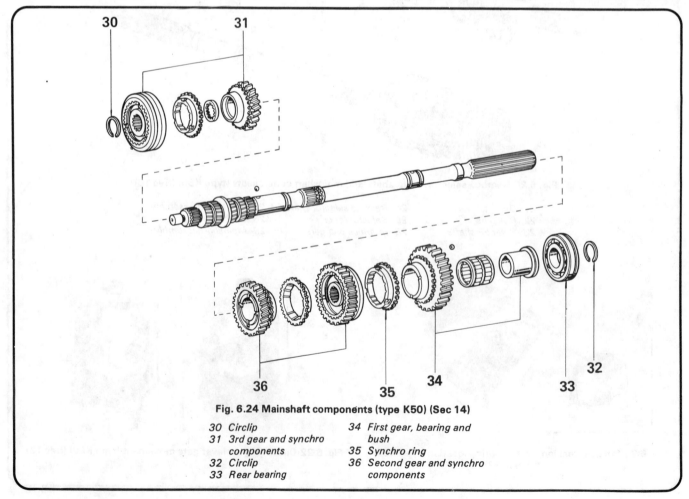

Fig. 6.24 Mainshaft components (type K50) (Sec 14)

30 Circlip
31 3rd gear and synchro
    components
32 Circlip
33 Rear bearing

34 First gear, bearing and
    bush
35 Synchro ring
36 Second gear and synchro
    components

each synchro ring; they are not interchangeable.

2   From the rear end of the mainshaft extract the circlip, and the bearing.

3   Now withdraw 1st gear bush, the needle roller bearing, 1st gear, the locking ball, synchro ring, 1st/2nd synchro unit, synchro ring and 2nd gear.

4   Servicing of the synchro units is as described in Section 7, paragraphs 16 to 25. See also Fig. 6.25.

5   Commence reassembly of the mainshaft by fitting onto the rear end the following components: 2nd gear, synchro ring (with wide cut-out), 1st/2nd synchro unit, locking ball, synchro ring (with narrow cut-out), needle roller bearing, 1st gear, and 1st gear bush. Make sure that the bush locates correctly on the locking ball, and that the synchro ring slots engage with the sliding keys.

6   Press on the mainshaft rear bearing so that the bearing outer track circlip groove is nearer the rear of the shaft.

7   Select a circlip which is the closest fit in the shaft groove from the thicknesses available (see the Specifications).

8   Using feeler blades check that the 1st and 2nd gear endfloat is in accordance with that given in the Specifications. Check the clearances against the mainshaft and first speed gear bush flanges; if the endfloat is excessive, wear is indicated in the synchro rings, gear cones, or first speed gear bush flange.

9   To the front of the mainshaft fit 3rd gear, the synchro ring, spacer and 3rd/4th synchro unit, with the taper on the synchro sleeve facing forwards. Make sure that the sliding keys engage with the slots.

10   Press the synchro hub onto the mainshaft with the fingers and use a feeler gauge to check that the 3rd gear endfloat is within the specified limits. If it is not, select a spacer to give the correct clearance and fit it.

11   Fit the circlip to the front of the mainshaft. The 3rd/4th synchro hub must have zero endfloat and if this is not the case, the circlip must be changed for one of suitable thickness.

15   Countergear (type K50) – servicing

1   Extract the countershaft and needle roller cage from the countergear.

2   Examine the countergear, shaft and needle roller bearings for wear and damage. Similarly check the 5th gear and the two shaft thrust washers. Renew the components as necessary.

3   Dip the front needle roller cage in gearbox oil and insert it into the countergear bore. Insert the countershaft into the countergear.

16   Gearbox (type K50) – reassembly

1   With all components clean, the gearbox is ready for reassembly.

2   Refit the mainshaft assembly through the front of the gearbox and secure the rear bearing after expanding the circlip.

3   Locate the 4th speed synchro ring on the gear cone and refit the input shaft assembly with a new gasket, making sure that the sliding keys engage the slots in the ring.

4   Smear the retaining bolt threads with jointing compound and tighten them to the specified torque in diagonal sequence.

5   Move the 1st/2nd synchro sleeve to 2nd gear position, engage the 1st/2nd shift fork in the groove, and rotate it to its normal position.

6   Engage the 3rd/4th shift fork with the groove in the 3rd/4th synchro sleeve and rotate it to its normal position. Note that the roll pin bosses face rearwards.

7   Engage the reverse shift fork with the selector arm peg. Insert the shaft through the casing and fork so that the groove lower edge is flush with the casing.

8   Smear grease onto the locking ball and insert it through the reverse shift fork hole as shown in Fig. 6.28; access is gained through the aperture in the top of the gearbox.

9   Insert the reverse selector shaft through the casing and reverse selector fork, and position it with the central detent groove visible through the detent hole in the casing.

10   Insert the 3rd/4th selector shaft through the casing and 3rd/4th selector fork, and position it with the central detent groove visible through the detent hole in the casing.

11   Insert the 1st/2nd selector shaft through the casing and 1st/2nd selector fork, and position it with the dummy hole in alignment with the interlock hole in the casing (Fig. 6.30).

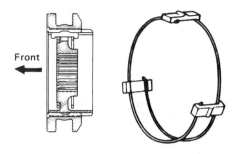

Fig. 6.25 Cross-section of 5th gear synchro unit (type K50) (Sec 14)

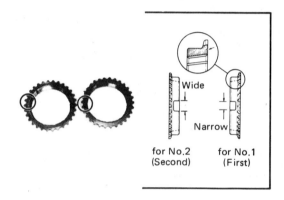

Fig. 6.26 Synchro ring identification (type K50) (Sec 14)

Fig. 6.27 Countergear and counter 5th gear (type K50) (Sec 15)

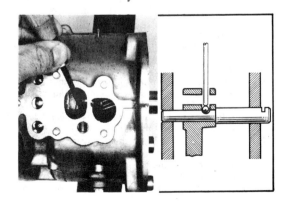

Fig. 6.28 Fitting the reverse shift fork locking ball (type K50) (Sec 16)

12 Lubricate the interlock plungers with grease and insert all three of them through the casing and selector shafts.

13 Using a screwdriver, make sure that the plungers are abutting each other, then move the 1st/2nd selector shaft to the neutral position with the central detent groove visible through the detent hole in the casing.

14 Check that the interlock plungers are correctly fitted by moving the central 3rd/4th selector shaft to the 3rd speed position; the remaining shafts should now be locked in position. Return the shaft to neutral after the check.

15 Tighten the interlock plug into the gearbox casing.

16 Align the selector fork holes with the shaft holes and tap the roll pins in until flush with the forks.

17 Lubricate the front countergear thrust washer with a little gearbox oil, and locate it over the countershaft with the oil groove side towards the countergear.

18 Lower the countergear assembly into the gearbox and through the rear bearing aperture, then insert the front of the shaft through the casing and locate the rectangular shaft and projection in the bearing retainer. With the shaft fitted correctly, the end of the countergear will be 0.37 in (9.5 mm) from the rear end of the shaft.

19 Expand the circlip and tap the countergear rear bearing outer track into the casing, then slide the needle roller cage onto the countergear.

20 Hold the reverse idle gear in position with the groove towards the rear of the gearbox and insert the shaft. Make sure that the selector arm is engaged in the groove.

21 With the dowel bolt holes in alignment, tighten the reverse gear shaft retaining bolt to the specified torque.

22 Locate the counter 5th gear over the end of the countergear with the grooved side towards the gearbox casing to give running clearance for the bearing outer track. Tap it fully onto the countergear and retain with a circlip selected to eliminate any movement of the 5th gear.

23 Place the thrust washer over the countergear shaft and temporarily fit the extension housing with a new gasket, tightening the retaining bolts to the specified torque.

24 Using a feeler gauge check the clearance between the front of the countergear and the thrust washer. If it is not within the specified limits, the rear thrust washer must be changed for one of suitable thickness. Remove the extension housing after making the check.

25 Slide the 5th gear and needle roller bearing over the end of the mainshaft and engage it with the counter 5th gear.

26 Locate the synchro ring on the gear cone, then slide the synchro hub and retainer ring onto the mainshaft splines, making sure that the sliding keys engage the slots in the ring. The tapered side of the synchro sleeve must face rearwards.

27 Fit the circlip to the mainshaft, then measure the 5th gear endfloat with a feeler gauge. If necessary substitute the circlip with a new one selected to give an endfloat within the specified limits.

28 Fit the 5th gear shift arm bracket and tighten the two crosshead retaining screws. Make sure that the selector fork is engaged with the groove in the synchro sleeve, the selector arm is engaged with the selector shaft, and the bracket base is entered in the reverse shaft slot.

29 Insert the four detent balls and springs and fit the top cover with a new gasket. Tighten the retaining nuts evenly.

30 With the reverse selector in neutral, check the clearance between the reverse idle gear and first speed gear teeth. If necessary, loosen the selector arm pivot locknut and turn the adjusting screw until the clearance is betweem 0.04 and 0.08 in (1.0 and 2.0 mm). Tighten the locknut.

31 Move the reverse/5th gear selector to 5th speed position and check the clearance between the synchro sleeve and the counter 5th gear teeth (Fig. 6.32). If necessary, loosen the selector arm pivot locknut and turn the adjusting screw until the clearance is between 0.04 and 0.08 in (1.0 and 2.0 mm). Tighten the locknut.

32 Fit the circlip, locking ball, speedometer drivegear and second circlip to the rear end of the mainshaft.

33 Check that the countergear rear thrust washer is in place with the oil groove towards the counter 5th gear.

34 With the gearbox on end, lower the extension housing into position. Make sure that the gear selector lever shaft engages with the selector fork shafts, and that the new gasket is located correctly.

35 Coat the threads of the retaining bolts with jointing compound, then insert and tighten them to the specified torque in diagonal sequence.

36 Fit a new gasket to the bottom cover and secure it with the nuts and washers, tightening them in diagonal sequence to the specified

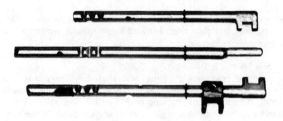

Fig. 6.29 The selector shafts (type K50) (Sec 16)

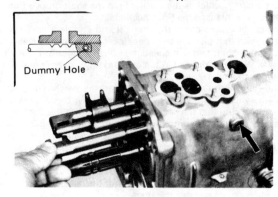

Fig. 6.30 1st/2nd selector shaft dummy hole location and interlock access hole – arrowed (type K50) (Sec 16)

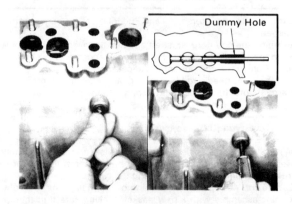

Fig. 6.31 Fitting the interlock plungers (type K50) (Sec 16)

Fig. 6.32 Adjusting the 5th gear synchro sleeve to countergear clearance A (type K50) (Sec 16)

torque.

37 Insert the speedometer driven gear to the extension housing and secure it with the clamp and bolt.

38 Refit the clutch release fork and bearing with reference to Chapter 5.

39 Fit the gearshift lever retainer with a new gasket and tighten the securing bolts in diagonal sequence.

40 Insert and tighten the reversing lamp switch.

41 Fit the rear mounting crossmember to the extension housing and tighten the retaining bolts.

42 Temporarily refit the gearstick and check that all gears are obtained with smooth operation.

17 Fault diagnosis – gearbox

Symptom	Reason/s
Ineffective synchromesh	Worn synchro rings or sliding keys Weak synchro springs
Jumps out of one or more gears	Weak detent springs Worn shift fork or selector shaft groove Worn synchro unit and engagement dogs
Noise, roughness, vibration or whining	Worn bearings or gears
Difficult gear engagement	Worn selector components Clutch fault

Chapter 7 Propeller shaft

For modifications, and information applicable to later models, see Supplement at end of manual

Contents

Specifications

Type .... Tubular steel, one-piece

Maximum spider side-play .... 0.002 in (0.05 mm)

Maximum run-out .... 0.010 in (0.25 mm)

Spider circlip sizes
Plain .... 0.047 in (1.20 mm)
Brown .... 0.049 in (1.25 mm)
Blue .... 0.051 in (1.30 mm)

Torque wrench settings	lbf ft	kgf m
Flange nuts and bolts (gold)	15	2.2

1 General description

1 The drive from the gearbox to the rear axle is transmitted by a tubular propeller shaft. Due to the variety of angles caused by the up and down motion of the rear axle in relation to the gearbox, universal joints are fitted to each end of the shaft.

2 As the movement also increases and decreases the distance between the rear axle and the gearbox, the forward end of the propeller shaft has a splined sleeve which is a sliding fit over the rear of the gearbox splined mainshaft.

3 The splined sleeve runs in an oil seal in the gearbox mainshaft rear cover, and is supported with the mainshaft on the gearbox rear bearing.

4 The splines are lubricated by oil in the rear cover coming from the gearbox.

5 The universal joints each comprise a four-way trunnion, or spider, each leg of which runs in a needle roller bearing race, preloaded with grease and fitted in the bearing journal yokes of the sliding sleeve and the propeller shaft and flange.

2 Propeller shaft – removal and refitting

1 Jack-up the rear of the car and support on firmly based axle stands.

2 The rear of the propeller shaft is connected to the rear axle pinion flange by four nuts and bolts. Mark the position of both flanges relative to each other, and then undo and remove the nuts and bolts (photo).

3 Move the propeller shaft forwards to disengage it from the pinion flange and then lower it to the ground.

4 Draw the other end of the propeller shaft, that is the splined sleeve, out of the rear of the gearbox rear cover (photo). The shaft is then clear for removal from the underside of the car.

5 Place a container under the gearbox rear cover opening so as to catch any oil which will certainly drip out.

6 Refitting the propeller shaft is the reverse sequence to removal but the following additional points should be noted:

   (a) *Ensure that the mating marks on the propeller shaft and differential pinion flange are lined up*

   (b) *Do not forget to check the gearbox oil level and top-up if necessary*

   (c) *Tighten the bolts holding the flange to the differential to the specified torque setting. Make sure that the nuts are towards the rear of the car*

3 Universal joints – testing for wear

1 Wear in the needle roller bearings is characterised by vibration in the transmission, 'clonks' on taking up the drive and in extreme cases

2.2 Propeller shaft rear universal joint and flange

2.4 Propeller shaft front universal joint and splined sleeve

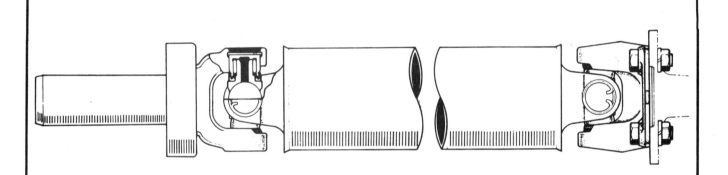
Fig. 7.1 Cutaway view of the propeller shaft (Sec 1)

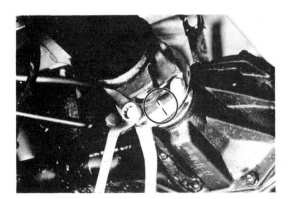

Fig. 7.2 Flange alignment marks (Sec 2)

Fig. 7.3 Removing a universal joint circlip (Sec 4)

Fig. 7.4 Removing a universal joint bearing cup (Sec 4)

Fig. 7.5 Using a socket and vice to press a universal joint bearing cup into the yoke (Sec 4)

of lack of lubrication, metallic squeaking, and ultimately grating and shrieking sounds as the bearings break up.

2   It is easy to check whether or not the needle roller bearings are worn with the propeller shaft in position by trying to turn the shaft with one hand, and the other hand holding the rear axle flange. Any movement between the propeller shaft and the flange is indicative of con-

siderable wear. If worn, the old bearings and spiders will have to be discarded and a repair kit comprising new universal joint spiders, bearings, circlips and oil seals purchased.

3   It is important to note that there could be difficulty in obtaining an overhaul kit in certain areas so ensure that one is to hand before commencing work.

4   The front needle roller bearings should be tested for wear using the same principle as described in paragraph 2.

5   To test the splined coupling for wear, lift the end of the shaft and note any movement in the splines.

6   Check the splined coupling dust cover for signs of damage or looseness on the shaft.

___

4   Universal joints – dismantling, inspection and reassembly

1   Clean away all traces of dirt and grease from the universal joint yoke. Using a pair of circlip pliers, compress the circlips and lift away. If the circlips are tight in their grooves tap the ends to shock move the bearing cups slightly.

2   Before disassembly, mark the two yokes to ensure correct reassembly and avoid vibration.

3   The bearing cups may be removed by one of two methods. Either hit the yoke (supported in the hand) adjacent to the bearing cup hole with a hammer or mallet until the cup begins to emerge or press the cup out in a vice using an old bearing cup on one side and tubular spacer or a large socket on the other to receive the ejected cup. With both methods, screw the cups out of their seats once they have emerged far enough to be able to grip them with a self-locking wrench.

4   Repeat the procedure on the other bearing cups and free the spider from the yoke.

5   Clean all parts thoroughly and check the yoke bearing apertures for damage. Any small nicks should be smoothed down carefully with a fine file. If the yokes are cracked or badly damaged they must be renewed ie, exchange propshaft.

6   If possible check the maximum shaft runout at the centre using V-blocks and a dial indicator gauge. The runout should not exceed the amount specified.

7   Slide the splined section onto the gearbox mainshaft and check for spline wear both radially and vertically.

8   If the needle bearings are worn it is probable that the spider trunnions are worn also, necessitating renewal.

9   The old circlips should be discarded and new ones obtained. However, in order to ascertain the spider side-play, they may be refitted initially and if the amount is within the specified limits, new circlips of the same size should be obtained. Refer to the Specifications for details of the various sizes available. Always fit circlips of the same thickness at opposite ends of the spider.

10   Check that new needle roller bearings and cups are free from dirt and the grease seals are in position.

11   Make sure the marks on each yoke are aligned and, with the spider in position, press the cups through each yoke aperture using an old bearing cup or socket onto the respective spider arm.

12   Check carefully that the needle rollers remain in the correct position. If necessary, add a little more grease inside the cup to hold the rollers in place.

13   Lock the cups in position with the new circlips. Check the spider movement, and if it is tight try tapping the yokes with a hammer. If this does not do the trick then something is amiss requiring investigation.

___

5 Fault diagnosis – propeller shaft

Symptom	Reason/s
Propeller shaft vibration	Propeller shaft distorted or out of balance Universal joints worn Splined sleeve worn Loose flange securing bolts
Knock or clunk when taking up drive or changing gear	Universal joints worn Splined sleeve worn Loose flange securing bolts

Chapter 8 Rear axle

For modifications, and information applicable to later models, see Supplement at end of manual

Contents

Specifications

Type .... Semi-floating, hypoid

Ratio 3.909:1

Axleshaft
Oil seal fitting depth .... 0.22 in (5.6 mm)
Run-out limit midway along shaft .... 0.08 in (2.0 mm)
Flange run-out limit on end face .... 0.01 in (0.2 mm)

Pinion
Oil seal fitting depth .... 0.04 in (1.0 mm)
Starting preload:
    Old bearing .... 3.5 to 6.1 lbf in (4.0 to 7.0 kgf cm)
    New bearing .... 5.6 to 10.9 lbf ft (6.5 to 12.5 kgf cm)

Lubricant capacity .... 1.8 Imp pints (1.0 litres)

Torque wrench settings

	lbf ft	kgf m
Axleshaft bearing retainer nuts	50	6.9
Pinion flange nut (maximum initial tightening)	80	11.1
Differential carrier to axle tube	25	3.5
Shock absorber lower mounting bolts	30	4.1
Upper control arm mounting bolts	100	13.8
Lower control arm mounting bolts	70	9.7

1 General description

1 The rear axle is of hypoid semi-floating type. The differential and hypoid gear pinion are carried on taper roller bearings, and are housed in a differential casing which is bolted to the banjo type axle tube.

2 The axle tube (or housing) is located both laterally and longitudinally by two upper and two lower control arms attached to the body underframe. Two coil springs support the weight of the body, and gas-filled telescopic shock absorbers dampern the up and down movement of the axle assembly.

3 The axleshafts (or halfshafts) are splined into the differential side gears and are supported at the ends of the axle tubes by ball bearings held by the bearing retainer plates.

2 Axleshaft (halfshaft) – removal, overhaul and refitting

1 Chock the front wheels, jack-up the rear of the car and support it with axle stands. Remove the roadwheels.

2 Remove the brake drum (see Chapter 9).

3 Unscrew and remove the bearing retainer securing nuts with a socket inserted through the axleshaft flange holes (Fig. 8.3).

4 The axleshaft and bearing must now be removed from the axle casing. This is best carried out using a slide hammer attached to the studs in the flange, but if the bearing is not too tight the roadwheel can be refitted to the studs and the axleshaft pulled out carefully. Failing this, insert two suitable length bolts from the rear of the backplate through the axle casing with nuts next to the outer face of the backplate. Screw the bolts in against the flange until the bearing is removed.

5 Remove the axleshaft from the axle tube, being careful not to allow oil to drip onto the brake shoes, then remove the gasket.

6 Examine the oil seal in the axle tube and, if necessary, renew it by prising it out and fitting the new one to the specified depth using a drift of suitable diameter (Fig. 8.4).

7 Examine the bearing for wear and damage. Note that it is pre-packed with grease and should not therefore be cleaned with any solvent.

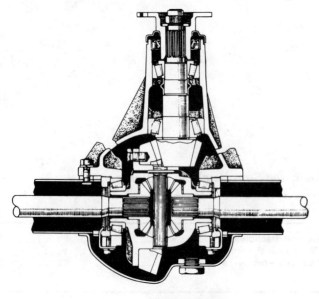

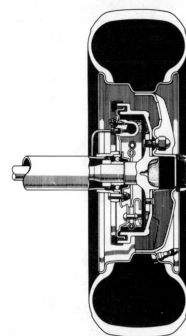

Fig. 8.1 Cutaway view of the differential assembly (top) and axleshaft bearing (bottom) (Sec 1)

8   If it is necessary to fit a new bearing, obtain a new one together with a retaining ring.

9   Grind away the retaining ring at one point through three quarters of its thickness, then use a cold chisel to sever the ring (Fig. 8.6). Make sure that the axleshaft is not damaged.

10   Press the bearing off the axleshaft and remove the retainer plate.

11   Clean the components and wipe them dry.

12   Slide the retainer and new bearing onto the axleshaft. Drive the shaft fully into the bearing with the bearing inner race supported on a vice (Fig. 8.7).

13   Heat the new bearing retaining ring to 150°C (300°F) in an oven or an oil bath, then quickly drive the shaft fully into the ring using the procedure described in paragraph 12.

14   When the ring has cooled wipe the complete shaft clean.

15   Smear the new gasket with a liquid sealer and place it on the retainer plate with the gasket cut-out and retainer oil channel in alignment (Fig. 8.9).

16   Apply a little multi-purpose grease to the seal lip and bearing outer race.

17   Insert the axleshaft into the axle tube, being careful not to damage the oil seal and internal oil deflector. Make sure that the retainer oil channel is facing downwards.

18   Drive the bearing into the axle tube by tapping the end of the axleshaft with a mallet, then tighten the retaining nuts in diagonal sequence to the specified torque.

19   Refit the brake drum and roadwheel, and lower the car to the ground.

3   Pinion oil seal – removal and refitting

1   Jack-up the rear of the car and support it on axle stands.

2   Mark the propeller shaft and pinion flanges in relation to each other and remove the four retaining bolts. Tie the propeller shaft to one side.

3   Bolt a length of flat steel to two adjacent holes in the pinion flange.

4   Mark the pinion, pinion nut, and pinion flange in relation to each other. This is necessary in order to maintain the pinion bearing preload. Failure to take this precaution will necessitate removing the front bearing and renewing the collapsible spacer.

5   Using a chisel, tap the staked part of the pinion nut from the end of the pinion.

6   Unscrew the nut with a socket, counting the number of turns to remove it.

7   Pull the flange from the pinion splines and ease the oil seal from the differential casing with a screwdriver.

8   Refitting is a reversal of removal, but the following points should be noted:

   (a) *Drive in the oil seal to the specified depth and lubricate its lip with a little grease*
   (b) *Apply grease to the pinion threads before tightening the nut to its exact original position. Do not exceed the specified initial tightening torque*
   (c) *Lock the nut by staking, and use a torque wrench to check that the starting preload is within the specified limits*
   (d) *Make sure that the previously made marks on the propeller shaft and pinion flanges are aligned*

4   Differential assembly – removal and refitting

   Note: *Due to the specialist equipment and tools required to overhaul the differential unit, overhaul is outside the scope of the home mechanic. Where the unit is excessively worn and noisy, it is recommended that a reconditioned or new assembly be purchased. Remove the differential carrier in the following way.*

1   Remove both axleshafts as described in Section 2.

2   Remove the drain plug and drain the rear axle oil into a suitable container.

3   Mark the propeller shaft and pinion flanges in relation to each other, then remove the four retaining bolts. Tie the propeller shaft to one side.

4   Unscrew and remove the retaining nuts and washers and lift the differential assembly from the rear axle housing.

5   Remove the gasket from the retaining studs.

6   Refitting is a reversal of removal, but the following points should be noted:

   (a) *Wipe clean the mating surfaces of the differential and axle housing*
   (b) *Smear liquid sealer to both sides of the gasket*
   (c) *Fit the differential gasket with its projection uppermost and adjacent to the breather plug*
   (d) *Tighten all nuts to the specified torque*
   (e) *Refill the rear axle with the specified oil to the bottom of the filler plug aperture, and check the tightness of both plugs*

5   Rear axle – removal and refitting

1   Jack-up the rear of the car and place axle stands beneath the body underframe next to the lower control arm mountings on each side.

2   Support the weight of the axle with a trolley jack.

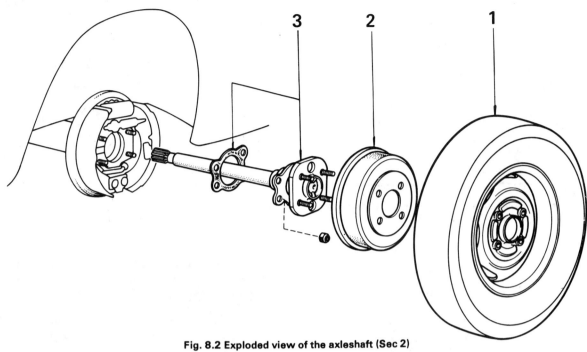

Fig. 8.2 Exploded view of the axleshaft (Sec 2)

1 Roadwheel
2 Brake drum

3 Axleshaft and retainer
   plate and gasket

Fig. 8.3 Unscrewing the bearing retainer plate nuts (Sec 2)

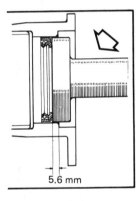

5.6 mm

Fig. 8.4 Axleshaft oil seal fitting (fitting tool arrowed) (Sec 2)

Fig. 8.5 Checking the axleshaft bearing (Sec 2)

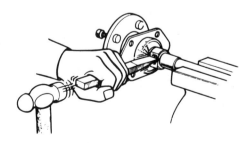

Fig. 8.6 Removing the axleshaft bearing retaining ring (Sec 2)

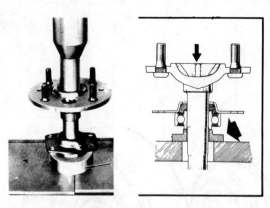

Fig. 8.7 Fitting the axleshaft bearing using a distance piece (arrowed) (Sec 2)

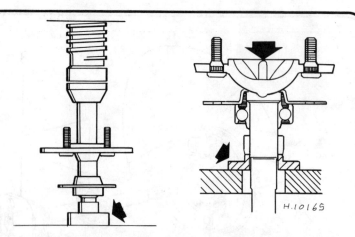

Fig. 8.8 Fitting the axleshaft bearing retaining ring using a distance piece (arrowed) (Sec 2)

Fig. 8.9 Axleshaft bearing retainer plate oil channel and gasket cutout (arrowed) (Sec 2)

Fig. 8.11 Staking the pinion nut (Sec 3)

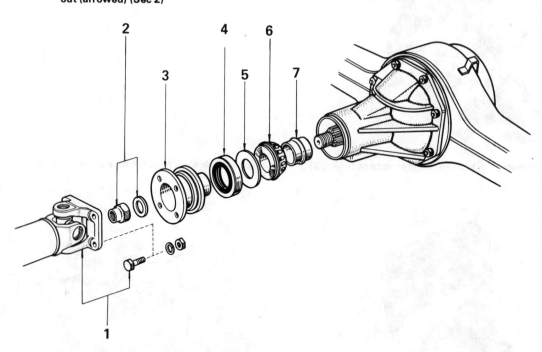

Fig. 8.10 Exploded view of the differential assembly front bearing and pinion oil seal (Sec 3)

1 Propeller shaft and bolt
2 Pinion nut and washer
3 Pinion flange
4 Pinion oil seal
5 Oil thrower
6 Front bearing
7 Collapsible spacer

3   Remove the roadwheels, then loosen the control arm mountings on the rear axle and body underframe.

4   Mark the propeller shaft and pinion flanges in relation to each other, and remove the four retaining bolts. Tie the propeller shaft to one side.

5   Drain the rear axle oil into a suitable container and retighten the drain plug.

6   Unscrew and remove the control arm mounting bolts from the axle housing and swivel the control arms away.

7   Temporarily remove the brake drums and disconnect the handbrake cables from the brake shoe levers (see Chapter 9); the handbrake lever must first be released.

8   To reduce the loss of brake fluid, seal the reservoir cap vent hole with adhesive tape or seal the edge of the cap to the reservoir body, again using adhesive tape.

9   Unscrew the union on top of the axle casing, disconnect the brake hose, and plug both ends.

10 Unscrew and remove the shock absorber lower mounting bolts and lower the rear axle to release the coil spring tension.

11 Support the rear axle and remove the coil springs and seats. The rear axle may now be lowered and removed from beneath the car.

12 Refitting is a reversal of removal, but the following additional points must be observed:

  (a) *Delay fully tightening the control rod mounting bolts until the weight of the car is on the axle*

  (b) *Remove the adhesive tape from the brake fluid reservoir and*

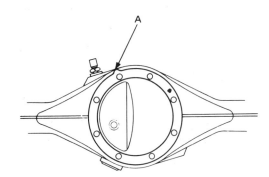

Fig. 8.12 Correct location of the differential gasket protrusion (A) when viewed from the front (Sec 4)

   bleed the brakes as described in Chapter 9
  (c) *With the car on level ground, refill the rear axle with the specified oil to the bottom of the filler plug aperture, then insert and tighten the filler plug*
  (d) *Check that the coil springs are positioned correctly in their seats*

6   Fault diagnosis – rear axle

Symptom	Reason/s
Vibration	Worn axleshaft bearing
	Loose pinion flange bolts
	Roadwheels out of balance (usually evident only at high speeds)
	Propeller shaft out of balance
	Worn crownwheel and pinion
Excessive noise	Worn axleshaft, differential or pinion bearings
	Incorrect pinion bearing preload
	Lack of oil or incorrect grade
Clunk on acceleration or deceleration	Worn crownwheel and pinion
	Loose pinion flange bolts
Frequent renewal of oil seals	Blocked axle housing breather

Chapter 9 Braking system

For modifications, and information applicable to later models, see Supplement at end of manual

Contents

Specifications

Type . . . . 4-wheel dual circuit hydraulic, servo-assisted (in UK), discs front, self-adjusting drums rear. Handbrake mechanical to rear wheels

Discs
Standard thickness . . . . 0.39 in (10.0 mm)
Minimum thickness . . . . 0.35 in (9.0 mm)
Maximum runout . . . . 0.006 in (0.15 mm)
Minimum pad lining thickness . . . . 0.04 in (1.0 mm)

Drums
Maximum inside diameter . . . . 7.95 in (202 mm)
Minimum lining thickness . . . . 0.04 in (1.0 mm)
Handbrake lever to shoe web clearance . . . . 0.014 in (0.35 mm)
Shoe to drum clearance . . . . 0.02 in (0.6 mm)

Pedal adjustment
Height from floorpan waterproof covering to pad (released) . . . . . . 6.91 to 6.95 in (175.5 to 176. 5 mm)
Free play:
    With servo . . . . 0.12 to 0.23 in (3.0 to 6.0 mm)
    Without servo . . . . 0.02 to 0.20 in (0.5 to 5.0 mm)

Servo
Pushrod to piston clearance:
    Nil vacuum . . . . 0.024 to 0.026 in (0.60 to 0.65 mm)
    Idling vacuum . . . . 0.004 to 0.02 in (0.1 to 0.5 mm)

Handbrake
Normal travel . . . . 3 to 6 notches

Torque wrench settings

	lbf ft	kgf m
Pedal shaft nut	30	4.1
Flexible hose to caliper	18	2.5
Hydraulic pipe union nut	13	1.8
Master cylinder stop bolt	10	1.4

Master cylinder check valve	35	4.8
Caliper mounting bolt	15	2.1
Disc to hub bolt	35	4.8
Disc backplate to steering knuckle	35	4.8
Rear axleshaft bearing retainer plate	50	6.9

1 General description

1   The braking system is of dual circuit hydraulic type, with discs at the front and self-adjusting drum brakes at the rear. A vacuum servo unit is fitted as standard equipment to UK models.

2   The pressure regulating valve is fitted in the hydraulic circuit to prevent the rear wheel locking in advance of the front wheels. The valve incorporates a differential pressure warning switch which illuminates the instrument panel warning light if low hydraulic pressure exists in either the front or rear braking system. The same warning light is operated if the master cylinder fluid level is low, or if the handbrake is applied.

3   The handbrake is mechanically operated on the rear wheels only.

4   The front disc calipers are of the single piston type.

2 Disc pads – inspection and renewal

1   Apply the handbrake, prise off the hub cover, slacken the wheel nuts, jack-up the front of the car and support it on axle stands. Remove the road wheel. Note that the disc pads should be renewed on one wheel at a time, otherwise a caliper piston may be displaced.

2   Measure the disc pad lining thickness through the inspection hole at the front of the caliper. Check both disc pads and if the lining is below the specified thickness, renew both pads.

3   To remove the pads, unscrew and remove the caliper mounting bolts while holding the bush hexagons stationary (photos). Withdraw the caliper from the disc and place it on the front anti-roll bar so that the flexible hose is not strained.

4   Remove the inner pad from the housing, then remove the outer pad together with the anti-squeal shim (photos).

5   Prise the anti-rattle springs and guides from the housing.

6   Remove the inner pad support spring from the caliper mounting.

7   Brush any dust or dirt from the caliper recesses, the housing, and springs. Do not inhale the dust as it is harmful. Using a piece of wood, press the piston into the caliper to accommodate the new linings. Keep an eye on the brake fluid level in the reservoir during this operation and, if necessary, syphon some out to prevent it overflowing.

8   Fitting of the new pads is a reversal of the removal procedure, but the following points must be observed:

   (a) Lift the anti-rattle springs to insert the outer disc pad and make sure that the anti-squeal shim is seated correctly on the outer pad

   (b) Make sure that the anti-squeal shim is fitted in the piston bore

   (c) Hold the bush hexagons stationary while tightening the caliper retaining bolts to the specified torque. If this precaution is not taken, uneven disc pad wear may occur

   (d) With the disc pads fitted, depress the footbrake pedal several times, and if necessary top-up the master cylinder fluid level

3 Rear brake shoes – inspection and renewal

1   Securely chock the front wheel, jack-up the rear of the car and remove the roadwheels. Fully release the handbrake lever. Support the car with axle stands placed beneath the axle tube.

2   Withdraw the brake drum from the wheel studs. If this proves difficult, extract the rubber plug from the brake backplate and use two

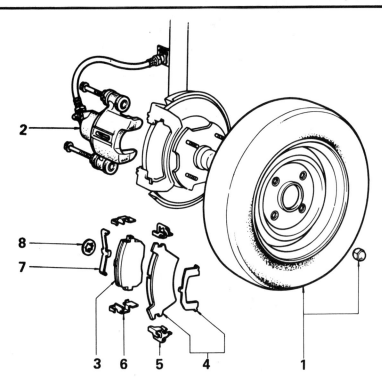

Fig. 9.1 Exploded view of a front disc caliper (Sec 2)

1 Wheel	4 Outer disc pad and anti-	6 Guide plate
2 Caliper	squeal shim	7 Support plate
3 Inner disc pad	5 Anti-rattle spring	8 Anti-squeal shim

2.3A Unscrewing the brake caliper mounting bolts

2.3B Removing the brake caliper mounting bolts

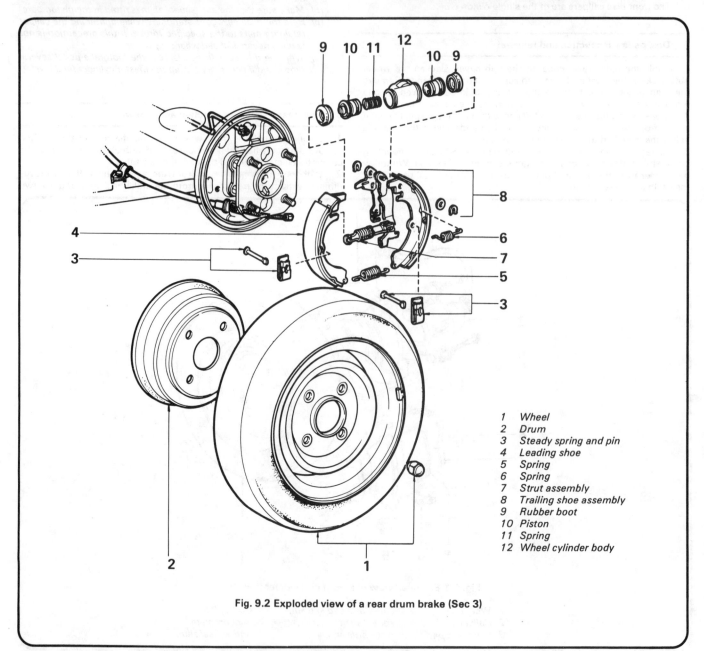

1 Wheel
2 Drum
3 Steady spring and pin
4 Leading shoe
5 Spring
6 Spring
7 Strut assembly
8 Trailing shoe assembly
9 Rubber boot
10 Piston
11 Spring
12 Wheel cylinder body

Fig. 9.2 Exploded view of a rear drum brake (Sec 3)

2.4A Removing the inner disc pad

2.4B Removing the outer disc pad

3.4 Trailing rear brake shoe components (right-hand side)

3.5A Rear brake automatic adjuster strut assembly (right-hand side)

3.5B Rear brake shoe lower anchor (right-hand side)

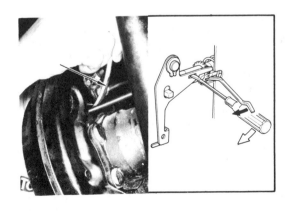

Fig. 9.3 Method of releasing rear brake shoes (Sec 3)

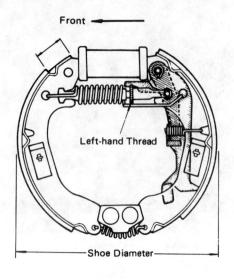

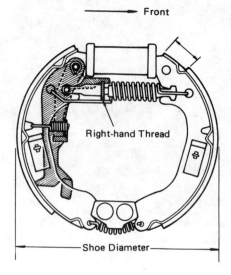

Fig. 9.4 Correct fitted positions of the rear brake shoes (Sec 3)

screwdrivers to lift the automatic adjuster lever and back off the toothed wheel on the adjuster strut (Fig. 9.3).

3   Brush away any accumulated dust, taking care not to inhale it, and inspect the linings. If the friction material is worn below the specified limit, renew the shoes as a complete axle set. If the linings are in good condition, clean and refit the drum.

4   To renew the shoes, first depress the shoe steady springs with a pair of pliers and turn them through 90° to release them from the pins (photo).

5   Disconnect the upper shoe return spring and expand the shoes over the lower anchor. Disconnect the lower shoe return spring (photos).

6   Remove the leading shoe and strut, then disconnect the spring and remove the strut.

7   Disconnect the handbrake cable from the lever and withdraw the trailing shoe.

8   Disconnect the short spring and extract the C-washer. The handbrake lever and automatic adjuster lever can now be transferred to the new shoe. If necessary, separate the two levers after extracting the retaining C-washer.

9   Turn the toothed wheel on the adjuster strut so that the strut is fully retracted.

10 Inspect the springs, levers and strut for wear, and renew them as necessary.

11 Using a feeler gauge, check the clearance between the trailing shoe web and the handbrake lever. If necessary, fit a shim between the C-washer and the shoe web to obtain the specified clearance.

12 Clean the brake backplate and check for oil leakage (see Chapter 8) or a leaking wheel cylinder. If evident, the fault should be rectified before proceeding.

13 Refer to Fig. 9.4 and note the position of the brake shoes in relation to the front of the car. The shoes must be assembled as shown.

14 Smear a little brake grease on the rubbing surfaces of the backplate and on the shoe web ends.

15 Connect the handbrake cable to the lever on the trailing shoe with the short return spring disconnected, then fit the spring.

16 Fit the strut and spring to the leading shoe, locate it on the backplate, then locate the trailing shoe on the backplate and refit the lower return spring. Make sure that both shoes are engaged correctly on the lower anchor.

17 Fit the upper return spring to the trailing shoe, making sure that the strut is located correctly and the shoe webs are engaged in the wheel cylinder piston grooves.

18 Fit the two shoe steady springs to the pins with the open ends facing upwards.

19 Centralise the brake shoes so that the lining contour matches that

of the backplate. Now expand the shoes by turning the toothed adjuster wheel until the point is reached where the brake drum will just slide over them and any further rotation of the adjuster wheel would obstruct the fitting of the drum.

20 Fit the brake drum, roadwheel, and backplate plug.

21 Repeat the procedure on the remaining rear brake, then operate the handbrake lever several times. With the lever applied, both rear wheels should be locked, and with it fully released both wheels should be free. If necessary adjust the handbrake as described in Section 15.

22 Lower the car to the ground.

---

4   Disc caliper – removal, servicing and refitting

1   Jack-up the front of the car and support it on axle stands. Remove the roadwheel.

2   Remove the disc pads as described in Section 2.

3   To prevent loss of hydraulic fluid during subsequent operations, either seal the master cylinder at the vent hole and round the rim of the cap with adhesive tape, or clamp the flexible hose with a suitable clamp, being careful not to damage the hose.

4   Loosen the flexible hose union at the caliper and unscrew the caliper from the hose. Retain the sealing washer, and plug the end of the hose to prevent entry of foreign matter.

5   With the caliper removed, clean the external surfaces.

6   Extract the spring retaining ring and prise out the dust excluder with a screwdriver.

7   Remove the piston from the caliper by applying air pressure to the union inlet with a footpump. Take care not to damage the piston.

8   Extract the piston seal from the caliper bore with a small screwdriver, being careful not to scratch the bore surface.

9   Press the mounting bushes from the caliper and remove the rubber boots and collars.

10 Clean all components in fresh brake fluid or methylated spirit and wipe dry with a lint-free cloth.

11 Discard the piston seal and dust excluder and obtain a repair kit. Inspect the surfaces of the piston and caliper bore; if any scratches or bright wear areas are evident, the complete caliper must be renewed.

12 Smear some rubber grease or brake fluid on the piston seal and locate it in the caliper bore groove using the fingers only.

13 Smear the piston with rubber grease or brake fluid and press it fully into the caliper through the seal.

14 Smear the dust excluder with rubber grease or brake fluid, locate it over the piston, and refit the retaining ring.

15 Fit the collars, rubber boots, and mounting bushes to the caliper. At the same time smear the components with rubber grease to ensure

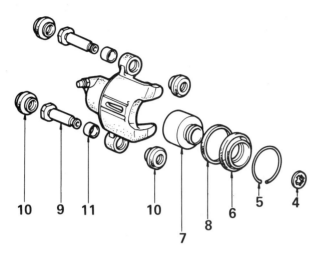

Fig. 9.5 Exploded view of the disc caliper cylinder assembly (Sec 3)

4 Anti-squeal shim	8 Seal
5 Retaining ring	9 Slide bush
6 Dust excluder	10 Boot
7 Piston	11 Collar

5.2 Removing the disc backplate housing (without the caliper)

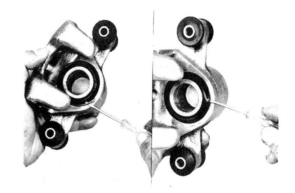

Fig. 9.6 Removing the retaining ring and dust excluder from the caliper (Sec 4)

Fig. 9.7 Removing a brake disc from the hub (Sec 5)

Fig. 9.8 Rear wheel cylinder components (Sec 6)

a free sliding action of the caliper.

16 Remove the plug from the flexible hose, locate the sealing washer, and screw the caliper onto the hose.

17 Refit the disc pads as described in Section 2.

18 Tighten the flexible hose union to the specified torque.

19 Remove the adhesive tape from the fluid reservoir or the clamp from the flexible hose, and bleed the hydraulic system as described in Section 14.

20 Refit the roadwheel and lower the car to the ground.

5 Brake disc – examination, removal and refitting

1 Jack-up the front of the car and support it on axle stands. Remove the roadwheel.

2 Unscrew and remove the disc backplate to steering knuckle retaining bolts, withdraw the assembly from the disc, and place it on the front anti-roll bar so that the flexible hose is not strained (photo).

3 Examine the disc for deep scoring or grooving. Light scoring is permissible but, if severe, the disc must be removed and either renewed or machined, provided the thickness will not be reduced below the

specified minimum.

4 Check the disc for run-out using feeler blades or a dial gauge. To be serviceable, the specified maximum disc run-out must not be exceeded. Take care not to confuse front wheel bearing endfloat with disc run-out.

5 If the disc is to be removed, first withdraw the hub/disc assembly as described in Chapter 11.

6 Unscrew and remove the four bolts securing the disc to the hub and separate the two components.

7 Refitting is a reversal of removal, but make sure that the mating surfaces are clean and tighten the disc and backplate retaining bolts to the specified torque. Adjust the front wheel bearings as described in Chapter 11.

6 Rear wheel cylinder – removal, servicing and refitting

1 Chock the front wheels, jack-up the rear of the car and support it on axle stands. Remove the roadwheel.

2 Remove the rear brake shoes as described in Section 3.

3 To prevent unnecessary loss of hydraulic fluid in subsequent

operations, seal the master cylinder reservoir cap or vent with adhesive tape to create a vacuum.

4   Prise the rubber boots from each end of the wheel cylinder.
5   Extract the pistons from the wheel cylinder bore.
6   Remove the internal spring.
7   Disconnect the hydraulic line and unbolt the wheel cylinder from the backplate. Plug the line to prevent entry of foreign matter. Remove the bleed screw.
8   Clean all components with fresh hydraulic fluid or methylated spirit. Inspect the surfaces of the pistons and cylinder bore; if any scoring or bright wear areas are evident, renew the complete assembly.
9   Prise the rubber seals from the pistons and discard them. Obtain a wheel cylinder repair kit.
10   Dip the pistons in clean hydraulic fluid and fit the new seals, using the fingers only to manipulate them into position. Make sure that the seal lips are facing the correct way (see Fig. 9.8).
11   Refitting is a reversal of removal, but the following points must be observed:

(a) Tighten the hydraulic line union to the specified torque
(b) Refit the brake shoes as described in Section 3
(c) Remove the adhesive tape from the master cylinder reservoir and bleed the hydraulic system as described in Section 14

7   Brake drum – inspection and renovation

1   After high mileages the brake drums should be examined for deterioration and wear. If excessive scoring is evident, the drum must either be renewed or ground by an engineering works. If the drum is to be ground, the specified maximum internal diameter must not be exceeded (photo).

8   Rear brake backplate – removal and refitting

1   Chock the front wheels, jack-up the rear of the car and support it on axle stands. Remove the roadwheel.
2   Remove the brake shoes as described in Section 3.
3   Remove the wheel cylinder as described in Section 6.
4   Remove the axleshaft (halfshaft) as described in Chapter 8.
5   Prise out the handbrake cable and withdraw the backplate and gasket from the axle tube.
6   Clean the mating surfaces of the axle tube and backplate.
7   Refitting is a reversal of removal, but the following points must be observed:

(a) One of two gasket thicknesses must be selected according to the thickness of the backplate flange. If the flange thickness is between 0·084 and 0·093 in (2·14 and 2·36 mm) a 0·024 in (0·6 mm) thick gasket must be fitted. If the flange thickness is between 0·3 and 0·097 in (2·36 and 2·46 mm) a 0·012 in (0·3 mm) thick gasket must be fitted
(c) Follow the refitting procedures given in Chapter 8 and in Sections 6 and 3 of this Chapter

9   Master cylinder – removal, servicing and refitting

1   The master cylinder is of tandem type and is mounted on the front face of the servo unit on UK models and on the bulkhead on some non-UK models (photo).
2   Disconnect the fluid level wiring at the plug.
3   Remove the reservoir cap and float and syphon out the hydraulic fluid (photo). Take care not to spill any fluid onto the paintwork.
4   Disconnect the brake pipes from the master cylinder and wipe

7.1 Rear drum maximum diameter detail location

9.1 Brake master cylinder location

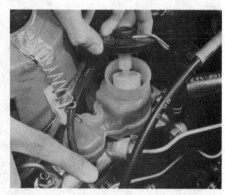
9.3 Removing the brake fluid reservoir cap

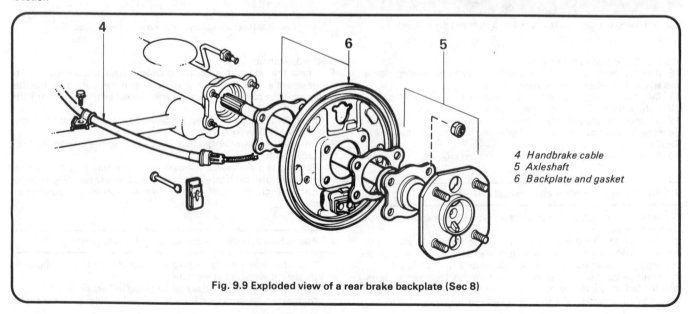

4 Handbrake cable
5 Axleshaft
6 Backplate and gasket

Fig. 9.9 Exploded view of a rear brake backplate (Sec 8)

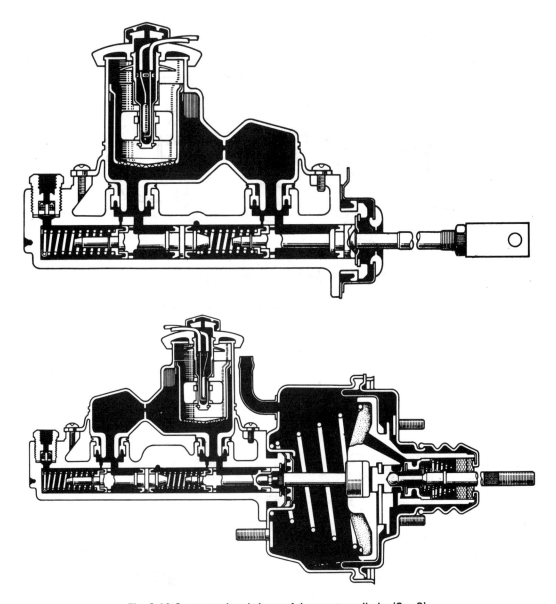

Fig. 9.10 Cross-sectional views of the master cylinder (Sec 9)

Top – without servo   *Bottom – with servo*

away any surplus fluid.

5   On non-UK models, disconnect the pushrod from the brake pedal.

6   Unscrew the retaining nuts and withdraw the master cylinder and gasket.

7   Unscrew the crosshead screws and withdraw the fluid reservoir.

8   Prise the seals from the master cylinder.

9   On UK models, detach the brake pipe and bracket.

10   Unscrew the unions and remove the check valves.

11   Push the pistons fully into the master cylinder and unscrew the stop pin (Fig. 9.13).

12   Extract the circlip from the end of the master cylinder. On non-UK models, remove the pushrod and washer.

13   Withdraw the primary piston and spring.

14   Tap the end of the cylinder on a block of wood to remove the secondary piston and spring. Identify each spring to ensure correct reassembly.

15   Examine the piston and cylinder bore surfaces for scoring or bright wear areas. Where these are evident, renew the complete master cylinder. If the surfaces are good discard the seals and obtain a master

cylinder repair kit. Wash all components with fresh hydraulic fluid or methylated spirit.

16   Fit the new seals to the pistons with reference to Fig. 9.14, using the fingers only to manipulate them into position.

17   Refit the pistons to the master cylinder body by reversing the removal procedure and similarly reassemble the remaining components. Tighten the stop bolt and unions to the specified torque.

18   Locate the rubber seals in the master cylinder and insert the reservoir. Tighten the crosshead retaining screws, noting that the clearance (A in Fig. 9.15) between the screw head and reservoir is intentional and no washers should be fitted.

19   Insert the float and press the cap onto the reservoir.

20   Where the master cylinder is mounted on a servo, the servo pushrod must be adjusted to achieve the specified fitted clearance. A special tool can be obtained from Toyota for this purpose, but if this is not available, proceed as follows. Unscrew the adjustment bolt until it can be felt to touch the primary piston when the master cylinder is mounted on the servo together with the gasket. Screw in the bolt until it just contacts the primary piston, then screw it in a further small

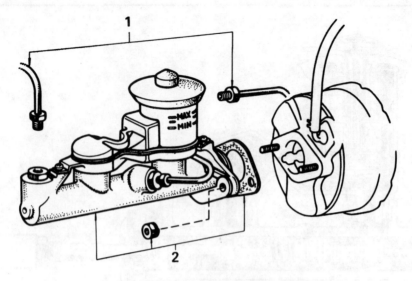

Fig. 9.11 Master cylinder location (Sec 9)

1 *Hydraulic lines*   2 *Master cylinder and gasket*

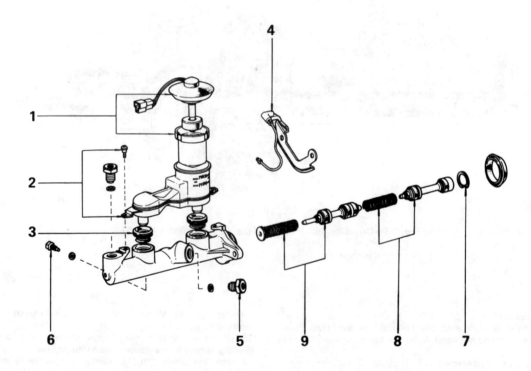

Fig. 9.12 Exploded view of the master cylinder (Sec 9)

1 *Cap and float*   6 *Stop bolt*
2 *Reservoir securing screw*   7 *Circlip*
3 *Seals*   8 *Primary piston and spring*
4 *Bracket and tube*   9 *Secondary piston and spring*
5 *Check valve*

Fig. 9.13 Removing the master cylinder stop bolt (Sec 9)

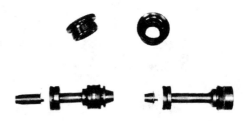

Fig. 9.14 Correct position of master cylinder seals (Sec 9)

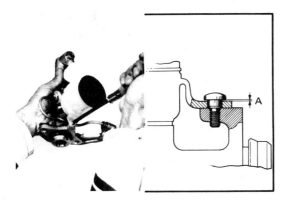

Fig. 9.15 Refitting the master cylinder reservoir, showing clearance A (Sec 9)

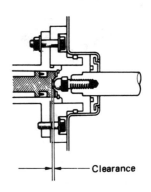

Fig. 9.16 Master cylinder pushrod clearance adjustment (Sec 9)

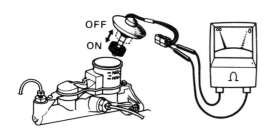

Fig. 9.17 Brake fluid level warning switch operation (Sec 11)

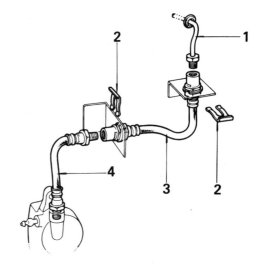

Fig. 9.18 Front brake flexible hose components (Sec 12)

1 Rigid line and grommet   *3 Upper flexible hose*
2 Clip   *4 Lower flexible hose*

amount to achieve the specified clearance (Fig. 9.16). Vernier calipers may be of use to measure the movement of the bolt.
21 Refit and tighten the retaining nuts to the specified torque.
22 The remaining refitting procedure is a reversal of removal, but it will be necessary to bleed the hydraulic system as described in Section 14.

10 Pressure regulating valve – removal and refitting

1 The valve is located on the bulkhead within the engine compartment (photo). If it develops a fault, it must be renewed complete.
2 To remove the valve, first seal the master cylinder reservoir vent or cap using adhesive tape. This will reduce the amount of hydraulic fluid loss by creating a vacuum.
3 Disconnect the hydraulic fluid lines.
4 Disconnect the pressure differential switch supply wire at the plug.

5 Unscrew the mounting bolts and withdraw the valve.
6 Refitting is a reversal of removal, but it will be necessary to bleed the hydraulic system as described in Section 14; remember to remove the adhesive tape from the master cylinder.

11 Brake fluid level warning switch – description and testing

1 The switch is an integral part of the master cylinder reservoir cap. Should the fluid level drop below the minimum limit, the switch contacts will operate the warning light on the instrument panel.
2 To test the switch, disconnect the supply wires at the plug and

10.1 Pressure regulating valve location

12.1 Front hydraulic line connection (flexible to rigid)

remove the cap. Connect a 12 volt test lamp, battery and leads to the two wires; with the float at the bottom of its stroke the lamp should glow, but with the float at the top of its stroke the lamp should be extinguished. If this is not the case, renew the cap and switch assembly.

12 Flexible hoses – inspection, removal and refitting

1   Regularly inspect the condition of the flexible hydraulic hoses. If they are perished, chafed, or swollen they must be renewed (photo).
2   To remove a flexible hose, first disconnect the rigid brake line unions while holding the hose stationary.
3   Extract the retaining clip(s) from the bracket(s) and withdraw the flexible hose.
4   Refitting is a reversal of removal, but take care to enter the union threads correctly and make sure that when fitted, the hose is not twisted and has sufficient clearance from surrounding components. Tighten the unions to the specified torque. Bleed the hydraulic system as described in Section 14.

13 Rigid brake lines – inspection, removal and refitting

1   At regular intervals wipe the steel pipes clean and examine them for signs of rust or denting caused by flying stones.
2   Examine the securing clips. Bend the tongues of the clips if necessary to ensure that they hold the brake pipes securely without letting them rattle or vibrate.
3   Check that the pipes are not touching any adjacent components or rubbing against any part of the vehicle. Where this is observed, bend the pipe gently away to clear.
4   Any section of pipe which is rusty or chafed should be renewed. Brake pipes are available to the correct length and fitted with end unions from most Toyota dealers and can be made to pattern by many accessory suppliers. When fitting the new pipes use the old pipes as a guide to bending and do not make any bends sharper than is necessary.
5   The hydraulic system will of course have to be bled when the circuit has been reconnected.

14 Hydraulic system – bleeding

1   Removal of all the air from the hydraulic system is essential to the correct operation of the braking system. Before undertaking this, examine the fluid reservoir cap to ensure that the vent hole is clear. Check the level of fluid in the reservoir and top-up as required.
2   Check all brake line unions and connections for possible leakage,

and at the same time check the condition of the flexible hoses.
3   If the condition of the caliper or wheel cylinders is in doubt, check for possible signs of fluid leakage.
4   If there is any possibility that incorrect fluid has been used in the system, drain all the fluid out and flush through with methylated spirit. Renew all piston seals and cups since they will be contaminated and could possibly fail under pressure.
5   One advantage of a dual line braking system is that if work is done to either the front or rear part of the system it will only be necessary to bleed half the system provided that the level of fluid in the reservoir has not fallen below half full.
6   Gather together a clean glass jar, a 12 inch (305 mm) length of tubing which fits tightly over the bleed screws and a tin of the correct brake fluid.
7   To bleed the system, clean the area around the rear left-hand wheel bleed screw which is furthest away from the master cylinder and remove the dust cap (photo).
8   Place one end of the tube in the clean jar, which should contain sufficient fluid to keep the end of the tube underneath during the operation, and the other end over the bleed nipple.
9   Open the bleed screw $\frac{1}{4}$-turn with the right sized spanner and have an assistant depress the brake pedal. When the brake pedal reaches the floor close the bleed screw and slowly return the pedal.
10   Open the bleed screw and continue the sequence in paragraph 9 until air ceases to flow from the end of the pipe. At intervals make certain that the reservoir is kept topped-up, otherwise air will enter at this point.
11   Finally press the pedal down fully and hold it there whilst the bleed screw is tightened.
12   Repeat this operation on the right-hand rear brake, and then the right and left front wheels (photos).
13   Wheel completed, check the level of the fluid in the reservoir and then check the feel of the brake pedal, which should be firm and free from any 'spongy' action – which is normally associated with air in the system.
14   Always discard fluid which has been expelled from the hydraulic system, and always top-up the level with fresh fluid which has remained unshaken for the previous 24 hours and has been stored in an airtight container.

15 Handbrake – adjustment

1   The handbrake is normally adjusted automatically by the action of the self-adjusting rear brake mechanism. However, due to cable stretch or when fitting a new cable, adjustment will be required to make sure that the handbrake is fully applied with the lever 3 to 6 notches from the released position.
2   Loosen the locknut located at the base of the handbrake lever; use

a spanner if it is tight (photo).
3   Turn the adjusting knob until the specified adjustment is achieved.
4   Tighten the locknut by hand.
5   If necessary, adjust the handbrake warning switch position.

16 Handbrake lever – removal and refitting

1   Chock the front and rear wheels and fully release the handbrake lever.
2   Unscrew and remove the adjusting knob and locknut from the end

of the cable.
3   Unscrew the mounting bolts and withdraw the handbrake lever. Note the location of the handbrake warning switch.
4   Refitting is a reversal of removal, but it will be necessary to adjust the handbrake as described in Section 15.

17 Handbrake cable – renewal

1   The handbrake cable is in three sections, any of which can if necessary be removed separately.

14.7 Rear wheel cylinder bleed screw location (arrowed)

14.12A Front caliper bleed screw location

14.12B Bleeding a front brake caliper

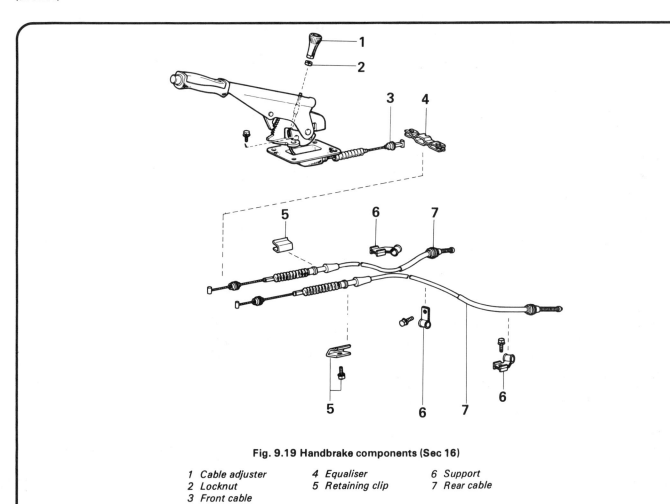

Fig. 9.19 Handbrake components (Sec 16)

1 *Cable adjuster*	4 *Equaliser*	6 *Support*
2 *Locknut*	5 *Retaining clip*	7 *Rear cable*
3 *Front cable*		

15.2 Handbrake adjusting knob location

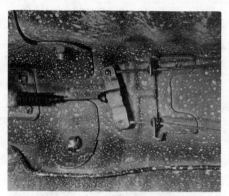

17.4 Handbrake cable equaliser location

19.2 Vacuum servo unit non-return valve location

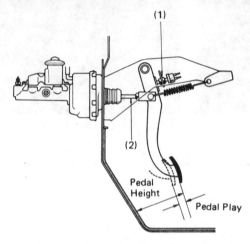

Fig. 9.20 Footbrake pedal adjustment points (Sec 18)

1 Stoplamp switch   2 Pushrod

2   Remove the handbrake lever as described in Section 16.
3   With the front wheels chocked, jack-up the rear of the car and support it on axle stands.
4   Reach over the propeller shaft and disconnect the front cable from the equaliser by turning the cable stop plate through 90° (photo). Withdraw the cable through the handbrake lever baseplate.
5   Prise the guide grommets at the front of the rear cables from the underframe brackets, then disconnect the equaliser.
6   Remove the rear brake shoes as described in Section 3.
7   Unbolt the rear cable from the suspension lower control arm and prise the cable out of the rear brake backplate.
8   Unscrew the bolts from the retainer mountings and withdraw the cable from beneath the car.
9   Refitting is a reversal of removal, but it will be necessary to refit the brake shoes as described in Section 3 and also to adjust the handbrake as described in Section 15.

18 Footbrake pedal – removal, refitting and adjustment

1   The brake and clutch pedals are located on the same shaft and the removal and refitting procedures are identical. Reference should therefore be made to Chapter 5.
2   After refitting the brake pedal, servo unit (UK models) or master cylinder (non-UK models), the pedal must be adjusted to achieve the specified height and free play.

Models with servo
3   Loosen the locknuts and back-off the stop lamp switch.
4   Loosen the locknut and turn the servo pushrod until the specified pedal height is achieved. Tighten the locknut.
5   Adjust the stoplamp switch so that its body just contacts the cushion on the brake pedal, then tighten the locknuts.

6   With the engine stopped depress the footbrake pedal several times to release the vacuum in the servo.
7   Using finger pressure only, check that the pedal free play is as specified. Note that the free play should only be measured to the point where the initial resistance is felt, not to the point where the servo piston starts to move. Provided the pedal height has been adjusted correctly, the free play should be correct.

Models without servo
8   Loosen the master cylinder pushrod locknut and the stop lamp switch locknuts.
9   Back off the stoplamp switch and pushrod until the specified pedal height is achieved with the pedal against the stoplamp switch body. Tighten the stoplamp switch locknuts.
10   Turn the master cylinder pushrod until the specified pedal free play is achieved. Tighten the locknut.

19 Vacuum servo unit – descrption and testing

1   A vacuum servo unit is fitted into the brake system on UK models, to provide assistance to the drive when the brake pedal is depressed. This reduces the effort required by the driver to operate the brakes under all braking conditions. It is mounted in series with the brake master cylinder.
2   The unit operates by vacuum obtained from the induction manifold and comprises basically a booster diaphragm and control valve assembly. The vacuum pipe from the induction manifold incorporates a non-return valve (photo).
3   The servo unit and hydraulic master cylinder are connected together so that the servo unit piston rod (valve rod) acts as the master cylinder pushrod. The driver's braking effort is transmitted through another pushrod to the servo unit piston and its built-in control system. The servo unit piston does not fit tightly into the cylinder, but has a strong diaphragm to keep its edges in constant contact with the cylinder wall, so ensuring an airtight seal between the two parts. The forward chamber is held under vacuum conditions created in the inlet manifold of the engine and, during periods when the brake pedal is not in use, the controls open a passage to the rear chamber so placing it under vacuum conditions as well. When the brake pedal is depressed, the vacuum passage to the rear chamber is cut off and the chamber opened to atmospheric pressure. The consequent rush of air pushes the servo piston forwards in the vacuum chamber and operates the main pushrod to the master cylinder.
4   The controls are designed so that assistance is given under all conditions. When the brakes are not required, vacuum is established in the rear chamber when the brake pedal is released.
5   Under normal operating conditions the vacuum servo unit is very reliable and does not require overhaul except at very high mileage. In this case it is far better to obtain an exchange or new unit, rather than attempt to repair the original unit.
6   To test the servo, first run the engine for 2 minutes, then stop it. Fully depress the pedal several times; the servo is in good condition if the pedal gradually rises after the first full depression. If the pedal remains at the same height, the servo is faulty.
7   Continue depressing the pedal until the vacuum is exhausted and

20.6 Vacuum servo unit mounting nuts

the pedal does not rise further. With the pedal depressed, start the engine and check that the pedal drops slightly. If not the servo is faulty.

8   Depress the pedal several times with the engine still running. Keep the pedal depressed and switch off the engine. The pedal height should remain unchanged for 30 seconds; if it rises during this period, the servo is faulty.

20 Vacuum servo unit – removal and refitting

1   Destroy the vacuum in the servo unit by repeated applications of the brake pedal.

2   Disconnect the vacuum hose from the servo unit.

3   Remove the master cylinder from the front face of the servo unit as described in Section 9.

4   Working inside the car, disconnect the stoplamp switch wire connector and remove the brake pedal return spring.

5   Disconnect the operating pushrod from the brake pedal by removing the clip and clevis pin.

6   Unscrew and remove the retaining nuts and washers, (accessible within the car,) and withdraw the servo unit from the bulkhead into the engine compartment (photo).

7   Refitting is a reversal of removal, but it will be necessary to adjust the footbrake pedal as described in Section 18. Refer to Section 9 for the master cylinder refitting procedure. Check the operation of the servo as described in Section 19.

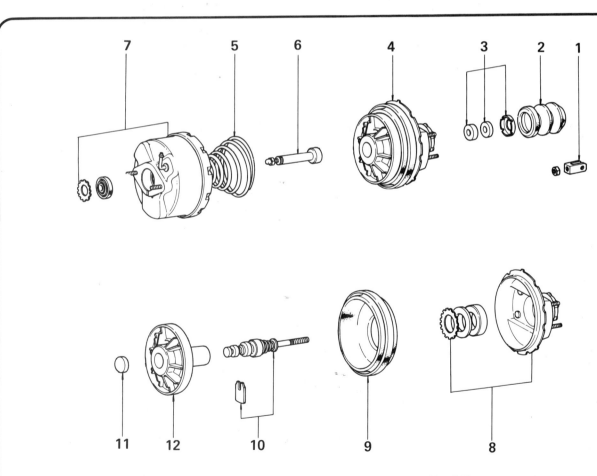

Fig. 9.21 Exploded view of the vacuum servo unit (Sec 22)

1	Clevis		plate	9	Diaphragm
2	Rubber boot	5	Spring	10	Operating rod and
3	Air filter elements and	6	Pushrod		stopper key
	retainer	7	Front shell and seal	11	Reaction disc
4	Rear shell with diaphragm	8	Rear shell and seal	12	Diaphragm plate

21 Vacuum servo unit air filter – removal

1   At intervals of 50 000 miles (80 000 km) the servo air filter should be renewed. In dusty climates renew it more frequently.
2   Working inside the car, disconnect the stoplamp switch connector and remove the brake pedal return spring.
3   Disconnect the operating pushrod from the brake pedal by removing the clip and clevis pin.
4   Loosen the locknut and remove the clevis and locknut.
5   Prise the rubber boot, retainer, and air filter elements from the end of the servo unit with a screwdriver.
6   Refitting is a reversal of removal, but adjust the footbrake pedal as described in Section 18.

22 Vacuum servo unit – overhaul

1   Before starting work, it will be necessary to obtain the special tools for separating the front and rear servo shells. If your local Toyota dealer or tool hire agent cannot provide the tool, it should be quite easy to make one out of angle iron. An overhaul repair kit should also be obtained.
2   With the servo unit on the bench, remove the air filter elements as described in Section 21.
3   Mark the front and rear shells in relation to each other.
4   Mount the servo unit and tool in a vice, and remove the rear shell from the front shell by turning the former anticlockwise.
5   Remove the spring and pushrod from the front shell, then drive out the retainer and seal.
6   Remove the diaphragm plate assembly from the rear shell.
7   Prise the retainer ring, bearing and seal from the rear shell.
8   Using the fingers only, remove the diaphragm from the diaphragm plate.
9   Depress the operating rod and extract the stopper key from the diaphragm plate; the operating rod can now be removed (Fig. 9.23).
10   Drive the reaction disc from the diaphragm plate.
11   Clean all components with methylated spirit, and inspect them for damage and deterioration. If components other than those supplied in the repair kit require renewal, it is recommended that the complete unit be renewed in the interests of economy.
12   Reassembly is a direct reversal of dismantling; but it is essential to coat the surfaces shown in Fig. 9.24 with the silicone grease supplied in the repair kit.

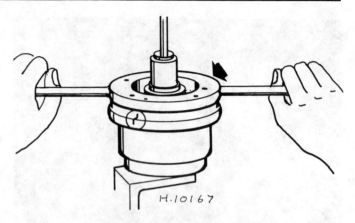

H.10167

Fig. 9.22 Removing the rear shell from the front servo shell, showing removal tool (arrowed) (Sec 22)

Fig. 9.23 Removing the servo stopper key (Sec 22)

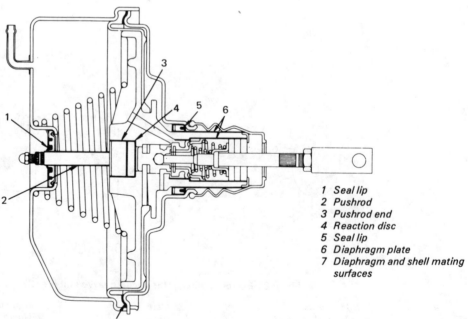

1 Seal lip
2 Pushrod
3 Pushrod end
4 Reaction disc
5 Seal lip
6 Diaphragm plate
7 Diaphragm and shell mating surfaces

Fig. 9.24 Surfaces to be coated with silicone grease when reassembling the brake servo unit (Sec 22)

23 Fault diagnosis – braking system

Symptom	Reason/s
Pedal travels almost to floor before brakes operate	Brake fluid too low Caliper leaking Master cylinder leaking (bubbles in master cylinder fluid) Brake flexible hose leaking Brake line fractured Brake system unions loose Rear brakes badly out of adjustment (automatic adjusters seized)
Brake pedal feels springy	New linings not yet bedded-in Brake discs or drums badly worn or cracked Master cylinder securing nuts loose
Brake pedal feels 'spongy' and 'soggy'	Caliper or wheel cylinder leaking Master cylinder leaking (bubbles in master cylinder fluid) Brake pipe line or flexible hose leaking Unions in brake system loose
Excessive effort required to brake car	Faulty vacuum servo unit Pad or shoe linings badly worn New pads or shoes recently fitted – not yet bedded-in Harder linings fitted than standard causing increase in pedal pressure Linings and brake drums contaminated with oil, grease or hydraulic fluid
Brake uneven and pulling to one side	Linings and discs or drums contaminated with oil, grease or hydraulic fluid Tyre pressures unequal Brake caliper loose or seized Brake pad or shoes fitted incorrectly Different type of linings fitted at each wheel Anchorage for front suspension or rear suspension loose Brake discs or drums badly worn, cracked or distorted
Brakes tend to bind, drag or lock-on	**Faulty pressure regulating valve** Air in system Handbrake cable over-tightened Wheel cylinder or caliper pistons seized
Brake warning light stays on	Leak in front or rear hydraulic circuits Faulty handbrake switch Faulty master cylinder fluid level switch

Chapter 10 Electrical system

For modifications, and information applicable to later models, see Supplement at end of manual

Contents

Specifications

System type . . . . 12 volt, negative earth

Battery capacity . . . . 40 or 60 amp-hours at 20 hour rate

Alternator
Output . . . . 30 or 45 amps
Rotor coil resistance . . . . 4.1 to 4.3 ohms
Brush length:
    Standard . . . . 0.49 in (12.5 mm)
    Minimum . . . . 0.22 in (5.5 mm)
Regulator control voltage . . . . 13.8 to 14.8 volts

Starter motor
Type . . . . Pre-engaged
Armature endfloat . . . . 0.04 in (1.0 mm)
Piston end clearance . . . . 0.04 to 0.16 in (1.0 to 4.0 mm)
Commutator segment undercut:
    Standard . . . . 0.020 to 0.032 in (0.5 to 0.8 mm)
    Minimum . . . . 0.008 in (0.2 mm)
Brush length:
    Standard . . . . 0.75 in (19.0 mm)
    Minimum . . . . 0.47 in (12.0 mm)

Fuses
In fusebox . . . . 2 x 5 amp, 5 x 15 amp, 1 x 20 amp
Fusible links . . . . 3 (RHD) or 2 (LHD)

Bulbs
                                                                      Wattage
Headlamps:
    Semi-sealed 45/50
    Sealed 40/50

Front parking	5
Direction indicator	21
Side repeater	5
Stop and tail	21/5
Reversing	21
Number plate	5
Interior	10

Torque wrench settings

	lbf ft	kgf m
Starter motor mounting bolts	11	1.5
Alternator mounting bolts	15	2.1

1 General description

1 The electrical system is of 12 volt negative earth type. The battery is charged by a belt-driven alternator. The voltage regulator is mounted on the left-hand side of the engine compartment.
2 The starter motor is of pre-engaged type, ie the solenoid engages the pinion with the flywheel ring gear before the motor is energised by internal contacts. A one-way clutch in the pinion prevents the engine turning the starter motor armature once the engine fires.
3 Although repair procedures are described in this Chapter, consideration should be given to obtaining new or exchange units, especially where the original equipment is well worn.

2 Battery – removal and refitting

1 The battery should be removed once every three months for cleaning and testing. Disconnect the negative, then the positive lead from the battery terminals by slackening the clamp bolts and lifting away the clamps (photo).
2 Undo and remove the nut and washer securing the battery clamp and lift away the clamp. Carefully lift the battery from its carrier and hold it upright to ensure that none of the electrolyte is spilled.
3 Refitting is a reversal of removal. Fit the positive, then the negative lead, and smear the terminals with petroleum jelly to prevent corrosion.

3 Battery – maintenance

1 Once a week the battery electrolyte level should be checked. On batteries with translucent cases, the level must be between the upper and lower lines. On other batteries the electrolyte must be level with the bottom of the cell filler tubes. If necessary top up each cell with distilled water (photo). Remember that electrolyte corrodes metal and if any is accidentally spilled, wash it away immediately with clean water.
2 As well as keeping the terminals clean and covered with petroleum jelly, the top of the battery, and especially the top of the cells, should be kept clean and dry. This helps to prevent corrosion and ensures that the battery does not become partially discharged by leakage through dampness and dirt.
3 Once every three months remove the battery and inspect the battery securing bolts, the clamp plate, tray and leads for corrosion. If any corrosion is found, clean off the deposits with ammonia, and paint over the clean metal with an anti-rust and acid paint.
4 If topping-up the battery becomes excessive and the case has been inspected for cracks that could cause leakage, but none are found, the battery is being overcharged and the voltage regulator will have to be checked and reset, or renewed.
5 With the battery on the bench at the three monthly interval check, measure the specific gravity with a hydrometer to determine the state of charge and condition of the electrolyte. There should be very little variation between the different cells and if a variation in excess of 0.025 is present it will be due to either:

(a) *loss of electrolyte from the battery at some time caused by spillage or a leak, resulting in a drop in the specific gravity of the electrolyte, when the deficiency was made up with distilled water instead of fresh electrolyte*
(b) *an internal short circuit caused by buckling of the plates or a similar malady pointing to the likelihood of total battery failure in the near future*

2.1 The battery and retaining clamp

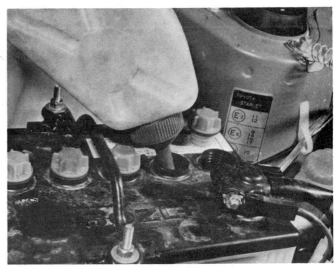

3.1 Topping-up the battery with distilled water

6 The specific gravity of the electrolyte for fully charged conditions at the electrolyte temperature indicated, is listed in Table A. The specific gravity of a fully discharged battery at different temperatures of the electrolyte is given in Table B.

Table A
Specific gravity – battery fully charged
1.268 at 100°F or 38°C electrolyte temperature
1.272 at 90°F or 32°C electrolyte temperature
1.276 at 80°F or 27°C electrolyte temperature
1.280 at 70°F or 21°C electrolyte temperature

1.284 at 60°F or 16°C electrolyte temperature
1.288 at 50°F or 10°C electrolyte temperature
1.292 at 40°F or 4°C electrolyte temperature
1.296 at 30°F or -1.5°C electrolyte temperature

Table B
Specific gravity – battery fully discharged
1.098 at 100°F or 38°C electrolyte temperature
1.102 at 90°F or 32°C electrolyte temperature
1.106 at 80°F or 27°C electrolyte temperature
1.110 at 70°F or 21°C electrolyte temperature
1.114 at 60°F or 16°C electrolyte temperature
1.118 at 50°F or 10°C electrolyte temperature
1.122 at 40°F or 4°C electrolyte temperature
1.126 at 30°F or -1.5°C electrolyte temperature

4   Electrolyte – replenishment

1   If the battery is in a fully charged state and one of the cells maintains a specific gravity reading which is .025 or more lower than the others, and a check of each cell has been made with a voltage meter to check for short circuits (a four to seven second test should give a steady reading of between 1.2 and 1.8 volts), then it is likely that electrolyte has been lost at some time from the cell with the low reading.
2   Have your garage drain and refill the battery cells with the correct acid/distilled water mixture.

5   Battery – charging

1   In winter time when heavy demand is placed upon the battery such as when starting from cold, and a lot of electrical equipment is continually in use, it is a good idea to occasionally have the battery fully charged from an external source at the rate of 3.5 to 4 amps.
2   Continue to charge the battery at this rate until no further rise in specific gravity is noted over a four hour period.
3   Alternatively, a trickle charger, charging at the rate of 1.5 amps, can be safely used overnight.
4   Specially rapid 'boost' charges which are claimed to restore the power of the battery in 1 to 2 hours are to be avoided as they can cause serious damage to the battery plates through overheating.
5   While charging the battery note that the temperature of the electrolyte should never exceed 100°F (37.8°C).
6   Always disconnect the battery leads when charging if the battery is still in the car.

6   Alternator – maintenance and special precautions

1   Occasionally wipe away any grit or grease which has accumulated on the outside of the unit and check the security of the leads.
2   Every 6000 miles (10 000 km) check the tension of the drivebelt and adjust if necessary as described in Chapter 2.
3   No lubrication is required as the bearings are sealed for life.

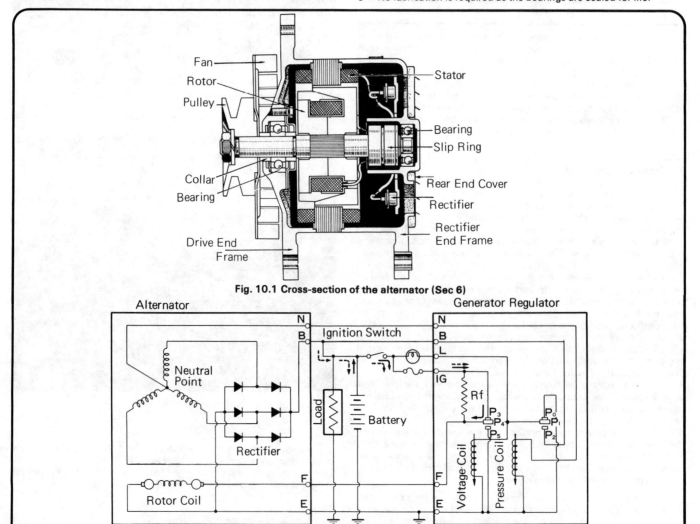

Fig. 10.1 Cross-section of the alternator (Sec 6)

Fig. 10.2 Diagram of the charging circuit (Sec 6)

4   The alternator incorporates silicon diodes which can easily be damaged when making circuit connections to the car. The following precautions must always be observed:

(a)   *Always ensure the correct polarity of wiring connections*
(b)   *Disconnect both battery terminals and the alternator plug before using electric arc-welding equipment*
(c)   *Disconnect both battery terminals when charging the battery*
(d)   *When using jumper leads, connect the identical terminals on each battery and avoid contact between the two vehicles*
(e)   *Comprehensive testing of the alternator is best carried out by a fully equipped automobile electrician*

7   Alternator – removal and refitting

1   Disconnect both battery terminals.
2   Remove the drivebelt as described in Chapter 2.
3   Remove the pivot and adjustment bolts and withdraw the alternator sufficient to disconnect the plug and lead from its rear face (photos). Note the lead support plate location.
4   Remove the alternator from the car.
5   Refitting is a reversal of removal, but adjust the drivebelt tension as described in Chapter 2.

8   Alternator – dismantling and reassembly

1   Mark the end brackets and stator in relation to each other to ensure correct reassembly.
2   Unscrew and remove the three tie-bolts.
3   Prise the drive end bracket and rotor from the stator and slip ring end bracket. Take care not to damage the stator coils.
4   Using a spanner and an Allen key, unscrew the pulley retaining nut and remove the washer (Fig. 10.4).
5   Remove the pulley, fan, key, and spacer from the rotor shaft.
6   Support the drive end bracket in a vice and drive the rotor through the front bearing with a plastic or hide mallet.
7   Unscrew the three retaining screws and remove the drive end bearing retainer plate.
8   Support the drive end bracket and drive out the bearing with a soft metal drift. Remove the cover and felt ring.
9   Using a suitable puller, remove the slip ring end bearing from the rotor shaft.
10 From the rear of the slip ring end bracket, unscrew and remove the three rectifier plate retaining nuts and the nut retaining the output terminal (B) insulator. Remove the insulator and withdraw the end cover plate.
11 Inspect the brushes for free movement in their guides and for length; if they are below the specified minimum length, renew them as

7.3A The alternator, showing pivot and adjustment bolts

7.3B Alternator plug and lead connections

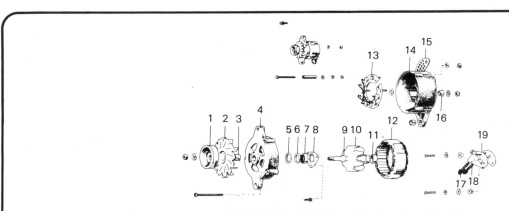

Fig. 10.3 Exploded view of the alternator (Sec 8)

1	Pulley	8	Retainer plate	14	Slip ring and bracket
2	Fan	9	Spacer	15	End cover
3	Spacer	10	Rotor	16	Insulator
4	Drive and bracket	11	Bearing	17	Brush
5	Felt	12	Stator	18	Spring
6	Cover	13	Rectifier plate	19	Brushholder
7	Bearing				

follows.

12 Remove the two crosshead screws retaining the brushholder to the rectifier plate together with the insulators.

13 Note the location of the three wires. Move the earth lead terminal with a screwdriver, then remove the insulator and extract the neutral lead terminal from the brushholder.

14 Unsolder the brush leads from their terminals, remove the brushes and insert the new ones. Solder the new leads so that the brushes protrude 0.5 in (12.5 mm) from the brush holder (Fig. 10.6), then cut off any excess wire. Check that the brushes move freely in their guides.

15 Examine the surfaces of the slip rings, which should be smooth and clean. If not, clean them with white spirit.

16 If an ohmmeter is available, connect it across the slip rings and check that the resistance is as specified. A low reading indicates a short circuit between coils, a high reading could be due to dirty slip rings, and a reading of infinity means an open circuit.

17 To test the stator, connect an ohmmeter between the neutral terminal and each remaining lead. There should be zero resistance in each test indicating continuity. If not, the stator should be renewed.

18 Both rotor and stator windings may be tested for continuity using a battery test lamp with a low wattage bulb and leads.

19 Test the rotor coils for earthing by connecting leads between each slip ring and the rotor poles. Similarly test the stator coils by connecting leads between the coil leads and the stator core.

20 To test the rectifier plate diodes, connect an ohmmeter or test lamp between each diode terminal and the baseplate and note the result. Now reverse the test lead positions and note the result again. Each diode should pass current in one direction but not in the other, and the results must be identical with the diodes mounted on each plate half. If not, renew the faulty plate half as necessary.

21 Check the rotor bearings for wear and renew them if necessary. Before fitting them, pack them with wheel bearing grease.

22 Clean and check the end brackets for deterioration.

23 Reassembly is a reversal of dismantling but the following points must be observed:

   (a) *Make sure that the insulators are located in their correct positions, in particular over the output terminal*

   (b) *Delay tightening the brushholder retaining screws until the rectifier plate is located in the slip ring and bracket*

   (c) *Locate the felt cover with its raised side facing in the direction of the pulley.*

   (d) *Hold the brushes away from the slip rings when inserting the rotor, with a piece of wire entered through the special hole in the slip ring end bracket. Remove the wire after reassembly*

9 Alternator regulator – description

1 The alternator regulator is mounted on the left hand side of the engine compartment and contains two coils and contact points (photo). The voltage relay coil points operate when a predetermined amount of current passes through the relay coil. This action extinguishes the ignition warning light and allows current to pass through the regulator coil.

2 The regulator coil points operate to control the field current in the rotor windings. This maintains the generated voltage at a constant value irrespective of the battery condition and state of charge.

3 Current to the alternator regulator is protected by the 20 amp fuse in the fuse block, and should this fuse blow, for example as a result of a short circuit in the engine cooling fan circuit, the alternator will not operate. The ignition warning lamp is also protected by a 5 amp in-line fuse (photo).

10 Starter motor – description

1 The starter motor comprises a solenoid, a lever, starter drive gear and the motor. The solenoid is fitted to the top of the motor. The plunger inside the solenoid is connected to a centre pivoting lever, the other end of which is in contact with the drive sleeve and drivegear.

2 When the ignition switch is operated, current from the battery flows through the series and shunt solenoid coils thereby magnetizing the solenoid. The plunger is drawn into the solenoid so that it operates the lever and moves the drive pinion into engagement with the starter ring gear. The solenoid switch contact close after the drive pinion is

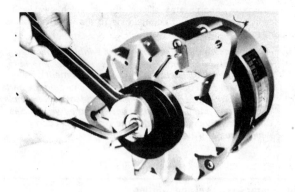

Fig. 10.4 Removing alternator pulley (Sec 8)

Fig. 10.5 Removing alternator brush holder (Sec 8)

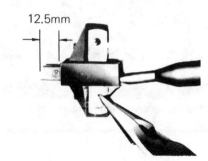

12.5mm

Fig. 10.6 Alternator brush fitting dimension (Sec 8)

Voltage Regulator

Voltage Relay

Fig. 10.7 Alternator regulator with cover removed (Sec 9)

engaged with the starter ring gear.

3   When the solenoid switch contacts are closed the starter motor rotates the engine while at the same time cutting current flow to the series coil in the solenoid. The shunt coil's magnetic pull is now sufficient to hold the pinion in mesh with the ring gear.

4   When the engine starts and the ignition switch is released, the solenoid plunger moves back under spring pressure and the internal contacts separate; the starter motor then stops.

5   An overrun clutch in the starter pinion prevents the armature being rotated by the engine once it has fired.

11 Starter motor – removal and refitting

1   Disconnect the battery negative terminal.

2   Unscrew the two terminal nuts and disconnect the leads from the starter solenoid.

3   Unscrew the retaining bolts and withdraw the starter motor from the gearbox bellhousing and engine rear plate (photo).

4   Refitting is a reversal of removal

12 Starter motor – dismantling, servicing and reassembly

1   Disconnect the field coil lead from the solenoid main terminal.

2   Undo and remove the two screws securing the solenoid to the starter housing and then withdraw the solenoid far enough for it to be unhooked from the drive engagement lever fork.

3   Undo and remove the two screws and spring washers securing the bearing cover to the commutator end frame. Lift away the bearing cover.

4   Remove the lockplate, spring and seal washer from the end of the armature.

5   Undo and remove the two through bolts, spring and plain washers securing the starter yoke and commutator endframe to the starter housing. Withdraw the commutator endframe and brush holder followed by the yoke from the starter housing.

6   Undo and remove the engagement lever pivot bolt from the side of the starter housing and then detach the rubber buffer and its backing plate. Remove the armature assembly complete with drive engagement lever from the starter housing.

7   Using a tubular drift, drive the pinion stop collar up the armature shaft far enough to enable the circlip to be removed. Pull the stop collar from the shaft and slide off the clutch assembly.

8   Check for wear in the armature shaft bearings. The specified clearance between shaft and bearing is between 0.0037 and 0.0053 in (0.095 and 0.135 mm) with a maximum of 0.008 in (0.2 mm). Normally the bearings will require renewal by pressing out the old ones from the starter housing and commutator endframe and pressing in the new ones. Before doing this check the diameter of the armature

9.1 Alternator regulator location

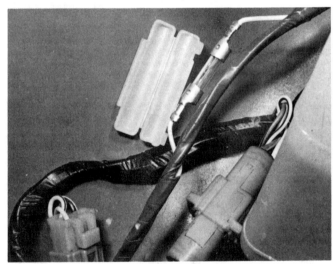

9.3 Ignition warning lamp in-line fuse location

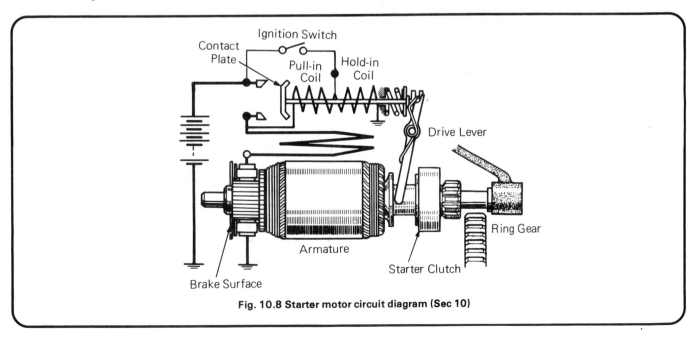

Fig. 10.8 Starter motor circuit diagram (Sec 10)

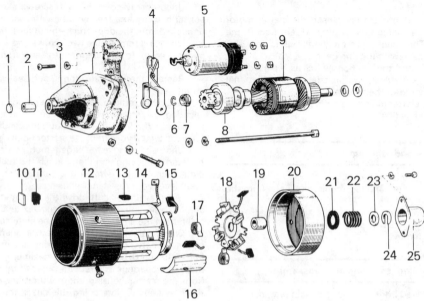

Fig. 10.9 Exploded view of the starter motor (Sec 12)

1	Plug	6	Circlip	10	Plate	14	Field coil	18	Brush holder	22	Spring
2	Bush	7	Pinion stop nut	11	Rubber	15	Brush	19	Bush	23	Washer
3	Starter housing	8	Clutch	12	Yoke	16	Pole core	20	Commutator endframe	24	Lockplate
4	Engagement lever	9	Armature	13	Insulation	17	Brush spring	21	Rubber	25	Cover
5	Solenoid switch										

11.3 Removing the starter motor

Fig. 10.10 Starter motor commutator segment undercut dimension (Sec 12)

shaft which should be 0.490 in (12.5 mm). If this is worn it can be re-ground and an undersize bearing fitted, (see following paragraphs).
9   Armature shaft rear bearings are available in standard and undersizes as follows:

Standard	0.4935–0.4945 in (12.535–12.560 mm)
Undersize (1)	0.4817–0.4827 in (12.235–12.260 mm)
(2)	0.4738–0.4748 in (12.035–12.060 mm)

Front bearings must be reamed to conform with the armature shaft fitting diameter and the specified running clearance.
10   Check the armature shaft for distortion or ovality and renew if evident.
11   Check the commutator segments and undercut the mica insulators using a hacksaw blade ground to the correct thickness. If the commutator is burnt or discoloured, clean it with a piece of fine glass paper (**not** emery or carborundum) and finally wipe with a petrol moistened cloth.

12   With the starter motor dismantled, test the four field coils for open circuit. Connect a 12 volt battery with a 12 volt bulb in one of the leads between the field terminal post and the tapping points of the field coils to which the brushes are connected. An open circuit is proved by the bulb not lighting.
13   If the bulb lights, it does not necessarily mean that the field coils are in order, as there is a possibility that one of the coils has earthed to the starter yoke or pole shoes. To check this, remove the lead from the brush connector and place it against a clean area of the starter yoke. If the bulb lights the field coils are earthing. Renewal of a field coil calls for the use of a wheel operated screwdriver, a soldering iron, caulking and riveting operations and is beyond the scope of the majority of owners. The starter yoke should be taken to a reputable automobile electrical engineering works for new field coils to be fitted. Alternatively, purchase an exchange starter motor.
14   If the armature is damaged this will be evident after visual inspection. Look for signs of discolouration of the wires.
15   Check the insulation of the brush holders and the length of the brushes. If these have worn below the specified limit, renew them. Before refitting them to their holders, dress them to the correct contour by wrapping a piece of emery cloth round the commutator and rotating the commutator back and forth.
16   Check the starter clutch assembly for wear, sticky action, or

chipped pinion teeth, and renew the assembly if necessary.

17 Locate the centre bearing and brake components on the armature shaft. Grease them and see that the brake spring ends are engaged in the holes in the centre bearing support plate and brake spring holder. Fit the clutch assembly to the armature shaft followed by a new pinion stop collar and circlip. Pull the stop collar forward and stake the collar rim over the circlip. Grease all sliding surfaces.

18 Locate the drive engagement lever to the armature shaft with the spring towards the armature and the steel washer up against the clutch.

19 Apply grease to all sliding surfaces and locate the armature assembly in the starter housing. Refit the drive engagement lever pivot bolt, well greased.

20 Fit the rubber buffer together with its backing plate and then align and offer into position the yoke to the starter housing.

21 Fit the brush holder to the armature and then insert the brushes.

22 Grease the commutator endframe bearing and then fit the end frame into position. Insert and tighten the two through bolts, spring and plain washers.

23 Fit the seal, washer and endcover (half-packed with multi-purpose grease). Check the armature endfloat. If this exceeds the tolerances specified, remove the endcover and fit an additional thrust washer. Retain in position with the lockplate.

24 Fit the solenoid switch making sure that its hook engages *under* the spring of the engagement lever fork.

25 Reconnect the field coil lead to the solenoid main terminal.

26 Connect up a 12 volt battery to the solenoid so that it is energised and insert a feeler gauge between the endface of the clutch pinion and the pinion stop collar. The pinion end clearance should be within the specified limits. If the clearance is incorrect, remove the solenoid switch and adjust the length of the adjustable stud by loosening its locknut.

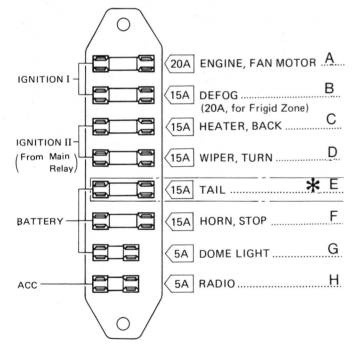

✱ For West Germany

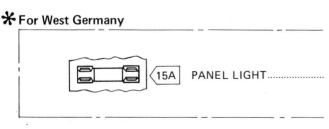

Fig. 10.11 Fusebox application chart (Sec 13)

13 Fuses and fusible links

1 The fusebox is located next to the bonnet release handle under the facia panel and contains eight fuses (photo).

2 The application of each fuse is as follows with reference to Fig. 10.11 (photo):

(A) *Cooling fan relay, voltage regulator, fuel cut solenoid*

(B) *Heated rear window, oil pressure warning, fuel gauge, water temperature gauge, brake warning light, main relay*

(C) *Heater, reversing light*

(D) *Direction indicator and warning light, headlight washer, windscreen wiper and washer*

(E) *Number plate light, instrument panel light, side and tail lights (Note – for West Germany, panel light)*

(F) *Horn, stoplight*

(G) *Open door warning light, clock, interior light*

(H) *Radio*

3 Always renew a fuse with one of similar rating, and never renew it more than once without tracing the source of the trouble.

4 With the exception of the starter motor main feed, the entire electrical system is protected by three fusible links located next to the battery in the leads connected to the positive terminal. Should a short circuit occur, the fusible links will melt before the wiring harness is damaged. Always trace and rectify the fault before renewing the fusible link and never connect a by-pass wire across the link.

14 Ignition switch/steering lock – removal and refitting

1 Disconnect the battery negative terminal.

2 Unscrew the three retaining screws and remove the instrument surround.

3 Unscrew the retaining screws and remove the steering column upper and lower shrouds (photo).

4 Insert the ignition key and turn it to the accessory (ACC) position.

5 With a small drill or piece of wire, depress the retaining pin and at the same time pull the key and cylinder from the switch housing.

6 Unscrew the retaining screw and remove the ignition switch after separating the multiplug connector (photo).

7 Refitting is a reversal of removal, but make sure that the switch recess and tab are engaged correctly, and position the bracket as shown in Fig. 10.12 before inserting the key cylinder.

15 Steering column combination switches – removal and refitting

1 Remove the steering wheel as described in Chapter 11.

2 Unscrew the retaining screws and remove the steering column upper and lower shrouds.

3 Separate the multiplug connector from the wiring harness (photo).

4 Unscrew the crosshead retaining screws and remove the combination switch assembly.

5 To remove the wiper and washer switch, first unscrew the retaining screws and detach the switch from the base assembly.

6 Carefully note the position of the wires in the multiplug connector. Remove each wire from the connector by pushing in the terminal to release the tags, then use a tool similar to that shown in Fig. 10.15 to depress the tags so that the terminal can be withdrawn from the plastic connector.

7 To remove the light control switch, detach the plate and ball from the housing, then remove the clamp. Unscrew the pivot screw and withdraw the switch lever. Disconnect the wires from the multiplug connector using the procedure described in paragraph 6.

8 To remove the hazard warning switch and direction indicator switch, remove the retaining screws and withdraw the assembly from the switch base.

9 Refitting is a reversal of removal, but the following points should be observed:

(a) *Ensure that the light control switch ball and plate are fitted as shown in Fig. 10.16*

(b) *Before inserting the terminals in the plastic connector, bend out the metal tags so that they will fully engage*

13.1 Fusebox cover location

13.2 Fusebox with cover removed

14.3 Ignition switch and steering lock with shrouds removed

14.6 Ignition switch loom connections

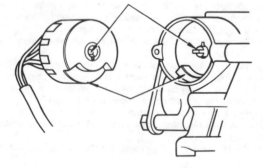

Fig. 10.12 Ignition switch engagement points (Sec 14)

(c) When refitting the shrouds, make sure that the self-tapping screws are used to connect the shrouds to each other, and the ordinary screws are used to secure the lower shroud to the column

16 Heated rear window and tailgate wiper switches – removal and refitting

1   Disconnect the battery negative terminal.
2   Disconnect the multiplug connector from the rear of the switch.
3   Depress the plastic tags and withdraw the switches from the fascia panel (photo).
4   Refitting is a reversal of removal

17 Reversing lamp switch – removal and refitting

1   The reversing lamp switch is screwed into the side of the gearbox casing on 4-speed models, and on the top of the casing on 5-speed models.
2   Disconnect the supply wires and unscrew the switch from the casing.
3   Refitting is a reversal of removal.

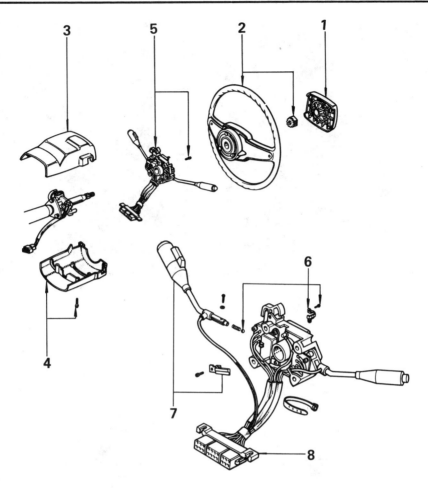

Fig. 10.13 Exploded view of the steering column combination switches (Sec 15)

1 Horn push
2 Steering wheel and nut
3 Upper shroud
4 Lower shroud

5 Combination switch
6 Plate, screw and ball
7 Light control switch
8 Multiplug connector

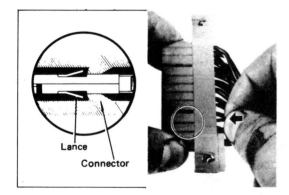

Fig. 10.14 Cross-sectional view of a multiplug connector (Sec 15)

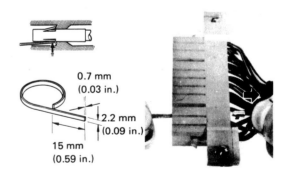

Fig. 10.15 Dimensions of tool for removing the multiplug terminals (Sec 15)

18 Relays – description and testing

1 The relays are located beneath the right-hand side of the fascia panel on RHD cars, and beneath the left-hand side on LHD cars. Their purpose is to prevent deterioration of switch contacts. When the switch is operated, an internal coil in the relevant relay is energised and independent contacts are closed electrically to provide current to the component.

2 To test the relay, first remove it from the mounting block. Check the coil windings for continuity using an ohmmeter or 12 volt test lamp and leads; the internal circuitry is shown in the wiring diagram at the end of this Chapter.

3 The internal contacts can be tested by connecting a 12 volt bulb across then and energising the coil windings. An audible /click' should also be heard indicating closure of the contacts.

4 A defective relay must be renewed as repair is not possible.

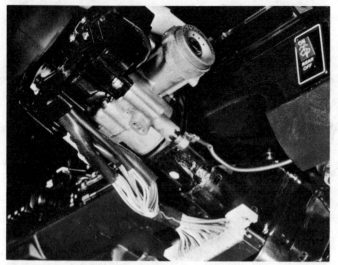

15.3 Steering column multiplug connector location

16.3 Removing the heated rear window and tailgate wiper switches

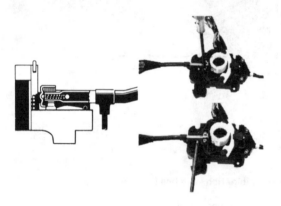

Fig. 10.16 Correct fitting of the light control switch (Sec 15)

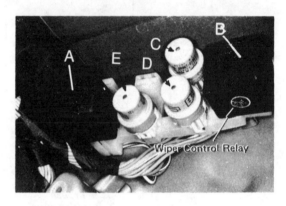

Fig. 10.17 Relays (RHD) (Sec 18)

A Turn signal and hazard warning	C Tail light
	D Headlights
B Wiper control	E Cooling fan

19 Direction indicator flasher unit – testing

1   The direction indicators should normally flash 70 to 100 times per minute when in use, but if an open circuit exists to one of the lamps, the rate will increase by 20 or 30 flashes per minute.

2   If the indicators fail to operate, first check the fuse. If it is blown, refer to the wiring diagram at the end of this Chapter for possible faults.

3   If current is reaching the B terminal lead to the flasher unit but it still fails to operate, it should be renewed.

20 Instrument panel cluster – removal and refitting

1   Disconnect the battery negative terminal.

2   Remove the retaining screws and withdraw the surround (photo).

3   Disconnect the speedometer cable at the gearbox and bend back the support clips.

4   Unscrew the retaining screws and withdraw the instrument panel cluster sufficiently to disconnect the multiplug connectors and speedometer cable (photo).

5   Remove the cluster from the fascia (photos).

6   Refitting is a reversal of removal.

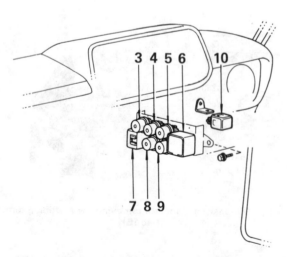

Fig. 10.18 Relays (LHD typical) (Sec 18)

3 Hazard warning (W. Germany, France)	7 Turn signal and hazard warning
4 Demister	8 Cooling fan
5 Tail light	9 Headlights
6 Wiper control	

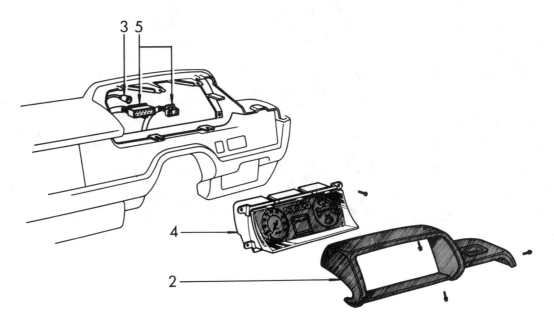

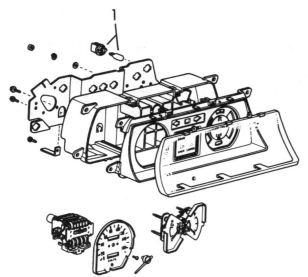

Fig. 10.19 Exploded view of the instrument panel cluster (Sec 20)

1 Warning light bulb and
  bulbholder
2 Surround

3 Speedometer cable
4 Instrument panel cluster
5 Multiplug connectors

20.2 Removing the instrument panel surround

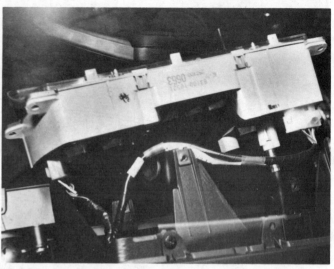

20.4 Removing the instrument panel cluster

20.5A Instrument panel cluster face view

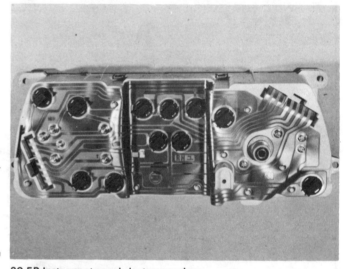

20.5B Instrument panel cluster rear view

3   Remove the headlamp bulb.
4   Refitting is a reversal of removal, but make sure that the projection on the bulb rim engages with the cut-out in the reflector.

Sealed beam type

5   Open the bonnet and disconnect the plug from the rear of the headlight. Remove the rubber cover.
6   Unscrew the crosshead screws and remove the headlight surround (photo).
7   Loosen the three rim retaining screws, turn the rim anti-clockwise and remove it while supporting the headlight (photo).
8   Withdraw the sealed beam unit.
9   Refitting is a reversal of removal, but make sure that the headlight is fitted with the TOP mark uppermost.

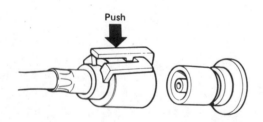

Fig. 10.20 Speedometer cable locking lever (Sec 20)

21 Headlamp bulb – renewal

Semi-sealed type

1   Open the bonnet and pull the connector from the rear of the headlight (photo).
2   Remove the rubber cover. Depress and turn the bulb retaining ring anticlockwise, then withdraw it (photos).

22 Headlamps – alignment

1   It is recommended that headlamp alignment is carried out by your dealer using modern beam setting equipment. However, in an emergency, the following procedure will provide temporary adjustment.
2   Position the car on level ground with the tyres correctly inflated, approximately 33 feet (10 metres) from a wall or a garage door.
3   Make two marks on the wall corresponding with the height above

21.1 The headlight wiring connector

21.2A The headlight rear cover

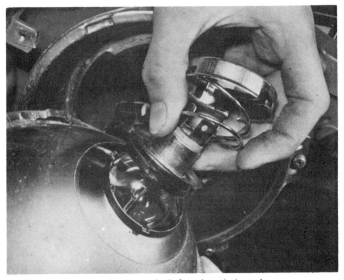

21.2B Removing the headlamp bulb (semi-sealed type)

21.6 Headlight surround

21.7 Headlight rim retaining screw

22.4 Headlight horizontal adjustment screw location

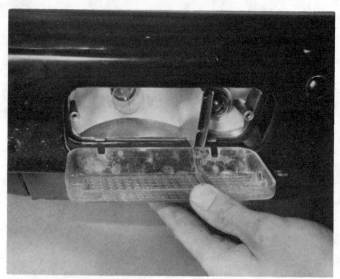

23.2 Removing the front indicator and parking light lens

23.3 Removing the side repeater light lens

23.4 Removing the number plate light cover and lens

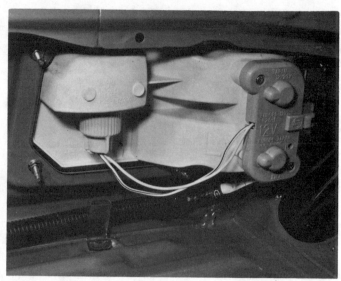

23.6A Tail light cluster interior view

23.6B Removing the tail light cluster bulbs

23.7 Removing the interior light lens

Fig. 10.21 Rear valance inner trim panel retaining screw locations (Sec 23)

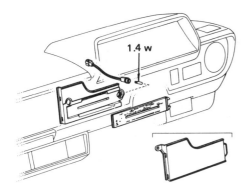

Fig. 10.22 Heater warning light bulb location (Sec 23)

the ground level of the headlamp centres, and the distance between the headlamp centres.

4 Switch the headlamps to main beam and check that the centres of height intensity are positioned over the previously made marks. If not, remove the headlamp surrounds and turn the alignment screws as necessary (photo).

5 During the adjustment make sure that the centre line of the car is at 90° to the wall surface and is in alignment with a point midway between the two marks.

6 Refit the surrounds when the adjustment is complete.

23 Bulbs (general) – renewal

1 The bulbs fitted to exterior lights are of the bayonet type and are

removed by depressing them and turning them anticlockwise. In the case of stop and tail lamp (twin filament) bulbs, the locating pins are staggered so that the bulb can only be fitted in one position.

Front indicator and parking lights
2 Loosen the two screws and withdraw the lens from the bumper (photo).

Side repeater lights
3 Loosen the two screws and withdraw the lens (photo).

Number plate light
4 Unscrew the retaining screws and remove the cover and glass lens (photo).

Tail light cluster
5 Open the tailgate and remove the rear valance inner trim panel; six screws are located along the top of the panel and two central screws at the bottom (Fig. 10.21).

6 The reversing lamp bulbholder can now be pulled from the body. Access to the remaining bulbs is gained by removing the retaining screws and withdrawing the combined bulbholder assembly (photos).

Interior light
7 Prise the lens from the light and remove the festoon type bulb from the light terminals (photo).

Heater warning light
8 Remove the heater control panel (see Chapter 12).

9 Pull out the bulbholder and extract the push-fit type bulb.

Heated rear window switch warning light
10 Remove the switch as described in Section 16.

11 Pull out the bulbholder and extract the push-fit type bulb.

Instrument panel warning lights
12 Remove the instrument panel cluster as described in Section 20.

13 Pull out the relevant bulbholder and extract the push-fit type bulb (photo).

Clock light
14 Pull off the radio control knobs and remove the surround.

15 Unscrew the retaining screw, withdraw the clock, and disconnect the multiplug connector.

16 Pull out the bulbholder and extract the bulb.

Refitting – all bulbs
17 Refitting of all bulbs is a reversal of removal, but make sure that the interior light terminals are tensioned sufficiently to hold the bulb firmly in position.

23.13 Instrument panel warning light bulb

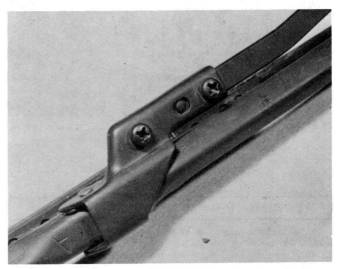

24.2 Wiper blade retaining screw

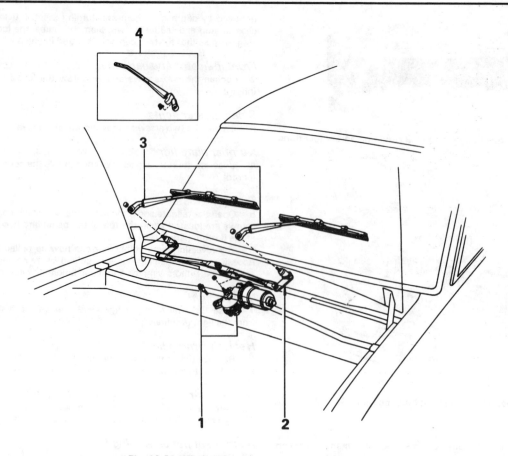

Fig. 10.23 Windscreen wiper components (Sec 25)

1 *Wiper motor and retaining*   3 *Wiper arm and blade*
   screw   4 *Wiper arm for LHD models*
2 *Linkage*

25.2 Removing a windscreen wiper arm

25.3A A windscreen wiper spindle with arm removed

25.3B Windscreen wiper motor location

24 Wiper blades – renewal

1   Whenever the wiper blades no longer clean the windscreen or tailgate window effectively, the flexible inserts should be renewed.
2   Pull one end of the insert from the end slot, then slide the complete insert from the wiper blade. If necessary, separate the wiper blade from the arm (photo).
3   Refitting of the inserts is a reversal of removal.

25 Windscreen wiper motor and linkage – removal and refitting

1   Disconnect the battery negative terminal.
2   Unscrew the retaining nuts and withdraw the wiper arms from the spindles (photo).
3   Disconnect the linkage from the motor spindle arm and detach it from the air grille valance. Withdraw it from the car (photos).
4   Unscrew the mounting bolts and remove the wiper motor from the

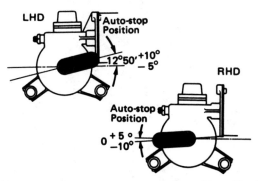

Fig. 10.24 Wiper motor arm auto-stop positions (Sec 25)

bulkhead. Note the position of the earth wire.
5   Refitting is a reversal of removal, but before fitting the linkage, temporarily reconnect the battery and turn on the ignition switch and wiper switch. To make sure that the wiper motor is in its auto-stop position (see Fig. 10.24), switch off the wiper motor using the wiper switch.

26 Tailgate wiper motor and linkage – removal and refitting

1   Disconnect the battery negative terminal.

2   Lift the hinged cap and unscrew the retaining nut to withdraw the wiper arm from the spindle (photo).
3   Using a screwdriver, carefully prise out the retaining clips and withdraw the trim cover.
4   Unscrew the retaining screws, remove the circular inspection cover, and separate the multiplug connector (photo).
5   Unscrew the securing screws and withdraw the wiper motor and linkage from the tailgate (photo).
6   Refitting is a reversal of removal, but before fitting the wiper arm, temporarily reconnect the battery and switch on the ignition switch and wiper switch. To make sure that the wiper motor is in its auto-stop position, switch off the wiper motor using the wiper switch.

27 Windscreen, tailgate window and headlight washers – maintenance

1   The washer components are shown in Figs. 10.27, 10.28 and 10.29 (photo).
2   The reservoir levels should be checked weekly and topped-up as necessary. Always use special cleaning solvent together with water, as this will assist the cleaning action and prevent freezing during winter. Do not use engine anitfreeze as this will damage the paintwork.
3   Removal and refitting of the washer components is straight-forward, but with the tailgate washer it will be necessary to remove the rear compartment right-hand side panel and the rear headlining trim for access to the washer hose. The rear valance inner trim panel must also be removed for access to the washer motor. Note that headlight washers are not fitted to UK models.

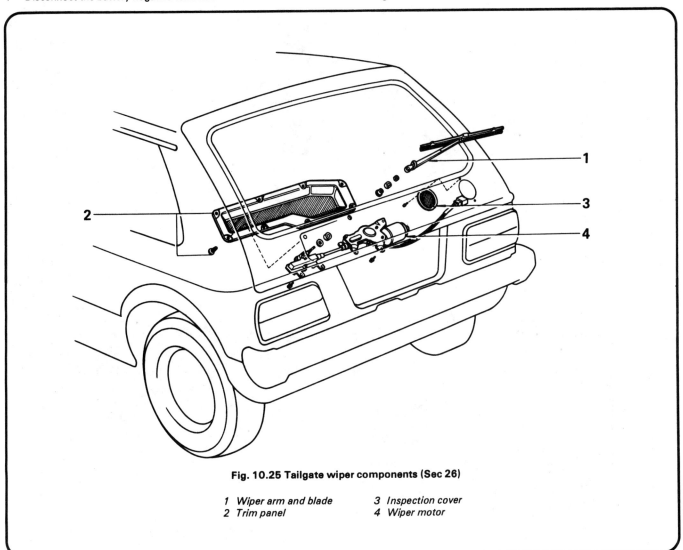

Fig. 10.25 Tailgate wiper components (Sec 26)

1 Wiper arm and blade	3 Inspection cover
2 Trim panel	4 Wiper motor

26.2 Tailgate window wiper arm retaining nut

26.4 Tailgate window wiper motor multiplug connector

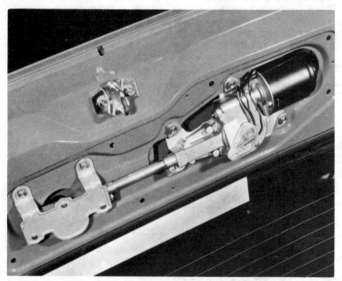

26.5 The tailgate wiper motor and linkage

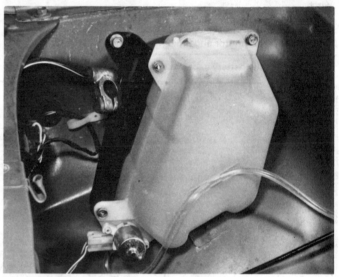

27.1 Windscreen washer reservoir and motor

28.1 Horn location

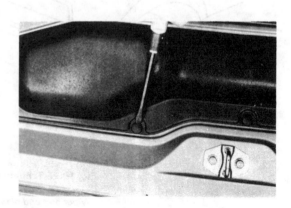

Fig. 10.26 Removing the tailgate inner trim panel (Sec 26)

28 Horn – testing, removal and refitting

1   The horn is located in front of the battery, and access to it is gained by removing the radiator grille (photo).

2   Should the horn fail to operate, first check the terminals for security, then check the relevant fuse. If this proves to be in order, check that current is reaching the green and red supply wire to the horn using a voltmeter or 12 volt test lamp and leads.

3   If current is reaching the horn, connect a lead from the other horn terminal to earth. The horn itself is faulty if it still fails to work, but the horn switch or horn switch earth is faulty if the horn operates during this test.

4   Access to the horn push and contacts is gained by removing the steering wheel (see Chapter 11).

5   To remove the horn, disconnect the battery negative terminal and horn leads, then unscrew the mounting. Refitting is a reversal of removal.

29 Radio – removal and refitting

1   Disconnect the battery negative terminal.

2   Pull the two knobs from the splined spindles.

3   Unscrew and remove the retaining nuts and washers, and the retaining screw, and withdraw the surround from the radio and clock.

4   Remove the retaining screw, withdraw the clock, and disconnect the multiplug.

5   Unscrew the securing screws and withdraw the radio, at the same time disconnecting the aerial and electrical wires from the rear of the radio.

6   Refitting is a reversal of removal.

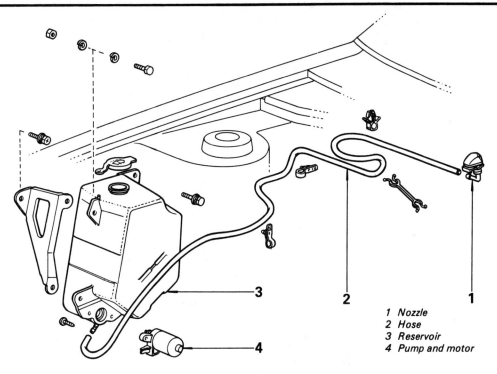

1 Nozzle
2 Hose
3 Reservoir
4 Pump and motor

Fig. 10.27 Windscreen washer components (Sec 27) (Above)

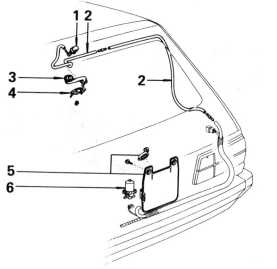

1 Nozzle
2 Hose
3 Grommet
4 Holder
5 Reservoir
6 Pump and motor

Fig. 10.28 Tailgate washer components (Sec 27)

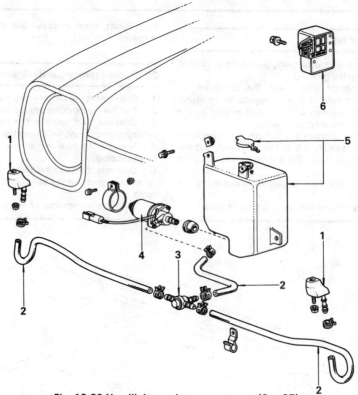

Fig. 10.29 Headlight washer components (Sec 27)

1 Nozzles   4 Pump and motor
2 Hose   5 Reservoir
3 Joint   6 Relay

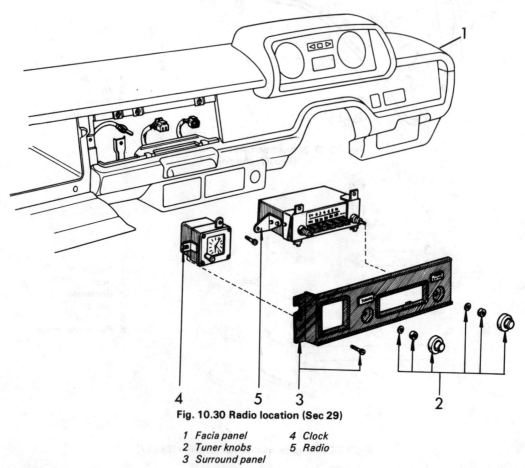

Fig. 10.30 Radio location (Sec 29)

1 Facia panel   4 Clock
2 Tuner knobs   5 Radio
3 Surround panel

30 Fault diagnosis – electrical system

Symptom	Reason/s
Ignition light stays on, battery runs flat	20 amp fuse blown
	Alternator drivebelt loose or missing
	Alternator brushes worn or sticking
	Alternator brush springs weak or broken
	Alternator slip rings dirty or worn
	Alternator winding(s) faulty
Ignition light not operating	5 amp in-line fuse blown
	Bulb blown
	Fusible link blown
	Faulty regulator
Starter motor fails to turn engine	
No electricity at starter motor	Battery discharged
	Battery defective internally
	Battery terminal leads loose or earth lead not securely attached to body
	Starter motor solenoid faulty
Electricity at starter motor	Starter brushes worn, sticking, or brush wire loose
	Commutator dirty, worn or burnt
	Starter motor armature faulty
	Field coils earthed
Starter motor turns engine very slowly	
Electrical defects	Battery in discharged condition
	Starter brushes badly worn, sticking, or brush wires loose
	Loose wires in starter motor circuit
Starter motor engages but does not turn engine	
Mechanical defect	Pinion or flywheel gear teeth broken or worn
Electrical defect	Battery almost completely discharged
	Solenoid internal contacts faulty
Starter motor noisy or excessively rough engagement	
Lack of attention or mechanical damage	Pinion or flywheel gear teeth broken or worn
	Starter motor retaining bolts loose
Battery will not hold charge for more than a few days	
Wear or damage	Battery defective internally
	Electrolyte level too low or electrolyte too weak due to leakage
	Plate separators no longer fully effective
	Battery plates severely sulphated
Insufficient current flow to keep battery charged	Battery plates severely sulphated
	Drivebelt slipping
	Battery terminal connections loose or corroded
	Alternator not charging
	Alternator regulator unit not working correctly
Horn	
Horn operates all the time	Horn push either earthed or stuck down
	Horn cable to horn push earthed
Horn fails to operate	Blown fuse
	Cable or cable connections loose, broken or disconnected
	Horn has an internal fault
Horn emits intermittent or unsatisfactory noise	Cable connections loose, or horn requires adjustment
Lights	
Lights do not come on	If engine not running, battery discharged
	Light bulb filament burnt out or bulbs broken
	Wire connections loose, disconnected or broken
	Light switch shorting or otherwise faulty, causing blown fuse
Lights come on but fade out	If engine not running, battery discharged
Lights give very poor illumination	Lamp glasses dirty
	Lamps badly out of adjustment

Symptom	Reason/s
Lights work erratically – flashing on and off, especially over bumps	Battery terminal or earth connection loose Lights not earthing properly Contacts in light switch faulty

Wipers

Symptom	Reason/s
Wiper motor fails to work	Blown fuse Wire connections loose, disconnected or broken Brushes badly worn Armature worn or faulty Field coils faulty
Wiper motor works very slowly and takes excessive current	Commutator dirty, greasy or burnt Armature bearings dirty, or unaligned Armature badly worn or faulty
Wiper motor works slowly and takes little current	Brushes badly worn Commutators dirty, greasy or burnt Armature badly worn or faulty
Wiper motor works but wiper blades remain static	Wiper motor gearbox parts badly worn

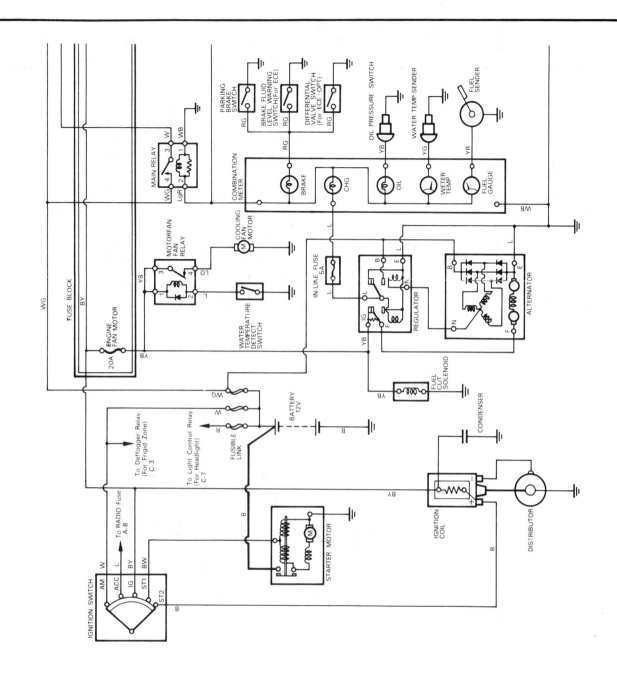

Fig. 10.31 Wiring diagram for the Toyota Starlet – early models (colour code on page 149)

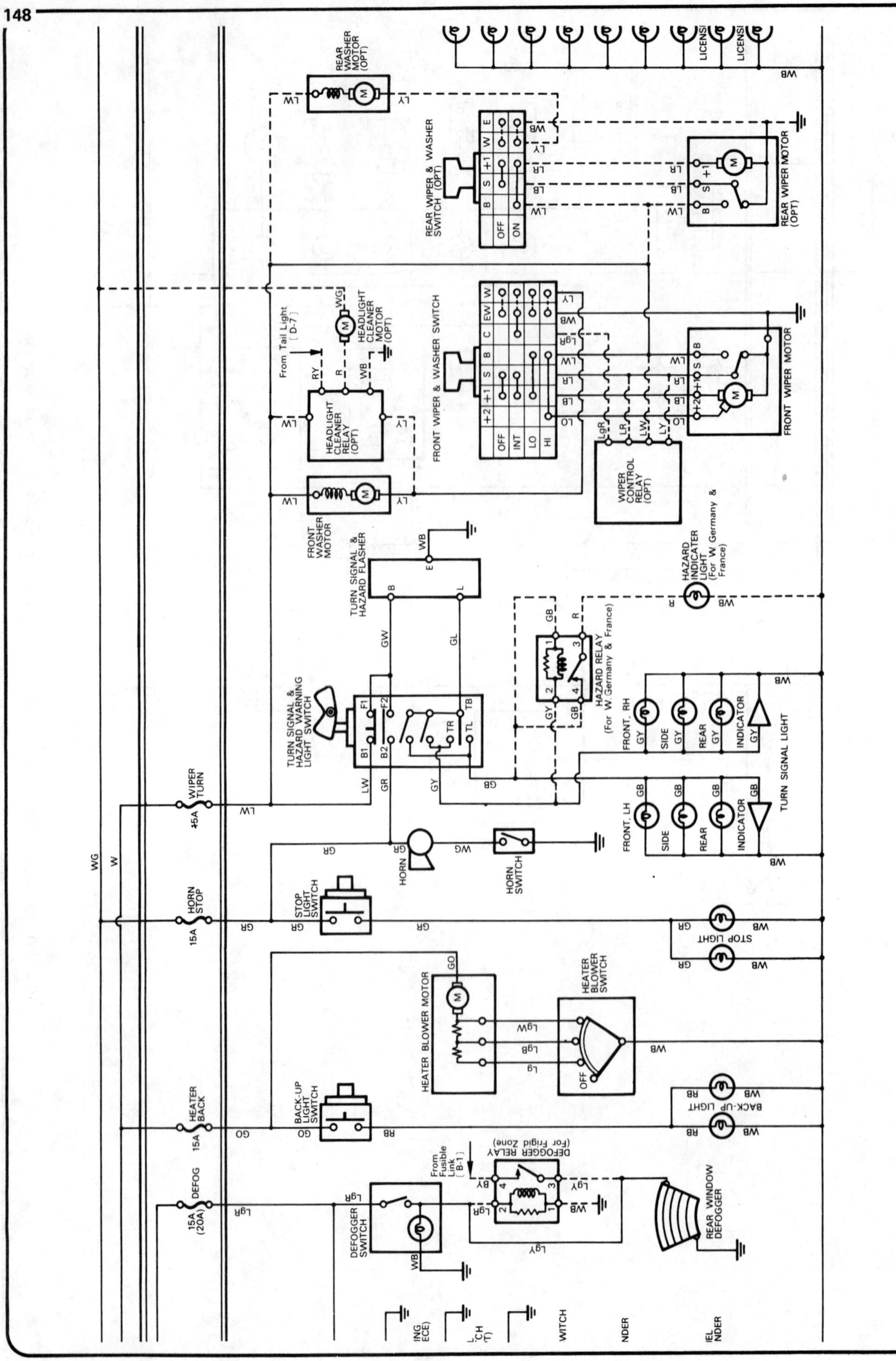

Fig. 10.31 Wiring diagram for the Toyota Starlet – early models (continued)

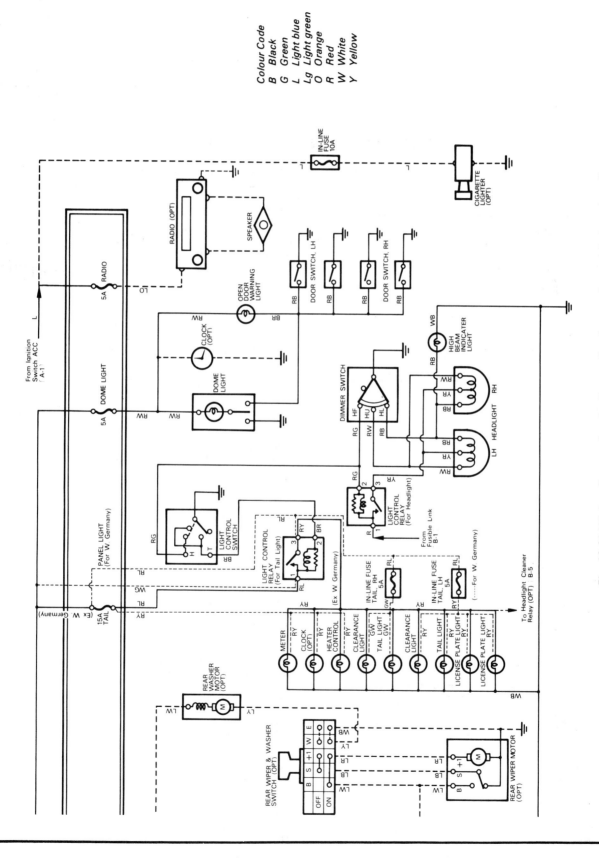

Fig. 10.31 Wiring diagram for the Toyota Starlet – early models (continued)

Chapter 11 Suspension and steering

For modifications, and information applicable to later models, see Supplement at end of manual

Contents

Specifications

Front suspension

Type . . . . Independent, MacPherson strut, with lower arm integral hydraulic telescopic shock absorbers, and anti-roll bar

Wheel bearing preload (turning) . . . . 0.6 to 1.5 lbf (0.3 to 0.7 kgf) at stud
Fluid capacity in front strut . . . . 9 fl oz (250 ml)
Front wheel alignment:
    Camber . . . . $0° 50' \pm 45'$ (left to right error 30')
    Caster . . . . $1° 20' \pm 45'$ (left to right error 30')
    Steering axis inclination . . . . $8° 25' \pm 45'$ (left to right error 30')
    Toe-in . . . . 0 to $\frac{5}{16}$ in (0 to 8.0 mm)
    Inside turning angle . . . . $35° 50' \pm 1°$
    Outside turning angle . . . . $34° 50' \pm 1°$
Vehicle height from lower arm inner bush centre to ground:
    6.00 x 12 4PR tyres (non UK models) . . . . 9.409 in (239.0 mm)
    155SR13 tyres . . . . 9.370 in (238.0 mm)
    155SR12 tyres . . . . 8.858 in (225.0 mm)
    145SR13 tyres . . . . 9.173 in (233.0 mm)

Rear suspension

Type . . . . Four link trailing arm with coil springs, gas filled telescopic shock absorbers
Vehicle height from lower control arm front bush centre to ground:
    6.00 x 12 4PR tyres (non UK models) . . . . 9.449 in (240.0 mm)
    155SR13 tyres . . . . 9.409 in (239.0 mm)
    155SR12 tyres . . . . 8.898 in (226.0 mm)
    145SR13 tyres . . . . 9.213 in (234.0 mm)

Steering

Type . . . . Rack and pinion, two-section column, collapsible main column
Steering wheel free play . . . . 0 to 1.2 in (0 to 30.0 mm)
Maximum rack run-out . . . . 0.01 in (0.3 mm)
Pinion bearing preload:
    Without rack . . . . 1.4 to 2.1 lbf in (1.5 to 2.5 kgf cm)
    Rack fitted . . . . 6.7 to 7.8 lbf in (7.0 to 9.0 kgf cm)
Ratio 15.9:1

Wheels and tyres

Roadwheels	Pressed steel, 4½J x 13 in (UK) or 4½J x 12 in
Tyres:	
Crossply	6.00 x 12 4PR
Radial	155SR12, 145SR13, 155SR13
Tyre pressures (front and rear):	
Crossply	21 lbf in² (1.5 kgf/cm²)
Radial	24 lbf/in² (1.7 kgf/cm²)

Note: *Increase the above pressures by 4.0 lbf/in² (0.3 kgf/cm²) for sustained speeds in excess of 65 mph (100 kph)*

Torque wrench settings

	lbf ft	kgf m
Front suspension		
Strut gland nut	100	13.8
Lower arm inner pivot	50	6.9
Lower balljoint to steering knuckle	60	8.3
Strut pinion rod nut	35	4.8
Upper suspension mounting	20	2.8
Strut to steering knuckle	50	6.9
Crossmember to body	70	9.7
Anti-roll bar to lower arm	85	11.8
Track-rod end	50	6.9
Track-rod adjusting clamp	15	2.1
Rear suspension		
Shock absorber to body	20	2.8
Shock absorber to axle tube	30	4.1
Upper control arm pivot bolts	100	13.8
Lower control arm pivot bolts	70	9.7
Steering		
Column upper mounting bolts	30	4.1
Steering wheel nut	25	3.5
Intermediate shaft clamps	25	3.5
Pinion bearing locknut	70	9.7
Rack guide spring cap – initial	18	2.5
Rack guide spring cap locknut	45	6.2
Rack end balljoints	60	8.3
Track-rod end locknut	15	2.1
Rack mounting bolts	30	4.1

1 General description

1   The front suspension is of independent MacPherson strut type, incorporating coil springs and hydraulic telescopic shock absorbers.
2   The lower balljoints and suspension arms cannot be serviced separately as they are a complete assembly. The suspension arms are mounted to the crossmember at their minor ends.
3   The anti-roll bar is attached to the suspension arms and mounted on the body underframe by rubber bushes.
4   The rear suspension is of trailing arm and coil spring type. Longitudinal movement of the rear axle is controlled by the lower control arm, and side to side movement by the upper arms. The gas-filled telescopic shock absorbers are attached to brackets on the axle tube at their lower ends, and to the body underframe at their upper ends.
5   The steering gear is of rack and pinion type, and is mounted on the front suspension crossmember. An intermediate shaft is attached to the main steering shaft and steering gear, and torque is transmitted through two universal joints.

2 Maintenance and inspection

1   Every 6000 miles (10 000 km), inspect the condition of all flexible gaiters, balljoint dust excluders and rubber suspension bushes. Renew any that have split or deteriorated, as described in the appropriate Section of this Chapter.
2   At the same time, check the tightness of all steering and suspension nuts and bolts in accordance with the torque figures listed in the Specifications.
3   At the intervals specified in Routine Maintenance, adjust or lubricate the front hubs and check the front wheel alignment.

3 Front hub – servicing and adjustment

1   Jack-up the front of the car and support it on axle stands. Remove the roadwheel.
2   Remove the brake caliper as described in Chapter 9.
3   Prise off the dust cap and withdraw the split-pin (photo).
4   Remove the adjusting cap.
5   Unscrew and remove the hub nut and extract the thrust washer (photo).
6   Pull the hub/disc assembly slightly outwards. This will eject the outer bearing which can then be removed. Now withdraw the hub/disc assembly from the stub axle (photos).
7   Lower the oil seal from the inner hub recess, and withdraw the inner roller bearing.
8   Wipe all old grease from the bearings and hub recesses and wash them with paraffin. Thoroughly wipe them until dry. Examine all components for wear and deterioration and renew them as necessary.
9   If the bearings are to be renewed, drive out the outer tracks with a soft metal drift. Do not mix bearing components if they are to be refitted as they are supplied as matched sets.
10 Pack lithium based grease into the roller bearings, and into the hub recesses and dust cap as shown in Fig. 11.3.
11 After fitting the outer tracks and inner bearing, drive a new oil seal squarely into the hub with suitable tubing. Smear a little grease on the oil seal lip (photo).
12 Locate the hub/disc on the stub axle and fit the outer bearings, thrust washer and hub nut. The bearing preload must now be adjusted in the following manner.
13 Tighten the hub nut to 22 lbf ft (3·0 kgf m) while turning the hub/disc forwards and backwards. Loosen the nut fully and tighten it again to the same torque. Loosen it fully again and tighten the socket using only the fingers and thumb.

3.3 Front hub nut locking cap and split-pin

3.5 Removing the front hub nut and thrust washer

3.6A Removing the front hub outer bearing

3.6B Removing the hub/disc assembly

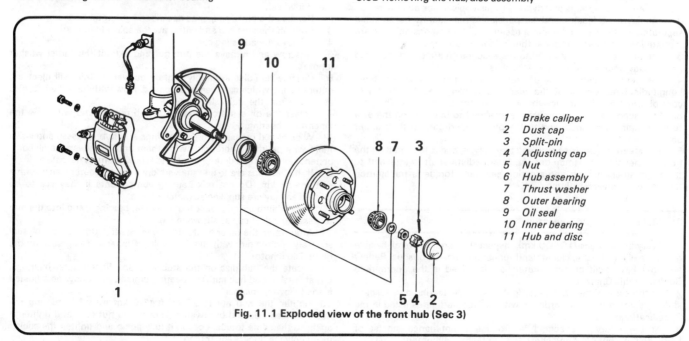

1	Brake caliper
2	Dust cap
3	Split-pin
4	Adjusting cap
5	Nut
6	Hub assembly
7	Thrust washer
8	Outer bearing
9	Oil seal
10	Inner bearing
11	Hub and disc

Fig. 11.1 Exploded view of the front hub (Sec 3)

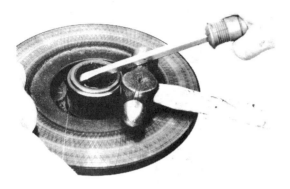

Fig. 11.2 Removing the hub oil seal (Sec 3)

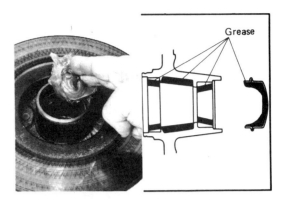

Fig. 11.3 Grease location in the front hub (Sec 3)

Fig. 11.4 Checking the front hub bearing preload with a spring balance (Sec 3)

3.11 Front hub oil seal

14 Refit the nut locking cap and align the holes. If necessary tighten the nut by a minimal amount to achieve this. Insert the split-pin and secure it by bending its legs.
15 Check that the hub revolves smoothly and, if available, use a spring balance to check the specified turning preload.
16 Refit the dust cap, and refer to Chapter 9 for the brake caliper refitting procedure.
17 Refit the roadwheel and lower the car to the ground.

4 Front suspension strut – removal and refitting

1 Jack-up the front of the car and support it on axle stands. Remove the roadwheel.
2 Seal the brake master cylinder filler cap by using adhesive tape over the vent hole or round the rim. This will reduce the loss of hydraulic fluid during subsequent operations by creating a vacuum in the reservoir.
3 Disconnect the flexible brake hose from the bracket beneath the front wing.
4 Support the suspension strut with a trolley jack. Unscrew and remove the upper mounting nuts and washers.
5 Refer to Section 3 and remove the front hub assembly.
6 Unscrew and remove the strut to suspension arm mounting bolts and washers.
7 Lower the trolley jack and push the suspension arm and knuckle

arm from the strut to disengage the locating dowels.
8 Withdraw the suspension strut from the car.
9 Unbolt the disc backplate from the strut (photo).
10 Using a spring compressor, compress the coil spring until it is detached from the upper seat.
11 Prise the dust cover from the upper support, then unscrew and remove the retaining nut from the end of the piston rod while holding the upper spring seat stationary. If necessary, the special tool for holding the seat may be hired from a Toyota dealer or tool hire agent.
12 Withdraw the upper support, dust seal and spring seat from the piston rod.
13 Lift off the flexible dust cover and spring bumper, then remove the coil spring (still compressed). If the spring is to be renewed, release the compressor gently, otherwise it can remain in position.
14 Clean all components and check them for wear and deterioration. In particular, check the strut for leaks or weak operation and the support bearing for roughness and excessive play. Renew the components as necessary and overhaul the strut as described in Section 5 if necessary.
15 Refitting is a reversal of removal, but the following additional points should be noted:

(a) Renew coil springs only as a pair, and fit them with the smallest diameter or the paint mark downwards (Fig. 11.7).
(b) Make sure that the spring seat locates on the piston rod flats correctly

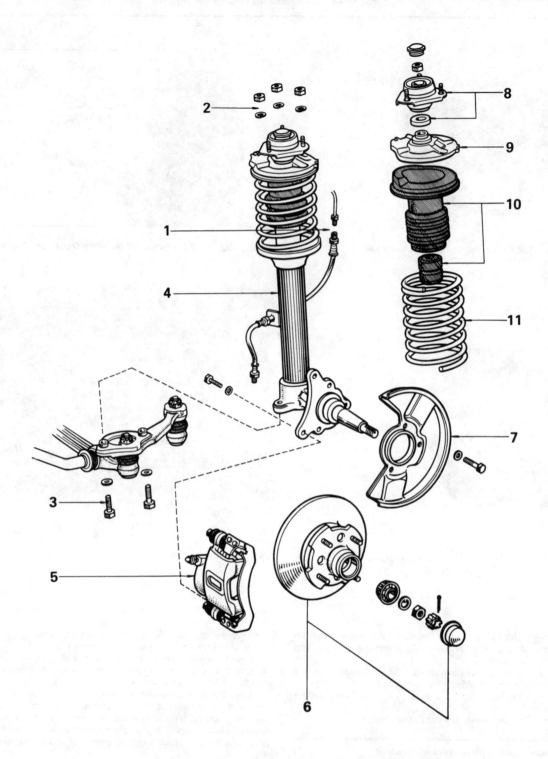

Fig. 11.5 Front suspension strut components (Sec 4)

1	Brake hydraulic line	7	Backplate
2	Upper support retaining nuts	8	Upper support and dust seal
3	Lower retaining bolts	9	Spring upper nut
4	Strut	10	Dust cover and spring bumper
5	Brake caliper		
6	Hub and disc assembly	11	Coil spring

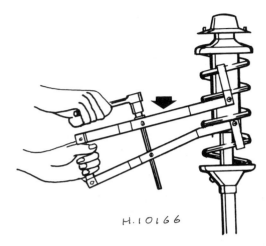

Fig. 11.6 Using a spring compressor (arrowed) on the front coil spring (Sec 4)

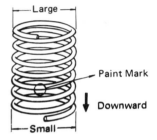

Fig. 11.7 Front coil spring fitting direction (Sec 4)

4.9 Disc backplate

(c) Always fit a new piston rod retaining nut

(d) Pack the support bearing with grease before refitting the dust cover

(e) Tighten all nuts and bolts to the specified torque

(f) Adjust the front hub as described in Section 3

(g) Remove the adhesive tape and bleed the hydraulic system as described in Chapter 9

5 Front suspension strut – overhaul

1 Remove the front suspension strut as described in Section 4 and thoroughly clean the outer shell.

2 It is important that the strut is dismantled and reassembled in a clean area, since the piston rod assembly has a precision surface which can easily be damaged, causing fluid leakage.

3 Temporarily reinsert the lower strut retaining bolts, then clamp them in a vice and unscrew the strut ring (upper gland) nut. If a suitable spanner is not available, grip the nut in the vice and lever on the stub axle.

4 Prise out the O-ring seal from the ring nut.

5 Withdraw the piston rod and cylinder assembly from the suspension strut. Place the strut in a container which will hold the fluid to be drained later.

6 Remove the seal rebound stopper and guide from the piston rod.

7 Using a suitable length of metal dowel, drive the base valve from the bottom of the cylinder.

8 Note that no attempt should be made to remove the valve from the bottom of the piston rod.

9 Empty the fluid from the suspension strut.

10 Clean all the components and wipe dry with a lint-free cloth.

11 Carefully examine all the components for wear and deterioration. Renew any components which are unserviceable, and obtain a new ring nut oil seal and fresh shock absorber fluid.

12 Press the new oil seal into the ring nut in a soft-jawed vice, making sure that it enters squarely.

13 Drive the base valve into the bottom of the cylinder, and locate the cylinder centrally in the strut.

14 Push the piston rod fully down into the cylinder, then fill the strut and cylinder with the specified amount of fresh shock absorber fluid.

15 Locate the rebound stopper and guide over the piston rod and press them down into the cylinder and strut shell.

16 Insert the new seal between the rod guide and strut shell.

17 Smear the ring nut oil seal lip with multi-purpose grease and lower the nut over the piston rod. Take care not to damage the seal; wrap a piece of adhesive tape around the piston rod shoulders so that the seal lip can slide onto the main piston and diameter.

18 With the suspension strut held firmly in a vice, tighten the ring (gland) nut to the specified torque. At the same time position the piston rod so that it protrudes 3·1 to 3·5 in (80·0 to 90·0 mm) from the strut.

6 Front suspension arm and balljoint – checking for wear, removal and refitting

1 Jack-up the front of the car and support it on axle stands. Apply the handbrake.

2 Raise the suspension arm approximately 1·0 in (25 mm) then grip the top and bottom of the wheel and attempt to rock it in the vertical plane. Provided the front hub bearings are not worn, and provided they are adjusted correctly, any slackness indicates a worn balljoint. The balljoints and suspension arms cannot be separated, and if wear is evident they must be renewed as complete assemblies, as described in the following paragraphs.

3 Remove the roadwheel.

4 Extract the split-pin and unscrew the nut from the track-rod end. Using a universal balljoint separator, detach the track-rod end from the knuckle arm.

5 Unscrew and remove the anti-roll bar to suspension arm retaining nut, washer, cover and rubber.

6 Unscrew and remove the strut lower mounting bolts, and lever the knuckle arm from the strut.

7 Unscrew the inner pivot bolt nut, then raise the suspension arm and twist it against the anti-roll bar until the pivot bolt can be removed.

8 Lower the suspension arm and withdraw it from the crossmember and anti-roll bar. Make sure that the rubber bush, cover, and caster spacer remain in place on the anti-roll bar.

9 Extract the split-pin and unscrew the knuckle arm retaining nut. Using a universal balljoint separator, detach the suspension arm and balljoint from the knuckle arm.

10 Check the components for wear and deterioration and renew them as necessary. If the suspension arm is still serviceable, the inner bush may if necessary be renewed using suitable tubing and a bench vice.

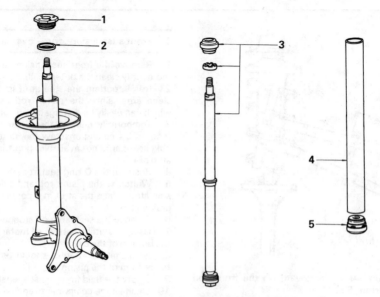

Fig. 11.8 Exploded view of a front suspension strut (Sec 5)

1 Ring (gland) nut
2 Seal
3 Piston rod, guide and

rebound stopper
4 Cylinder
5 Base valve

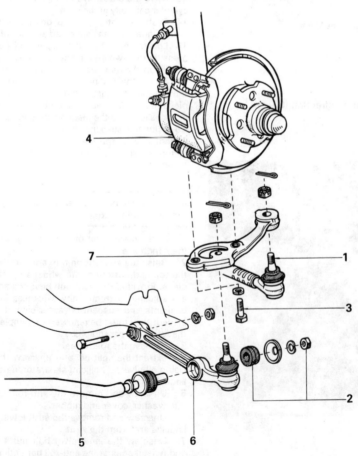

Fig. 11.9 Front suspension arm and balljoint components (Sec 6)

1 Track-rod end
2 Anti-roll bar mounting
3 Strut lower retaining bolts
4 Strut and caliper

5 Inner pivot bolt
6 Suspension arm
7 Knuckle arm

Make sure that the mating surfaces are scrupulously clean before fitting the bush.

11 Refitting is a reversal of removal, but the following additional points should be noted:

(a) Tighten all nuts and bolts to the specified torque, but delay tightening the anti-roll bar nut and inner pivot bolt until the weight of the car is fully on the suspension
(b) Make sure that the split-pin is not trapped between the knuckle arm and strut mating surfaces
(c) Check the front wheel alignment as described in Section 16

7 Front anti-roll bar – removal and refitting

1 Jack-up the front of the car and support it on blocks placed under the front tyres. Apply the handbrake. Mark the anti-roll bar for position.
2 Unbolt the front brackets from the underframe.
3 Unscrew and remove the anti-roll bar to suspension arm retaining nuts, washers, covers and rubber bushes (photo).
4 Lever one end of the anti-roll bar inwards and at the same time pull it from the suspension arm. The complete bar can now be withdrawn from the car.
5 Remove the sleeves, rubber bushes, covers and caster spacers from the anti-roll bar. Carefully note the location and number of caster spacers.
6 Remove the front bracket rubber bushes.
7 Examine the bush components for wear and renew them as necessary.
8 Refitting is a reversal of removal, but the following additional points should be noted:

(a) Tighten the nuts and bolts to the specified torque with the full weight of the car on the suspension
(b) Make sure that the caster spacers are returned to their original poisitons
(c) Check the front wheel alignment as described in Section 16

8 Front crossmember – removal and refitting

1 Jack-up the front of the car and support it on axle stands.
2 Remove the steering gear as described in Section 14.

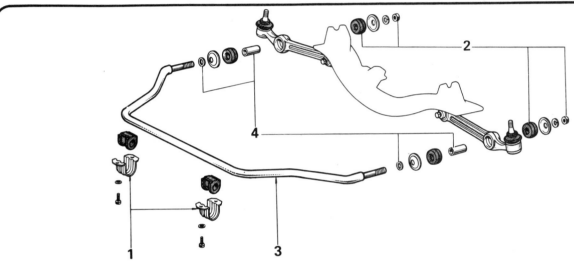

Fig. 11.10 Front anti-roll bar components (Sec 7)

1 Brackets
2 Mounting rubber components
3 Anti-roll bar

4 Mounting sleeves, rubbers, and caster spacers

Fig. 11.11 Removing an anti-roll bar caster spacer (Sec 7)

7.3 Anti-roll bar to suspension arm mounting

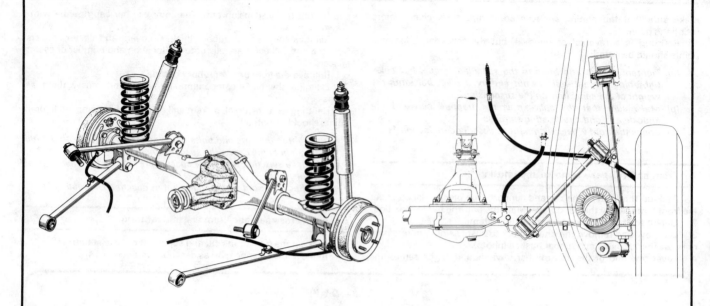

Fig. 11.12 Rear suspension layout (Sec 9)

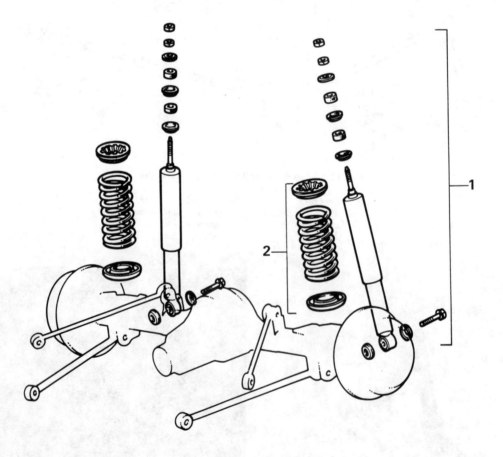

Fig. 11.13 Rear shock absorber (1) and coil spring (2) components (Sec 9)

3   Remove the front engine guard.
4   Remove the anti-roll bar as described in Section 7.
5   Remove the suspension arm inner pivot bolts and disconnect the arms from the crossmember.
6   Support the weight of the engine, either with a hoist or by a trolley jack and block of wood beneath the engine.
7   Unscrew and remove the engine front mounting nuts and washers.
8   Unscrew the mounting bolts and lower the crossmember from the body underframe.
9   Refitting is a reversal of removal, but the following additional points should be noted:

(a) Tighten all nuts and bolts to the specified torque, but delay tightening the anti-roll bar and suspension arm nuts until the full weight of the car is on the suspension
(b) Check the front wheel alignment as described in Section 16.

9   Rear shock absorber – removal, testing, and refitting

1   Jack-up the rear of the car and support it with axle stands placed under the axle tube. Remove the roadwheel.
2   Working inside the rear of the car, unscrew and remove the locknut, retaining nut and mounting components from the top of the shock absorber (photo). Note the order of removal to ensure correct refitting.
3   Unscrew the shock absorber lower mounting bolt from the axle tube, recover the spacers, and withdraw the shock absorber from beneath the car (photo).
4   Grip the lower shock absorber mounting in a vice with the shock absorber vertical, then fully extend and retract the unit ten or twelve times. The resistance should be smooth in both directions without any squelching noises. Renew the unit if it is proved unserviceable.
5   Refitting is a reversal of removal, but check that the upper mounting is assembled as shown in Fig. 11.14 and only tighten the mounting nuts and bolt with the full weight of the car on the suspension.

10   Rear coil spring – removal and refitting

1   Jack-up the rear of the car and support it with axle stands placed beneath the underframe.
2   Support the axle tube with a trolley jack and remove the shock absorber as decribed in Section 9.
3   Lower the axle tube until the coil spring and seats can be lifted out. Remove the spring bumper where fitted.
4   Refitting is a reversal of removal, but make sure that the spring is located correctly in the seats and refer to Section 9 for the shock absorber refitting procedure.

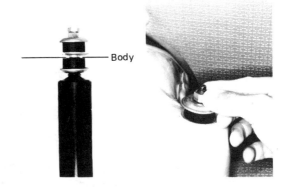

Fig. 11.14 Rear shock absorber upper mounting (Sec 9)

11   Rear upper and lower control arms – removal and refitting

1   Jack-up the rear of the car and support it with axle stands placed beneath the axle tube. Support the front of the differential casing with a trolley jack. Remove the roadwheel.
2   Unscrew and remove the mounting bolts from the control arm. When removing the lower control arm, it will be necessary to detach the shock absorber lower mounting and handbrake cable support.
3   Remove the control arm and examine it for damage and deterioration. If the bushes in the lower control arm need renewing, they can be removed and refitted in a vice using suitable tubing. Note that a chamfer is cut on one side of the control arm to facilitate fitting. No lubricant should be used.
4   Refitting is a reversal of removal, but the following additional points should be noted:

(a) The lower control arm must be located with the handbrake cable mounting nearer the axle tube
(b) The control arm and shock absorber mounting bolts must initially be assembled finger tight, then fully tightened to the specified torque with the full weight of the car on the suspension

12   Steering wheel – removal and refitting

1   Set the front roadwheels in the straight-ahead position. Disconnect the battery negative terminal.

9.2 Rear shock absorber upper mounting

9.3 Rear shock absorber lower mounting

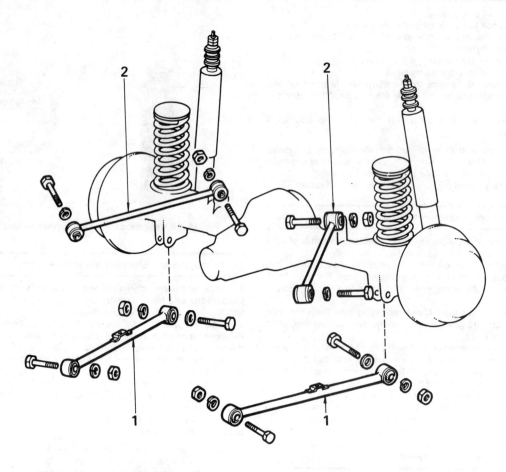

Fig. 11.15 Rear suspension lower control arm (1) and upper control arm (2) components (Sec 11)

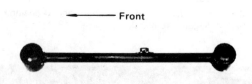

← Front

Fig. 11.16 Rear suspension lower control arm fitting positions (Sec 11)

2   With a screwdriver, prise the pad from the centre of the steering wheel.

3   Unscrew and remove the steering wheel retaining nut with a socket or box spanner (photo).

4   Mark the relative position of the wheel to the steering shaft by dot punching the end faces.

5   Pull the steering wheel from the shaft splines; do not attempt to jar it off as this may damage the shaft shear pins. If it is very tight, a puller will have to be used.

6   Refitting is a reversal of removal, but make sure that the steering wheel engages the direction indicator cancelling cam and that the previously made marks are aligned. Tighten the retaining nut to the specified torque.

Note: *Access to the horn contacts is gained by removing the covers (photo).*

13   Steering column – removal, overhaul and refitting

1   Remove the steering wheel as described in Section 12.

2   Unscrew the universal joint clamp bolts, pull the intermediate steering shaft from the steering gear, then withdraw the shaft from the main steering shaft universal joint.

3   Remove the steering column switches as described in Chapter 10.

4   Disconnect the ignition switch wiring plug.

5   Unscrew the bolts securing the hole cover to the bulkhead.

6   Unscrew the upper column mounting bolts and nut, remove the earth lead and wedge, and withdraw the column from inside the car. Recover the hole cover spacer.

7   Remove the ignition key cylinder as described in Chapter 10.

8   Unscrew the securing bolts and withdraw the retainer plate from the main steering shaft.

9   Using circlip pliers extract the circlip, then unbolt the upper bearing bracket from the steering column.

10 Withdraw the upper bearing bracket and upper tube from the steering shaft.

11 Prise the dust cover from the hole cover and remove it from the shaft.

12 Mount the hole cover in a vice and press the steering shaft into it while prising the spring clip from its groove.

13 Withdraw the hole cover and spring over the universal joint.

14 Remove the upper retainer from the shaft. Extract the bearing

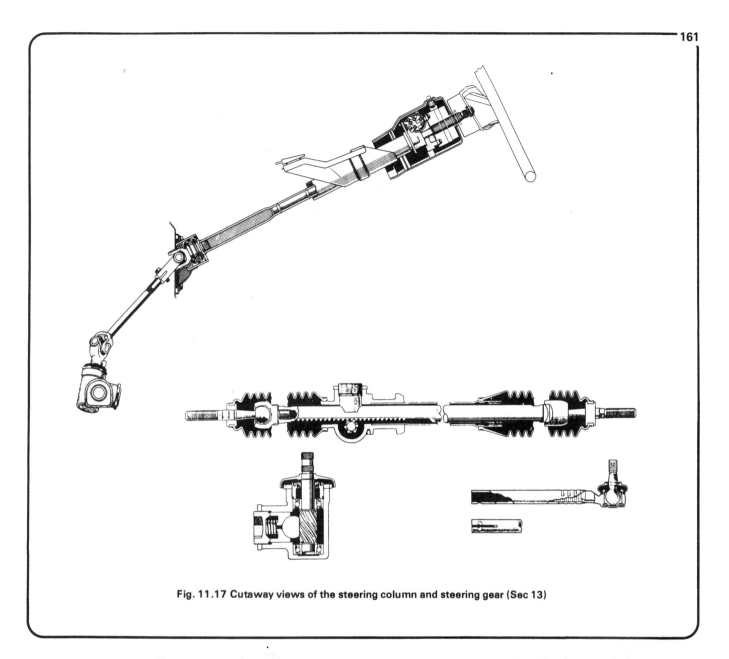

Fig. 11.17 Cutaway views of the steering column and steering gear (Sec 13)

12.3 Steering wheel retaining nut

12.6 Horn contact location in the steering wheel

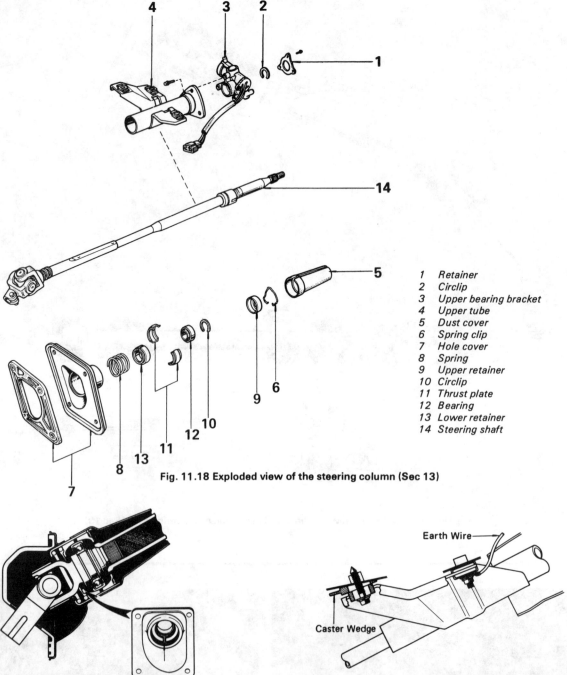

1 Retainer
2 Circlip
3 Upper bearing bracket
4 Upper tube
5 Dust cover
6 Spring clip
7 Hole cover
8 Spring
9 Upper retainer
10 Circlip
11 Thrust plate
12 Bearing
13 Lower retainer
14 Steering shaft

Fig. 11.18 Exploded view of the steering column (Sec 13)

Fig. 11.19 Steering column lower bearing retainer slot location
(Sec 13)

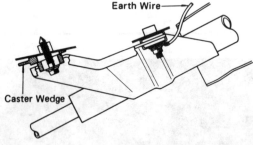

Fig. 11.20 Steering column upper tube and wedge location
(Sec 13)

retaining circlip using circlip pliers.

15 Remove both halves of the bearing thrust plate. Drive the bearing from its location shoulder and withdraw it.

16 Remove the lower retainer from the shaft.

17 Drive the upper bearing from the upper bracket with a soft metal drift of suitable diameter.

18 Clean all components in paraffin, wipe them dry, and examine them for wear and deterioration. Check the steering shaft shear pins for slackness and if evident, renew the shaft assembly. Renew all components which are unserviceable.

19 Reassembly and refitting procedures are a reversal of dismantling and removal, but the following additional points should be noted:

(a) Smear the upper and lower retainers with multi-purpose grease before fitting them, and locate the lower retainer with

the slot facing downwards (Fig. 11.19). Similarly smear the thrust plate with grease

(b) The wedge must be located between the upper column and bulkhead so that the tube of the upper column is concentric with the steering shaft (photo)

(c) Fit the intermediate shaft with the steering wheel and roadwheels in the straight-ahead position

(d) Tighten all nuts and bolts to the specified torque

---

14 Steering gear – removal, overhaul and refitting

1 Jack-up the front of the car and support it on stands. Remove the roadwheels.

Fig. 11.21 Steering gear location and cross sectional view of strut/hub assembly (Sec 14)

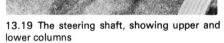

13.19 The steering shaft, showing upper and lower columns

14.3 Steering track-rod end (left-hand side)

14.4A Steering gear and mounting clamp (pinion side)

14.4B Steering gear bellows and mounting clamp

2   Unscrew and remove the intermediate steering shaft clamp bolts. Pull the shaft from the steering gear and withdraw it from the main steering shaft universal joint.

3   Extract the split-pins and unscrew the track-rod end nuts (photo). Disconnect the track-rod ends from the steering knuckle arms using a suitable separator.

4   Unscrew and remove the steering gear mounting clamp bolts and remove the clamps (photos).

5   Lift the steering gear from the front crossmember and withdraw it from beneath the car.

6   Clean the exterior of the steering gear and grip it in a soft-jawed vice around the grooved mounting.

7   Mark the position of the track-rod ends on the rack ends, and also mark each track-rod end for location. Loosen the pinch-bolts and unscrew the track-rod ends.

8   Remove the spring and hose clips from the rubber bellows. Withdraw the bellows and dust seals from the rack ends and mark the bellows left-hand and right-hand sides as they are diferent.

9   Bend up the tab washers and mark the rack ends left-hand and right-hand sides.

10 Hold the rack steady, then unscrew and remove the rack ends and tab washers.

11 Unscrew and remove the rack guide thrust bearing locknut and the spring cap, using a hexagon key for the latter.

12 Extract the spring and thrust bearing.

13 Prise the dust cover from the pinion and unscrew the adjusting screw locknut.

14 Unscrew the pinion bearing adjusting screw, using the special tool available or a suitable pin wrench. The tool incorporates two pegs for locating in the screw, and if necessary one can easily be made out of flat steel and two bolts of suitable diameter.

15 Pull the rack from the pinion end of the steering gear until the pinion is located in the recess and is not in mesh with the teeth.

16 Extract the pinion and bearing using a pair of pliers and a hammer as shown in Fig. 11.26. Take care not to damage the splines. Remove the spacer from the base of the pinion.

17 Withdraw the rack from the pinion end of the steering gear.

18 Using a screwdriver, lever the oil seal from the pinion bearing adjusting screw.

19 Using a suitable puller, remove the upper bearing from the pinion. Alternatively support the bearing in a vice and drive the pinion through it. Recover the spacer and note its location for correct reassembly.

20 Heat the pinion end of the steering gear in boiling water, then tap it on a piece of wood to release the lower pinion bearing.

21 Wash all components in paraffin and wipe them dry with lint-free cloth. Examine the components for wear and deterioration and renew them as necessary. If the bush in the end of the steering gear housing requires renewal, it can be driven out using a length of metal rod. Fully drive in the new bush using a suitable tubular drift.

22 Commence reassembly by fitting the pinion lower bearing into the housing after having heated the housing in boiling water. Refer to Fig. 11.27 and make sure that the bearing is located the correct way round.

23 Wipe away any traces of water, then pack the pinion lower bearing and housing as shown in Fig. 11.27 with a lithium based grease. Smear grease also on the housing bush. The housing should be approximately half full of grease.

24 Grease the rack teeth and insert it into the pinion end of the housing until the recess is in line with the pinion aperture.

25 Locate the spacer on the pinion and fully drive on the bearing using suitable tubing. Take care to position the bearing with the seal facing downwards.

26 Grease the pinion teeth and bearing and locate the lower spacer on the pinion shoulder. Tap the pinion and bearing into the housing.

27 Drive the new oil seal into the pinion adjusting screw, leaving it protruding by 0·02 in (0·5 mm).

28 Grease the oil seal lip, then insert and tighten the adjusting screw until the pinion turning torque is 3·5 lbf in (4·0 kgf cm) measured with a torque wrench. A special adaptor will be required to check the torque. Now loosen the screw until the specified preload (without rack) is obtained plus 0·4 lbf in (0·5 kgf cm).

29 Smear some liquid sealer on the base of the locknut, then tighten it onto the adjusting screw to the specified torque, holding the adjusting screw with the pin wrench. Check that the pinion turning torque is now reduced to within the specified limits.

30 Push the rack into its normal central position and at the same time mesh it with the pinion.

31 Grease the thrust bearing and insert it through the housing

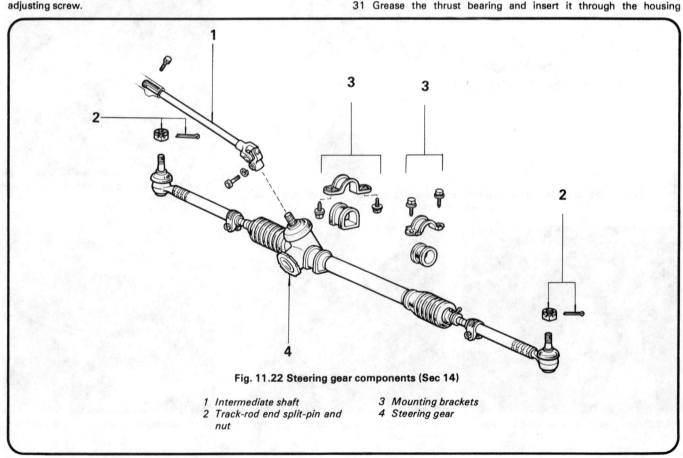

Fig. 11.22 Steering gear components (Sec 14)

1 Intermediate shaft
2 Track-rod end split-pin and nut
3 Mounting brackets
4 Steering gear

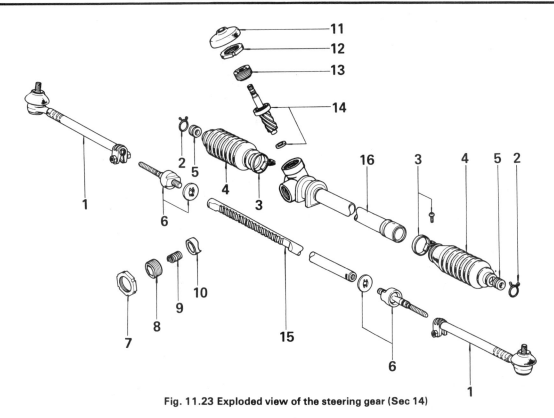

Fig. 11.23 Exploded view of the steering gear (Sec 14)

1	Track-rod end	7	Locknut	13	Adjusting screw
2	Spring clip	8	Spring cap	14	Pinion, bearing and
2	Bellows clip	9	Spring		spacer
4	Rubber bellows	10	Thrust bearing	15	Rack
5	Dust seal	11	Dust cover	16	Housing
6	Rack end and tab washer	12	Locknut		

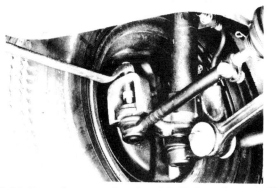

Fig. 11.24 Removing a track-rod end balljoint using a balljoint separator (Sec 14)

Fig. 11.25 Mounting the steering gear in a vice (Sec 14)

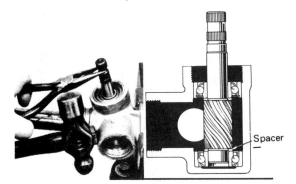

Fig. 11.26 Method of removing steering gear pinion and bearing (Sec 14)

Fig. 11.27 Grease location in the steering gear, showing correct fitting of the pinion lower bearing (Sec 14)

aperture.

32 Refit the spring and cap and tighten the cap to the initial specified torque. From this position loosen the cap between 25° and 30°.

33 Smear some liquid sealer on the base of the spring cap locknut, then tighten it onto the cap to the specified torque.

34 Check that the pinion turning torque is now within the specified limits (rack fitted).

35 Fit the rubber dust cover.

36 Grease the rack end balljoints, locate the tab washers, and screw the rack ends into the rack. With the tab washers located in the rack grooves, tighten the rack ends to the specified torque and bend over the tab washers. A special adaptor will be needed for the torque wrench (Fig. 11.29).

37 Fit the rack end dust seals and check that the pressure transfer holes in the housing are unobstructed (Fig. 11.30).

38 Refit the rubber bellows, spring and wire clips, and screw on the track-rod ends to their original positions. The distance from the balljoint centre to the dust seal on each side should be approximately 9·3 in (235·0 mm). Tighten the pinch-bolts.

39 Refit the steering gear to the front crossmember, locate the clamps, and tighten the retaining bolts.

40 Insert the track-rod ends into the steering knuckle arms. Tighten the nuts to the specified torque and fit the split-pins.

41 With the steering wheels in the straight-ahead position, refit the intermediate steering shaft and tighten the clamp bolts to the specified torque.

42 Refit the roadwheels and lower the car to the ground.

43 Adjust the front wheel alignment as described in Section 16.

---

15 Track-rod end balljoints – testing and renewal

1 The track-rod end balljoints should be examined for deterioration and wear at the intervals specified in Routine Maintenance.

2 Grip the track-rod near the balljoint and attempt to move it back and forth in a horizontal plane. Renew the track-rod end if any movement is evident.

3 Jack-up the front of the car and support it on axle stands. Remove the roadwheel.

4 Extract the split-pin and unscrew the nut. Use a balljoint separator to release the track-rod and from the steering knuckle arm.

5 Mark the position of the track-rod end on the rack end threads. Loosen the pinch-bolt and unscrew the track-rod end while holding the rack end stationary.

6 Refitting is a reversal of removal, but it will be necessary to check and adjust the front wheel alignment as described in Section 16.

---

16 Steering angles and front wheel alignment

1 Accurate front wheel alignment is essential for slow tyre wear and good steering. Before checking or adjusting the alignment, ensure that the tyres are correctly inflated, the front hub bearings are correctly adjusted, the front wheels are balanced and not buckled, the strut shock absorbers are serviceable, and that the track-rod ends are not worn.

2 Wheel alignment consists of four main factors:

(a) *Camber, the angle at which the front wheels are set from the vertical when viewed from the front of the car*

(b) *Caster, the angle at which the steering axis is set from the vertical when viewed from the side of the car*

(c) *Steering axis inclination, the angle at which the steering axis is set from the vertical when viewed from the front of the car*

(d) *Toe-in, the amount by which the distance between the front edges of the roadwheels (measured at hub height) is less than the corresponding distance between the rear edges of the front roadwheels*

3 Camber and steering axis inclination are not adjustable. Caster can be adjusted by varying the number of spacers fitted between the front anti-roll bar and the suspension arm. Toe-in can be adjusted by repositioning the track-rod ends on the rack ends.

4 Accurate checking of steering angles and wheel alignment is only possible with expensive equipment and is therefore best entrusted to

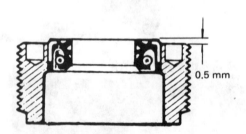

Fig. 11.28 Pinion adjusting nut oil seal protrusion dimension (Sec 14)

Fig. 11.30 Clearing the steering gear pressure transfer holes (Sec 14)

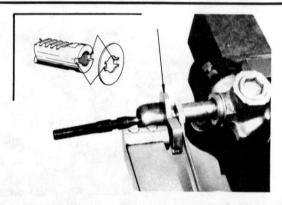

Fig. 11.29 Tightening the rack ends with a torque wrench (arrowed). Inset shows tab washer location (Sec 14)

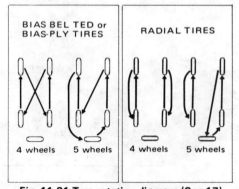

Fig. 11.31 Tyre rotation diagram (Sec 17)

your Toyota dealer. However, reasonable adjustment of toe-in is possible by using a home made adjustable trammel bar.

5   Drive the car onto level ground and adjust the trammel bar between the centres of the tyre tread on the rear of the front tyres. Mark the tyres with a small dot at the point where the trammel bar touches the tyres.

6   Move the car forwards so that the marks are now at hub height on the front of the tyres (wheel turned through 180°). Move the trammel bar to the front of the car without altering the adjustment. The distance between the two dots should now be less than the first distance by the specified amount of toe-in. If not, loosen the track-rod pinch-bolts and remove the steering gear bellows outer clips. Turn each rack end by equal amounts until the toe-in is correct (hold the track-rods quite still with a pair of grips), then tighten the pinch-bolts and refit the bellows clips.

17 Wheels and tyres – general care and maintenance

Wheels and tyres should give no real problems in use provided that a close eye is kept on them with regard to excessive wear or damage. To this end, the following points should be noted.

Ensure that tyre pressures are checked regularly and maintained correctly. Checking should be carried out with the tyres cold and not immediately after the vehicle has been in use. If the pressures are checked with the tyres hot, an apparently high reading will be obtained owing to heat expansion. Under no circumstances should an attempt be made to reduce the pressures to the quoted cold reading in this instance, or effective underinflation will result.

Underinflation will cause overheating of the tyre owing to excessive flexing of the casing, and the tread will not sit correctly on the road surface. This will cause a consequent loss of adhesion and excessive wear, not to mention the danger of sudden tyre failure due to heat build-up.

Overinflation will cause rapid wear of the centre part of the tyre tread coupled with reduced adhesion, harsher ride, and the danger of shock damage occurring in the tyre casing.

Regularly check the tyres for damage in the form of cuts or bulges, especially in the sidewalls. Remove any nails or stones embedded in the tread before they penetrate the tyre to cause deflation. If removal of a nail *does* reveal that the tyre has been punctured, refit the nail so that its point of penetration is marked. Then immediately change the wheel and have the tyre repaired by a tyre dealer. Do *not* drive on a tyre in such a condition. In many cases a puncture can be simply repaired by the use of an inner tube of the correct size and type. If in any doubt as to the possible consequences of any damage found, consult your local tyre dealer for advice.

Periodically remove the wheels and clean any dirt or mud from the inside and outside surfaces. Examine the wheel rims for signs of rusting, corrosion or other damage. Light alloy wheels are easily damaged by 'kerbing' whilst parking, and similarly steel wheels may become dented or buckled. Renewal of the wheel is very often the only course of remedial action possible.

The balance of each wheel and tyre assembly should be maintained to avoid excessive wear, not only to the tyres but also to the steering and suspension components. Wheel imbalance is normally signified by vibration through the vehicle's bodyshell, although in many cases it is particularly noticeable through the steering wheel. Conversely, it should be noted that wear or damage in suspension or steering components may cause excessive tyre wear. Out-of-round or out-of-true tyres, damaged wheels and wheel bearing wear/maladjustment also fall into this category. Balancing will not usually cure vibration caused by such wear.

Wheel balancing may be carried out with the wheel either on or off the vehicle. If balanced on the vehicle, ensure that the wheel-to-hub relationship is marked in some way prior to subsequent wheel removal so that it may be refitted in its original position.

General tyre wear is influenced to a large degree by driving style – harsh braking and acceleration or fast cornering will all produce more rapid tyre wear. Interchanging of tyres may result in more even wear, but this should only be carried out where there is no mix of tyre types on the vehicle. However, it is worth bearing in mind that if this is completely effective, the added expense of replacing a complete set of tyres simultaneously is incurred, which may prove financially restrictive for many owners.

Front tyres may wear unevenly as a result of wheel misalignment. The front wheels should always be correctly aligned according to the settings specified by the vehicle manufacturer.

Legal restrictions apply to the mixing of tyre types on a vehicle. Basically this means that a vehicle must not have tyres of differing construction on the same axle. Although it is not recommended to mix tyre types between front axle and rear axle, the only legally permissible combination is crossply at the front and radial at the rear. When mixing radial ply tyres, textile braced radials must always go on the front axle, with steel braced radials at the rear. An obvious disadvantage of such mixing is the necessity to carry two spare tyres to avoid contravening the law in the event of a puncture.

In the UK, the Motor Vehicles Construction and Use Regulations apply to many aspects of tyre fitting and usage. It is suggested that a copy of these regulations is obtained from your local police if in doubt as to the current legal requirements with regard to tyre condition, minimum tread depth, etc.

18 Fault diagnosis – suspension and steering

Symptom	Reason/s
Lost motion at steering wheel	Worn rack and pinion Worn track-rod end balljoints Worn suspension arm balljoints
Steering wander	Worn steering gear Worn track-rod end or suspension arm balljoints Incorrect front wheel alignment Incorrectly adjusted front hub bearings
Heavy or stiff steering	Dry or distorted steering rack Incorrect front wheel alignment Incorrect tyre pressures Seized suspension strut upper bearing
Wheel wobble and vibration	Roadwheels out of balance or buckled Weak shock absorbers Worn track-rod end or suspension arm balljoints
Excessive pitching or rolling	Weak shock absorbers Weak or broken coil spring

Chapter 12 Bodywork and fittings

For modifications, and information applicable to later models, see Supplement at end of manual

Contents

Specifications

Torque wrench settings

	lbf ft	kgf m
Front seat mounting bolts	35	4.8

1 General description

1   The compact body is of all-steel welded construction and incorporates galvanised underwing panels at the front. The body is designed to reduce wind resistance to a minimum and is corrosion-proofed at manufacture.
2   The front wings are bolted into position and are easily renewed in the event of a front end collision.
3   The substantial bumpers are fitted with end rubber quarter sections. A rubbing strip is fitted along the side panels and doors on each side.

2 Maintenance – bodywork and underframe

1   The general condition of a car's bodywork is the one thing that significantly affects its value. Maintenance is easy but needs to be regular and particular. Neglect, particularly after minor damage, can lead quickly to further deterioration and costly repair bills. It is important also to keep watch on those parts of the car not immediately visible, for instance the underside, inside all the wheel arches and the lower part of the engine compartment.
2   The basic maintenance routine for the bodywork is washing – preferably with a lot of water, from a hose. This will remove all the solids which may have stuck to the car. It is important to flush these off in such a way as to prevent grit from scratching the finish. The wheel arches and underbody need washing in the same way to remove any accumulated mud which will retain moisture and tend to encourage rust. Paradoxically enough, the best time to clean the underbody and wheel arches is in wet weather when the mud is thoroughly wet and soft. In very wet weather the underbody is usually cleaned of large accumulations automatically and this is a good time for inspection.
3   Periodically it is a good idea to have the whole of the underside of the car steam cleaned, engine compartment included, so that a thorough inspection can be carried out to see what minor repairs and renovations are necessary. Steam cleaning is available at many garages and is necessary for removal of accumulations of oily grime which sometimes collects thickly in certain areas near the engine, gearbox and back axle. If steam facilities are not available, there are one or two excellent grease solvents available which can be brush applied. The dirt can then be simply hosed off.
4   After washing paintwork, wipe off with a chamois leather to give an unspotted clear finish. A coat of clear protective wax polish will give added protection against chemical pollutants in the air and will survive several subsequent washings. If the paintwork sheen has dulled or oxidised, use a cleaner/polisher combination to restore the brilliance of the shine. This requires a little effort, but is usually caused because regular washing has been neglected! Always check that the door and

ventilator drain holes and pipes are completely clear so that water can drain out (photo). Brightwork should be treated the same way as paintwork. Windscreens and windows can be kept clear of the smeary film which often appears if a little ammonia is added to the water. If glasswork is scratched, a good rub with a proprietary metal polish will often clean it. Never use any form of wax or other paint or chromium polish on glass.

2.4 Door drain hole

3 Maintenance – upholstery and carpets

1   Mats and carpets should be brushed or vacuum cleaned regularly to keep them free of grit. If they are badly stained, remove them from the car for scrubbing or sponging and make quite sure they are dry before replacement. Seats and interior trim panels can be kept clean by a wipe over with a damp cloth. If they do become stained (which can be more apparent on light coloured upholstery) use a little liquid detergent and a soft nail brush to scour the grime out of the grain of the material. Do not forget to keep the headlining clean in the same way as the upholstery. When using liquid cleaners inside the car do not over-wet the surfaces being cleaned. Excessive damp could get into the upholstery seams and padded interior, causing stains, offensive odours or even rot. If the inside of the car gets wet accidentally it is worthwhile taking some trouble to dry it out properly, particularly where the carpets are involved. **Do not** leave oil or electric heaters inside the car for this purpose.

4 Minor body damage – repair

The photo sequences on pages 174 and 175 illustrate the operations detailed in the following sub-sections.

Note: *For more detailed information about bodywork repair, the Haynes Publishing Group publish a book by Lindsay Porter called The Car Bodywork Repair Manual. This incorporates information on such aspects as rust treatment, painting and glass fibre repairs, as well as details on more ambitious repairs involving welding and panel beating.*

Repair of minor scratches in the car's bodywork

If the scratch is very superficial, and does not penetrate to the metal of the bodywork, repair is very simple. Lightly rub the area of the scratch with a paintwork renovator, or a very fine cutting paste, to remove loose paint from the scratch and to clear the surrounding bodywork of wax polish. Rinse the area with clean water.

Apply touch-up paint to the scratch using a thin paint brush; continue to apply thin layers of paint until the surface of the paint in the scratch is level with the surrounding paintwork. Allow the new paint at least two weeks to harden, then blend it into the surrounding paintwork by rubbing the paintwork, in the scratch area with a paintwork renovator or a very fine cutting paste. Finally, apply wax polish.

Where the scratch has penetrated right through to the metal of the bodywork, causing the metal to rust, a different repair technique is required. Remove any loose rust from the bottom of the scratch with a penknife, then apply rust inhibiting paint to prevent the formation of rust in the future. Using a rubber or nylon applicator fill the scratch with bodystopper paste. If required, this paste can be mixed with cellulose thinners to provide a very thin paste which is ideal for filling narrow scratches. Before the stopper-paste in the scratch hardens, wrap a piece of smooth cotton rag around the top of a finger. Dip the finger in cellulose thinners and then quickly sweep it across the surface of the stopper-paste in the scratch; this will ensure that the surface of the stopper-paste is slightly hollowed. The scratch can now be painted over as described earlier in this Section.

Repair of dents in the car's bodywork

When deep denting of the car's bodywork has taken place, the first task is to pull the dent out, until the affected bodywork almost attains its original shape. There is little point in trying to restore the original shape completely, as the metal in the damaged area will have stretched on impact and cannot be reshaped fully to its original contour. It is better to bring the level of the dent up to a point which is about $\frac{1}{8}$ in (3 mm) below the level of the surrounding bodywork. In

cases where the dent is very shallow anyway, it is not worth trying to pull it out at all.

If the underside of the dent is accessible, it can be hammered out gently from behind, using a mallet with a wooden or plastic head. Whilst doing this, hold a suitable block of wood firmly against the impact from the hammer blows and thus prevent a large area of the bodywork from being 'belled-out'.

Should the dent be in a section of the bodywork which has double skin or some other factor making it inaccessible from behind, a different technique is called for. Drill several small holes through the metal inside the area – particularly in the deeper section. Then screw long self-tapping screws into the holes just sufficiently for them to gain a good purchase in the metal. Now the dent can be pulled out by pulling on the protruding heads of the screws with a pair of pliers.

The next stage of the repair is the removal of the paint from the damaged area, and from an inch (25.4 mm) or so of the surrounding 'sound' bodywork. This is accomplished most easily by using a wire brush or abrasive pad on a power drill, although it can be done just as effectively by hand using sheets of abrasive paper. To complete the preparation for filling, score the surface of the bare metal with a screwdriver or the tang of a file, or alternatively, drill small holes in the affected area. This will provide a really good 'key' for the filler paste.

To complete the repair see the Section on filling and respraying.

Repair of rust holes or gashes in the car's bodywork

Remove all paint from the affected area and from an inch or so of the surrounding 'sound' bodywork, using an abrasive pad or a wire brush on a power drill. If these are not available a few sheets of abrasive paper will do the job just as effectively. With the paint removed you will be able to gauge the severity of the corrosion and therefore decide whether to renew the whole panel (if this is possible) or to repair the affected area. New body panels are not as expensive as most people think and it is often quicker and more satisfactory to fit a new panel than to attempt to repair large areas of corrosion.

Remove all fittings from the affected area except those which will act as a guide to the original shape of the damaged bodywork (eg headlamp shells etc). Then, using tin snips or a hacksaw blade, remove all loose metal and any other metal badly affected by corrosion. Hammer the edges of the hole inwards in order to create a slight depression for the filler paste.

Wire brush the affected area to remove the powdery rust from the surface of the remaining metal. Paint the affected area with rust inhibiting paint; if the back of the rusted area is accessible treat this also.

Before filling can take place it will be necessary to block the hole in some way. This can be achieved by the use of aluminium or plastic mesh, or aluminium tape.

Polyurethane foam is best used where the hole is situated in a section of bodywork of complex shape, backed by a small box section (eg where the sill panel meets the rear wheel arch – most cars). The usual mixing procedure for this foam is as follows: put equal amounts of fluid from each of the two cans provided in the kit, into one container. Stir until the mixture begins to thicken, then quickly pour this mixture into the hole, and hold a piece of cardboard over the larger apertures. Almost immediately the polyurethane will begin to expand, gushing out of any small holes left unblocked. When the foam hardens it can be cut back to just below the level of the surrounding bodywork with a hacksaw blade.

Bodywork repairs – filling and respraying

Before using this Section, see the Sections on dent, deep scratch, rust holes and gash repairs.

Many types of bodyfiller are available, but generally speaking those proprietary kits which contain a tin of filler paste and a tube of resin hardener are best for this type of repair. A wide, flexible plastic or nylon applicator will be found invaluable for imparting a smooth and well contoured finish to the surface of the filler.

Mix up a little filler on a clean piece of card or board – use the hardener sparingly (follow the maker's instructions on the packet) otherwise the filler will set very rapidly.

Using the applicator apply the filler paste to the prepared area: draw the applicator across the surface of the filler to achieve the correct contour and to level the filler surface. As soon as a contour that approximates the correct one is achieved, stop working the paste – if you carry on too long the paste will become sticky and begin to 'pick up' on the applicator. Continue to add thin layers of filler paste at twenty-minute intervals until the level of the filler is just proud of the surrounding bodywork.

Once the filler has hardened, excess can be removed using a Surform plane or file. From then on, progressively finer grades of abrasive paper should be used, starting with a 40 grade production paper. Always wrap the abrasive paper around a flat rubber, cork, or wooden block – otherwise the surface of the filler will not be completely flat. During the smoothing of the filler surface the wet-and-dry paper should be periodically rinsed in water. This will ensure that a very smooth finish is imparted to the filler at the final stage.

At this stage the 'dent' should be surrounded by a ring of bare metal, which in turn should be encircled by the finely 'feathered' edge of the good paintwork. Rinse the repair area with clean water, until all of the dust produced by the rubbing-down operation has gone.

Spray the whole repair area with a light coat of primer – this will show up any imperfections in the surface of the filler. Repair these imperfections with fresh filler paste or bodystopper, and once more smooth the surface with abrasive paper. If bodystopper is used, it can be mixed with cellulose thinners to form a really thin paste which is ideal for filling small holes. Repeat this spray and repair procedure until you are satisfied that the surface of the filler, and the feathered edge of the paintwork are perfect. Clean the repair area with clean water and allow to dry fully.

The repair area is now ready for final spraying. Paint spraying must be carried out in a warm, dry, windless and dust free atmosphere. This condition can be created artificially if you have access to a large indoor working area, but if you are forced to work in the open, you will have to pick your day very carefully. If you are working indoors, dousing the floor in the work area with water will help settle the dust which would otherwise be in the atmosphere. If the repair area is confined to one body panel, mask off the surrounding panels; this will help to minimise the effects of a slight mis-match in paint colours. Bodywork fittings (eg chrome strips, door handles etc) will also need to be masked off. Use genuine masking tape and several thicknesses of newspaper for the masking operations.

Before commencing to spray, agitate the aerosol can thoroughly, then spray a test area (an old tin, or similar) until the technique is mastered. Cover the repair area with a thick coat of primer; the thickness should be built up using several thin layers of paint rather than one thick one. Using 400 grade wet-and-dry paper, rub down the surface of the primer until it is really smooth. While doing this, the work area should be thoroughly doused with water, and the wet-and-dry paper periodically rinsed in water. Allow to dry before spraying on more paint.

Spray on the top coat, again building up the thickness by using several thin layers of paint. Start spraying in the centre of the repair

area and then using a circular motion, work outwards until the whole repair area and about 2 inches (50 mm) of the surrounding original paintwork is covered. Remove all masking material 10 to 15 minutes after spraying on the final coat of paint. Allow the new paint at least two weeks to harden, then, using a paintwork renovator or a very fine cutting paste, blend the edges of the paint into the existing paintwork. Finally, apply wax polish.

5 Major body damage – repair

Where serious damage has occurred or large areas need renewal due to neglect, it means certainly that completely new sections or panels will need welding in and this is best left to professionals. If the damage is due to impact it will also be necessary to completely check the alignment of the bodyshell structure. Due to the principle of construction the strength and shape of the whole can be affected by damage to a part. In such instances the services of a Toyota garage with specialist checking jigs are essential. If a body is left misaligned it is first of all dangerous as the car will not handle properly and secondly uneven stresses will be imposed on the steering, engine and transmission, causing abnormal wear or complete failure. Tyre wear may also be excessive.

6 Maintenance – hinges, door catches, and locks

1   Oil the hinges of the bonnet, boot and doors with a drop or two of light oil periodically. A good time is after the car has been washed.
2   Oil the bonnet safety catch periodically.
3   Do not over-lubricate door latches and strikers. Normally one or two drops regularly applied is better than a lot at one go.

7 Doors – tracing rattles and rectification

1   Check first that the door is not loose at the hinges and that the latch is holding the door firmly in position. Check also that the door lines up with the aperture in the body.
2   If the hinges are loose or the door is out of alignment it will be necessary to reset the hinge position as described in Section 8.
3   If the latch is holding the door properly it should hold the door tightly when fully latched and the door should line up with the body. If it is out of alignment it needs adjustment, as described in Section 9. If loose, some part of the lock mechanism must be worn out and requiring renewal.
4   Other rattles from the door could be caused by wear or looseness in the window winder, the glass channels, weather strips, or the door buttons and interior latch release mechanism. All these are dealt with in subsequent Sections.

8 Door alignment – hinge adjustment

1   The hinges are adjustable both on the door and pillar mountings. Access to some of the bolts will require removal of trim and the use of a bent spanner.
2   When re-aligning is necessary, slacken the bolts holding the hinge to the door, reposition the door as required and make sure the bolts are thoroughly tightened up again. If the amount of movement on the door half of the hinge is insufficient it may be adjusted at the door pillar.
3   If the hinges themselves are worn at the hinge pin the door should be detached from the hinges, the hinges removed and new ones fitted.

9 Door latch striker – adjustment

1   Assuming that the door hinges are correctly aligned but the trailing edge of the door is not flush with the body when the door is fully latched, then the striker plate needs adjusting.
2   Slacken the two crosshead screws holding the striker plate to the door pillar just enough to hold the striker plate in position and then push the plate to the inner limit of its position. Try to shut the door, moving the striker plate outwards until the latch is able to engage fully.

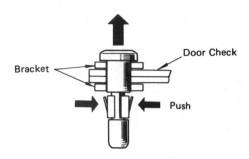

Fig. 12.1 Door check strap pivot pin removal (Sec 10)

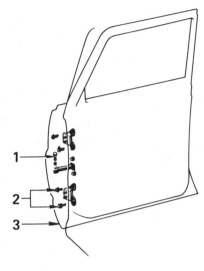

Fig. 12.2 Front door hinge positions (Sec 10)

1 Check strap pivot
2 Retaining bolts
3 Door panel

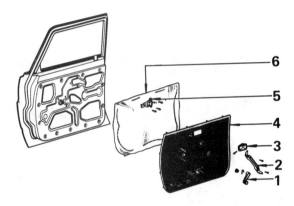

Fig. 12.3 Front door trim components (Sec 11)

1 Window regulator   4 Trim panel
2 Door pull   5 Handle
3 Bezel   6 Protective sheeting

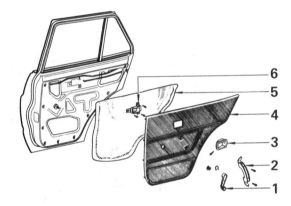

Fig. 12.4 Rear door trim components (Sec 11)

1 Window regulator   4 Trim panel
2 Door pull   5 Protective sheeting
3 Bezel   6 Handle

Fig. 12.5 Front door trim panel clip locations (Sec 11)

Fig. 12.6 Rear door trim panel clip locations (Sec 11)

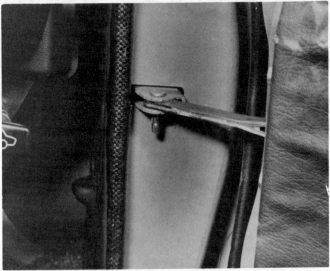

10.1 Door check strap

11.2A Removing the window regulator handle spring clip

11.2B Removing the window regulator handle and bezel

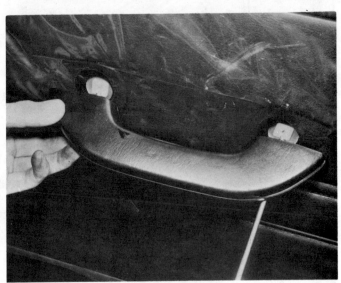

11.3 Removing the combined door pull/armrest

11.4A Removing the door interior handle bezel retaining screw

11.4B Removing the door interior handle bezel

3 Without pulling on the release handle but working inside the car, push the door outwards until it is flush with the bodywork. This will move the striker plate along with the latch.

4 Release the latch very carefully so as not to disturb the striker plate and open the door. Tighten down the striker plate securing screws.

10 Front and rear doors – removal and refitting

1 Open the door and depress the claw retaining the check strap pivot pin (Fig. 12.1). Remove the pin from the pillar bracket (photo).

2 Support the weight of the door, then unscrew and remove the hinge to door panel mounting bolts.

3 Withdraw the door from the car.

4 Refitting is a reversal of removal, but it will be necessary to carry out the adjustments described in Sections 8 and 9.

11 Front and rear door trim panel – removal and refitting

1 Fully lower the door glass.

2 Note the position of the window regulator handle, then, using a piece of bent wire, extract the spring clip and remove the handle and bezel (photos).

3 Unscrew the retaining screws and remove the door pull (photo).

4 Unscrew the door interior handle bezel retaining screw, and remove the bezel (photos).

5 Using a wide-bladed screwdriver, carefully lower the thin panel from the door, releasing the retaining clips indicated in Figs. 12.5 and 12.6.

6 Refitting is a reversal of removal. Fit the clip to the regulator handle before locking the handle to the regulator shaft by striking it a sharp blow with the hand.

12 Front door window glass – removal and refitting

1 Fully lower the door glass, and remove the door trim as described in Section 11.

2 Pull back the protective sheeting, and unscrew the glass channel to regulator retaining bolts (photo).

3 Prise out the door inner and outer weatherstrips.

4 Lift the glass from the door over the outside of the window aperture.

5 If necessary, the channel may be prised from the bottom of the glass and a new one fitted in accordance with the dimensions shown in Fig. 12.7. Use soapy water to fit the channel and tap it into place with a wooden or plastic mallet.

6 Refitting is a reversal of removal.

13 Front door window regulator – removal and refitting

1 Remove the door trim as described in Section 11.

2 Remove the front door window glass as described in Section 12.

3 Pull back the protective sheeting and unscrew the five retaining bolts (photos). The window regulator can now be withdrawn through the aperture.

4 Refitting is a reversal of removal, except that the regulator bracket retained by the two bolts must be tightened into position with the door glass upper edge parallel to the upper frame (Fig. 12.10).

14 Interior door handle – removal and refitting

1 Remove the door trim as described in Section 11.

2 Peel back the protective sheeting. Reach into the aperture and unclip the control link from the door handle.

3 Unscrew the retaining bolts and remove the door handle (photo).

4 Refitting is a reversal of removal, but the handle position must be adjusted as follows. With the retaining bolts loose, move the assembly forwards until resistance is felt, then move it rearwards by between 0·02 and 0·04 in (0·5 and 1·0 mm) (Fig. 12.11). Tighten the bolts with the handle in this position. Make sure that the protective sheeting is well secured before fitting the trim panel.

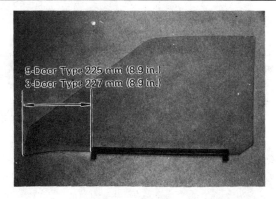

Fig. 12.7 Front door window glass channel location dimensions (Sec 12)

Fig. 12.8 Front door window regulator (Sec 13)

1 Inner and outer weatherstrips   2 Window glass
3 Channel retaining bolts

Fig. 12.9 Window regulator lubrication points (Sec 13)

Fig. 12.10 Correct front door window glass location (Sec 13)

This sequence of photographs deals with the repair of the dent and paintwork damage shown in this photo. The procedure will be similar for the repair of a hole. It should be noted that the procedures given here are simplified — more explicit instructions will be found in the text

In the case of a dent the first job — after removing surrounding trim — is to hammer out the dent where access is possible. This will minimise filling. Here, the large dent having been hammered out, the damaged area is being made slightly concave

Now all paint must be removed from the damaged area, by rubbing with coarse abrasive paper. Alternatively, a wire brush or abrasive pad can be used in a power drill. Where the repair area meets good paintwork, the edge of the paintwork should be 'feathered', using a finer grade of abrasive paper

In the case of a hole caused by rusting, all damaged sheet-metal should be cut away before proceeding to this stage. Here, the damaged area is being treated with rust remover and inhibitor before being filled

Mix the body filler according to its manufacturer's instructions. In the case of corrosion damage, it will be necessary to block off any large holes before filling — this can be done with aluminium or plastic mesh, or aluminium tape. Make sure the area is absolutely clean before ...

... applying the filler. Filler should be applied with a flexible applicator, as shown, for best results; the wooden spatula being used for confined areas. Apply thin layers of filler at 20-minute intervals, until the surface of the filler is slightly proud of the surrounding bodywork

Initial shaping can be done with a Surform plane or Dreadnought file. Then, using progressively finer grades of wet-and-dry paper, wrapped around a sanding block, and copious amounts of clean water, rub down the filler until really smooth and flat. Again, feather the edges of adjoining paintwork

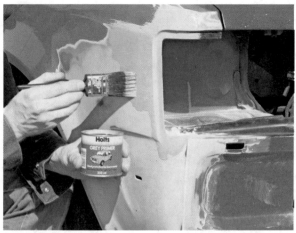

The whole repair area can now be sprayed or brush-painted with primer. If spraying, ensure adjoining areas are protected from over-spray. Note that at least one inch of the surrounding sound paintwork should be coated with primer. Primer has a 'thick' consistency, so will find small imperfections

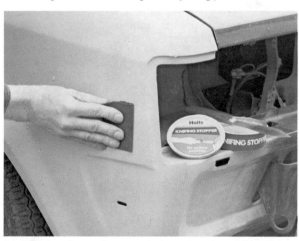

Again, using plenty of water, rub down the primer with a fine grade wet-and-dry paper (400 grade is probably best) until it is really smooth and well blended into the surrounding paintwork. Any remaining imperfections can now be filled by carefully applied knifing stopper paste

When the stopper has hardened, rub down the repair area again before applying the final coat of primer. Before rubbing down this last coat of primer, ensure the repair area is blemish-free – use more stopper if necessary. To ensure that the surface of the primer is really smooth use some finishing compound

The top coat can now be applied. When working out of doors, pick a dry, warm and wind-free day. Ensure surrounding areas are protected from over-spray. Agitate the aerosol thoroughly, then spray the centre of the repair area, working outwards with a circular motion. Apply the paint as several thin coats

After a period of about two weeks, which the paint needs to harden fully, the surface of the repaired area can be 'cut' with a mild cutting compound prior to wax polishing. When carrying out bodywork repairs, remember that the quality of the finished job is proportional to the time and effort expended

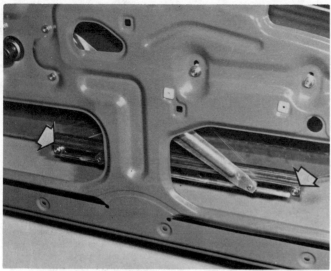

12.2 Front door glass channel to regulator retaining bolts (arrowed)

13.3A Front door window regulator retaining bolts

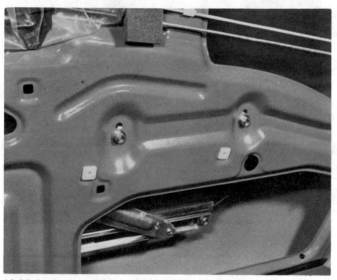

13.3B Front door window regulator retaining bolts

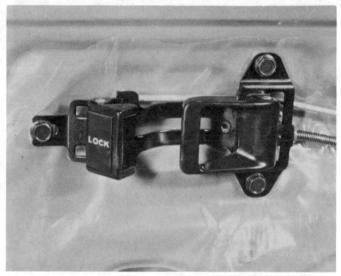

14.3 The front door interior door handle (bezel removed)

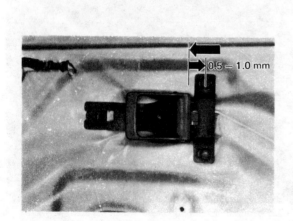

Fig. 12.11 Door interior handle adjustment dimension (Sec 14)

0.5 – 1.0 mm

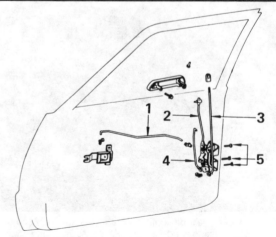

Fig. 12.12 Front door lock components (Sec 15)

1 Interior handle link   4 Exterior lock link
2 Exterior handle link   5 Screws
3 Interior lock link

15 Front door lock and exterior handle – removal and refitting

1 Remove the door trim as described in Section 11.
2 Unclip the control links from the interior door handle and the lock (photo).
3 Disconnect the control links from the exterior door handle and lock cylinder.
4 On 5 door versions, disconnect the interior lock control link.
5 Unscrew the mounting screws and withdraw the lock through the aperture.
6 If necessary the exterior door handle can be removed after unscrewing the mounting screws.
7 Refitting is a reversal of removal, but lubricate all moving parts with a little engine oil, and position the exterior handle 0·02 to 0·04 in (0·5 to 1·0 mm) up from its lowest position (see Fig. 12.13).

16 Rear door window glass – removal and refitting

1 Fully lower the door glass, and remove the door trim as described in Section 11.
2 Pull back the protective sheeting and unscrew the channel retainer lower mounting screw.
3 Prise the weatherstrip from the top of the door to gain access to the channel retainer upper mounting screws. Remove the screws.
4 Remove the upper section of the glass channel, followed by the channel retainer.
5 Pull the quarter glass and weatherstrip forward and withdraw them from the door.
6 Prise out the door inner and outer weatherstrips.

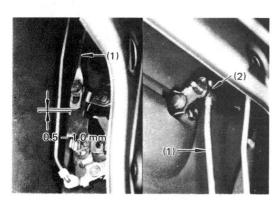

Fig. 12.13 Front door exterior handle adjustment (Sec 15)

1 Control link   2 Adjuster and pin

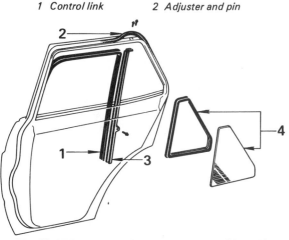
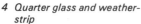

Fig. 12.14 Rear door window components (Sec 16)

1 Glass channel   4 Quarter glass and weather-
2 Weatherstrip   strip
3 Retainer

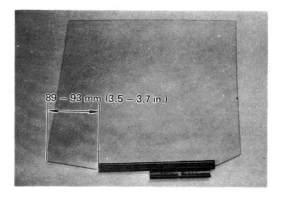

Fig. 12.15 Rear door window glass channel setting diagram (Sec 16)

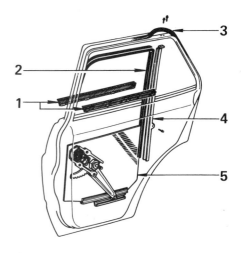

Fig. 12.16 Rear door window and regulator (Sec 16)

1 Inner and outer   3 Weatherstrip
   weatherstrips   4 Retainer
2 Glass channel   5 Window glass

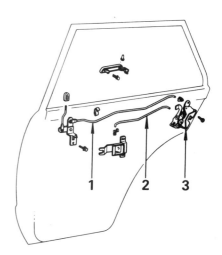

Fig. 12.17 Rear door lock components (Sec 18)

1 Interior lock link   2 Interior handle link
           3 Door lock

7   Temporarily refit the window regulator handle and wind the window up until it can be lifted from the door.
8   If necessary, the channel may be prised from the bottom of the glass and a new one fitted in the position shown in Fig. 12.15. Use soapy water and tap the channel into place with a plastic or hide mallet.
9   Refitting is a reversal of removal.

17 Rear door window regulator – removal and refitting

1   Fully lower the door glass and remove the door trim as described in Section 11.
2   Unscrew and remove the window regulator mounting bolts and tilt the glass to detach the regulator from the lower channel.
3   Withdraw the regulator through the aperture.
4   Refitting is a reversal of removal.

18 Rear door lock and exterior handle – removal and refitting

1   Remove the door trim as described in Section 11.
2   Disconnect the interior handle and locking links from the door lock.
3   Unscrew the mounting screws and remove the door lock through the aperture.
4   If necessary, remove the retaining screws and withdraw the exterior handle.
5   Refitting is a reversal of removal. Make sure that the child proof lever is released, and position the exterior handle so that there is a gap of 0·02 to 0·04 in (0·5 to 1·0 mm) between it and the lock lever (see Fig. 12.18).

19 Tailgate – removal and refitting

1   Disconnect the battery negative terminal.
2   Disconnect the supply wires to the heated rear window and wiper motor (where fitted). Disconnect the washer hose (see Chapter 10).
3   Fully open the tailgate and detach the gas-filled strut by unscrewing the pivot stud.
4   With the aid of an assistant, unbolt the tailgate from the hinges and lift it away.
5   Refitting is a reversal of removal, but before reconnecting the strut, the tailgate position within the body aperture must be adjusted. Since the strut will tend to move the tailgate lower edge away from it, the initial gap on the opposite edge should be increased by approximately 0·12 in (3·0 mm). Refer to Fig. 12.20. The adjustment is made at the hinges before tightening the bolts.

20 Tailgate lock – removal and refitting

1   Open the tailgate and unscrew the crosshead screw retaining the lock to the body panel.
2   Unclip the link and disconnect the return springs and cable.
3   Withdraw the lock from the body panel.
4   Refitting is a reversal of removal. If necessary, adjust the striker on the tailgate so that it enters the lock centrally.

21 Bonnet and lock – removal, refitting and adjustment

1   Mark the hinge positions with a pencil (photo).
2   Place some padding between the bonnet and the windscreen front valance. Disconnect the windscreen washer hose and unscrew the hinge bolts.
3   Withdraw the bonnet from the front of the car.
4   To remove the lock, unscrew the retaining bolts and disconnect the release cable (photo).
5   Refitting is a reversal of removal, but check the position of the bonnet in relation to the front wings and grille. Horizontal movement is made by repositioning the hinges on the bonnet, and vertical movement by adjusting the height of the rubber stops at the front of the engine compartment. Any vertical adjustment will necessitate repositioning the bonnet lock.

15.2 Front door lock control links

Fig. 12.18 Rear door exterior handle adjustment (Sec 18)

1 Adjustment screw   2 Lever

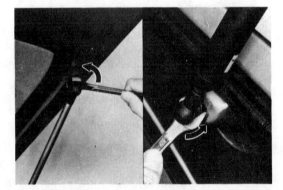

Fig. 12.19 Removing the tailgate strut (Sec 19)

22 Windscreen and tailgate glass – removal and refitting

1   Cover the interior of the car with sheeting to catch the pieces of glass if it has shattered. Adhesive sheeting is also useful to remove sections of the broken glass.
2   Remove the interior mirror and radio aerial if the windscreen is being removed complete, or disconnect the wire to the heated rear window if the tailgate glass is being removed.
3   Remove the wiper arm(s) and weatherstrip moulding.
4   Using a screwdriver, break the seal between the weatherstrip and

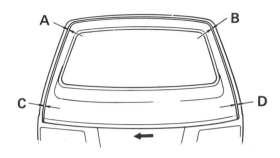

Fig. 12.20 Tailgate initial adjustment (Sec 19)

$A = B$ $\qquad C = D + 0.12 \text{ in } (3.0 \text{ mm})$

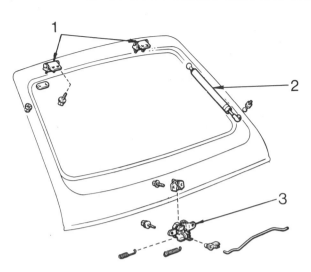

Fig. 12.21 Tailgate components (Sec 20)

1 Hinges 2 Strut
3 Lock

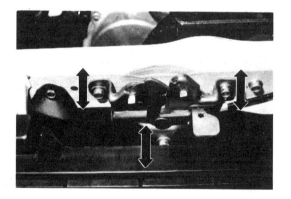

Fig. 12.22 Bonnet lock and adjustment (arrowed) (Sec 21)

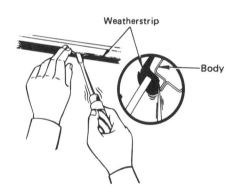

Fig. 12.23 Removing the windscreen or tailgate glass (Sec 22)

21.1 A bonnet hinge

21.4 Bonnet lock

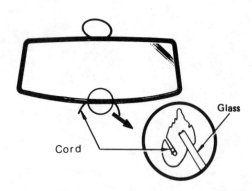

Fig. 12.24 Cord insertion for windscreen refitting (Sec 22)

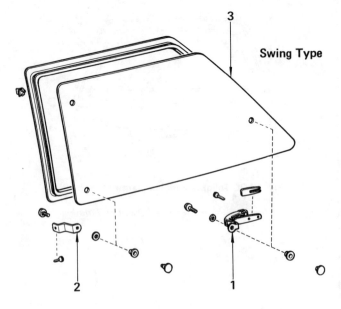

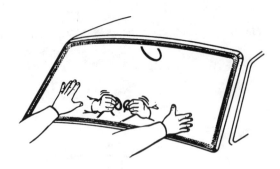

Fig. 12.25 Fitting the windscreen (Sec 22)

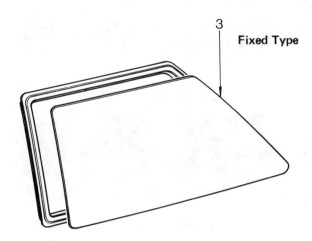

Fig. 12.26 Rear quarter window components (Sec 23)

1 Lock　　　　　　　2 Hinge
3 Window glass

the body aperture both inside and outside the car. Take care not to damage the paintwork.

5   Have an assistant support the glass on the outside, and then from inside the car ease the weatherstrip from the aperture flange using a wide blade screwdriver. The glass and weatherstrip can now be released from the flange by gentle pressure until the glass can be completely withdrawn from the car.

6   Examine the weatherstrip for signs of damage and deterioration and renew it if necessary. Clean away all traces of sealing compound, glass fragments and dirt from the body aperture and weatherstrip.

7   Brush a soapy water solution onto the weatherstrip and fit it to the edge of the glass.

8   Cut a length of cord and insert it into the weatherstrip groove as shown in Fig. 12.24.

9   Locate the glass centrally in the body aperture and have an assistant press firmly on the outside while the cord is pulled from the inside to engage the weatherstrip on the flange. Alternating between the upper and lower flanges will assist the operation and ensure that the glass is seated centrally.

10 Apply sealing compound between the weatherstrip and glass and weatherstrip and body aperture on the windscreen only (ie *not* the tailgate glass).

11 Refit the weatherstrip moulding and wiper arm(s) and the items removed in paragraph 2; use soapy water when refitting the moulding. Any excess sealing compound can be removed with paraffin or white spirit. Retrieve the licence disc from the old glass screen.

23 Rear quarter window – removal and refitting

1   The rear quarter window is only fitted to 3 door models and may be of the fixed or hinged type. In the former case, removal is identical to the procedure given in Section 22, but with the hinged type proceed as follows.

2   Remove the two screws securing the lock to the window glass and withdraw the lock together with the packing.

3   Unscrew the hinge to body retaining screws and lift the window

from the car. If necessary, unbolt the hinges from the window glass.

4   Refitting is a reversal of removal.

24 Facia panel and safety pad – removal and refitting

1   Disconnect the battery negative terminal.

2   Unscrew the retaining screws and withdraw the instrument surround panel and disconnect the air hose.

3   Pull off the radio control knobs, unscrew the two nuts, and withdraw the radio and clock panel.

4   Unscrew the mounting screws, disconnect the supply wires and aerial, and remove the radio and clock.

5   Unscrew the retaining screws and remove the glovebox lid stay and glovebox.

6   Unscrew the retaining screws and remove the under tray.

7   Unscrew the retaining screws and withdraw the safety pad. At the same time disconnect the air hose.

8   Remove the instrument pack as described in Chapter 10.

9   Remove the heater controls and panel as described in Section 31.

10 Detach the bonnet release from the facia panel.

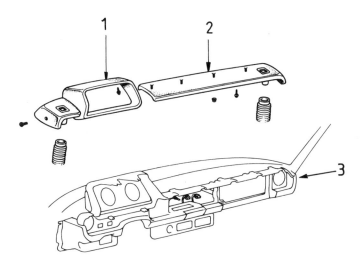

Fig. 12.27 Instrument surround (1), safety pad (2) and facia panel (3) – LHD model shown (Sec 24)

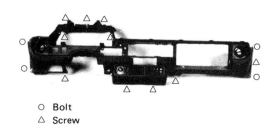

○ Bolt
△ Screw

Fig. 12.28 Facia panel bolt and screw locations – LHD model shown (Sec 24)

11 Detach the fuse block and choke control.
12 Detach the steering column upper bracket from the facia panel as described in Chapter 11.
13 Unscrew the mounting bolts and screws indicated in Fig. 12.28 and withdraw the facia panel.
14 With the panel removed, the air vent louvres, heater louvres, reinforcement frame and instrument panel finisher can be removed.
15 Refitting is a reversal of removal, but make sure that all electrical connections are re-made correctly before reconnecting the battery terminal.

25 Interior trim – removal and refitting

1 With the exception of the door weatherseals, all interior trim items are retained by screws and are easily removed and refitting. The weatherseals are pressed into position on the body/door closure flanges.
2 Removal and refitting of the headlining requires special adhesive and tools and it is not recommended that the home mechanic attempts this work. Your local Toyota dealer should be well equipped to make any repairs.

26 Bumpers – removal and refitting

Front bumper
1 Disconnect the battery negative terminal.
2 Disconnect the front sidelight and direction indicator multi-plugs on each side of the car.
3 Unbolt the bumper stays from the body underframe and withdraw the bumper forwards. The stays, quarter sections and lamp units can then be removed from the front bumper.
4 Refitting is a reversal of removal.

Rear bumper
5 Remove the spare wheel and fuel filler pipe shroud.
6 Unbolt the bumper stays from the body underframe and withdraw the bumper rearwards. The stays and quarter sections can then be removed from the rear bumper.
7 Refitting is a reversal of removal.

27 Front seat – removal and refitting

1 Move the seat fully forwards. Unscrew and remove the two mounting bolts from the rear of the tracks.
2 Move the seat rearwards and remove the two mounting bolts from the front of the tracks.
3 Remove the seat from the car.
4 Refitting is a reversal of removal, but check the track movement first and if necessary lubricate it with a little multi-purpose grease. Tighten the mounting bolts to the specified torque.

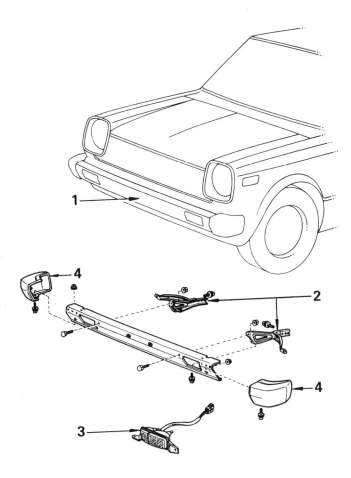

Fig. 12.29 Front bumper components (Sec 26)

1 Front bumper assembly   *3 Sidelight and indicator lamp*
2 Stays   *4 Quarter sections*

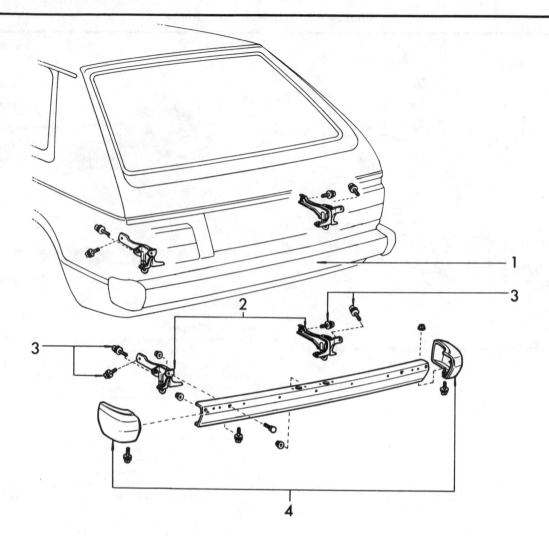

Fig. 12.30 Rear bumper components (Sec 26)

1 Rear bumper assembly   3 Retaining bolts
2 Stays   4 Quarter sections

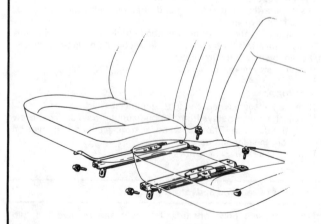

Fig. 12.31 Front seat track location (Sec 27)

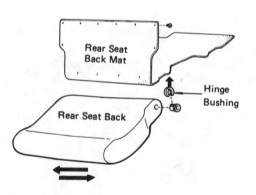

Rear Seat
Back Mat

Hinge
Bushing

Rear Seat Back

Fig. 12.32 Removing the rear seat – arrows indicate direction of removal for each rear seat backrest (Sec 28)

28 Rear seat – removal and refitting

1   Using a screwdriver, prise the rear seat cushion from the retaining clips and swivel it from the rear mounting hooks.
2   Unlock the rear seat backrests and fold them forwards. Prise out the retaining clips and pull the matting from the backrests.
3   Extract the clips and remove the hinge bushes. Release the backrests and withdraw them upwards.
4   Refitting is a reversal of removal.

29 Front wing – removal and refitting

1   Remove the front bumper as described in Section 26.
2   Remove the front headlight surround (three screws).
3   Disconnect the supply wire multi-plug from the direction indicator side repeater.
4   Unbolt the wing liner and front wing with reference to Fig. 12.33.
5   Refitting is a reversal of removal.

30 Heater motor – removal and refitting

1   Disconnect the battery negative terminal.
2   Disconnect the supply wire multi-plug located next to the heater motor.
3   Remove the three mounting screws and withdraw the motor from the heater unit, together with the packing.
4   If necessary, the fan can be removed from the motor shaft after unscrewing the retaining nut. Note the location of the washers and spacers.
5   Refitting is a reversal of removal.

31 Heater controls – removal and refitting

1   Remove the radio and clock as described in Chapter 10.
2   Detach the heater control knobs and multi-plug.
3   Pull off the heater switch knob and unscrew the panel retaining nut, then remove the heater control panel.

4   Note the location of the control cables and disconnect them from the heater unit, water valve and air duct (photo).
5   Detach and withdraw the heater control unit from the facia panel.
6   Refitting is a reversal of removal, but lubricate the control unit if necessary with a little grease, and position the outer cable ends as shown in Fig. 12.36. Check that the controls move smoothly throughout their full travel.

32 Heater unit – removal and refitting

1   Remove the heater controls as described in Section 31.
2   Drain the cooling systems as described in Chapter 2.
3   If fitted, remove the duct assembly from the heater to the rear compartment.

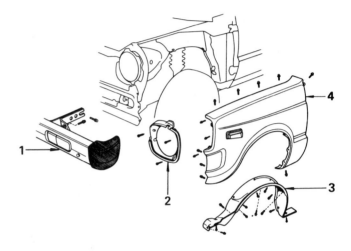

Fig. 12.33 Removing the front wing, showing bolt locations (Sec 29)

1 Front bumper   3 Wing liner
2 Headlight surround   4 Wing

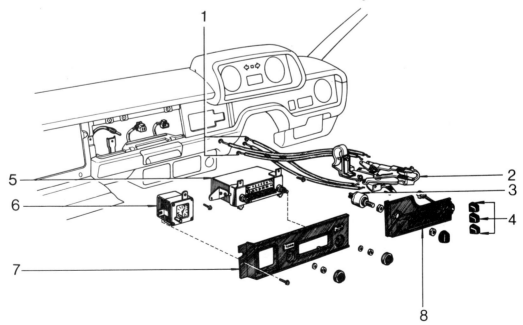

Fig. 12.34 Heater control location (Sec 31)

1 Cables   5 Radio
2 Controls   6 Clock
3 Switch   7 Facia panel
4 Knobs   8 Control panel

4   Remove the under tray, cowl trim and glovebox.
5   Remove the air damper assembly and air hose.
6   Disconnect the defroster hoses and interior air ducts from the heater unit.
7   Remove the ashtray and retainer plate (4 bolts).
8   From within the engine compartment, remove the ignition coil from the bulkhead (2 bolts).
9   Also within the engine compartment, loosen the two clamps and

remove the heater hoses noting their location. Remove the grommet with a screwdriver.
10   Detach the air duct from the heater unit, then withdraw the radiator assembly.
11   Unscrew the retaining bolts and lift the heater unit from the car. On LHD cars it will also be necessary to remove a small cover.
12   Refitting is a reversal of removal, with reference also to Section 31 and Chapter 2.

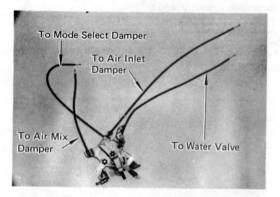

Fig. 12.35 Heater control unit cable locations (Sec 31)

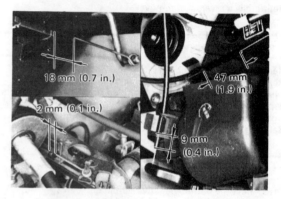

Fig. 12.36 Heater control cable fitting dimensions (Sec 31)

31.4 View of the heater controls with instrument panel removed

Toyota Starlet GL

Chapter 13 Supplement:
Revisions and information on later models

Contents

1 Introduction

This supplement contains information which is additional to, or a revision of, material given in the main Chapters. The Sections in this Supplement follow the same order as the main Chapters to which they relate. The Specifications are all grouped together for convenience, but they too follow Chapter order.

Before any work is undertaken, it is recommended that reference is made to any relevant Sections in this Supplement, and any changes to procedure or specification noted.

Basically, the Starlet has changed very little since its introduction.

The 993 cc (2K engine) KP 60 model has continued right through to 1985 when the RWD configuration was dropped in favour of FWD. The 1166 cc (3K-H engine) KP 62 model introduced in 1979 was replaced by the 1290 cc (4K engine) KP 61 model in 1982, which was itself discontinued in 1983.

Much of the information in this Supplement concerns the 1290 cc (4K) engined KP 60 model, although many of the improvements made to this model were subsequently incorporated into the other two models. When ordering new parts, it is important to supply the chassis and engine numbers to your dealer in order that components of the correct modification state are obtained.

2 Specifications

These Specifications are revisions of, or supplementary to, the Specifications at the beginning of each of the preceding Chapters.

4K engine
Where not as given in Chapter 1

General
Type	4-cylinder, in-line, OHV
Displacement	1290 cc
Bore and stroke	2.95 x 2.90 in (75 x 73 mm)
Firing order	1-3-4-2
Compression ratio:	
Up to 1982	9.0 to 1
1982 on	9.5 to 1
Maximum power (DIN)	44 kW at 5600 rev/min
Maximum torque (DIN)	68 lbf ft (93 Nm) at 3600 rev/min

Valves
Valve stem diameter (inlet)	0.3136 to 0.3142 in (7.965 to 7.980 mm)
Valve stem oil clearance	0.0012 to 0.0026 in (0.030 to 0.065 mm)

Camshaft
Bearing running clearance:	
No 1 and 4	0.0010 to 0.0026 in (0.025 to 0.066 mm)
No 2 and 3	0.0016 to 0.0030 in (0.040 to 0.076 mm)

All engines
Pistons for 3K and 4K series
Produced up to end 1982:	
Diameter	2.9504 to 2.9524 in (74.94 to 74.99 mm)
Piston-to-bore clearance	0.0020 to 0.0028 in (0.05 to 0.07 mm)
Produced 1983 on:	
Diameter	2.9512 to 2.9531 in (74.96 to 75.01 mm)
Piston-to-bore clearance	0.0012 to 0.0020 in (0.03 to 0.05 mm)

Piston ring end gap
2K series:	
Rings produced 1981 to 1984:	
Top (compression)	0.0075 to 0.0146 in (0.19 to 0.37 mm)
Middle (compression)	0.0059 to 0.0189 in (0.15 to 0.48 mm)
Bottom (oil control)	0.0079 to 0.0268 in (0.20 to 0.68 mm)
Rings produced 1984 on:	
Top compression	0.0075 to 0.0382 in (0.19 to 0.97 mm)
Middle (compression)	0.0059 to 0.0425 in (0.15 to 1.08 mm)
Bottom (oil control)	0.0079 to 0.0504 in (0.20 to 1.28 mm)
3K and 4K series:	
Rings produced 1981 to 1984:	
Top (compression)	0.0102 to 0.0153 in (0.26 to 0.39 mm)
Middle (compression)	0.0059 to 0.0165 in (0.15 to 0.42 mm)
Bottom (oil control)	0.0118 to 0.0401 in (0.30 to 1.02 mm)
Rings produced 1984 on:	
Top (compression)	0.0102 to 0.0390 in (0.26 to 0.99 mm)
Middle (compression)	0.0059 to 0.0402 in (0.15 to 1.02 mm)
Bottom (oil control)	0.0118 to 0.0638 in (0.30 to 1.62 mm)

Connecting rod
Big-end endfloat	0.0079 to 0.0120 in (0.200 to 0.304 mm)

Crankshaft
Maximum run-out	0.0016 in (0.040 mm)
Endfloat:	
Standard	0.0016 to 0.0095 in (0.040 to 0.242 mm)
Flywheel maximum run-out	0.004 in (0.1 mm)

Cooling system
Thermostat – 1983 on
Starts to open	179 to 190°F (82 to 88°C)

Fuel system
Idling speed
Manual transmission	750 rpm (cooling fan off)
Automatic transmission	850 rpm

Carburettor settings

Exhaust gas CO content	0.5 to 1.5% at idle
Accelerator pump stroke (1981 on)	0.191 in (4.85 mm)
Float level – 4K:	
Raised position	0.295 in (7.5 mm)
Lowered position	0.024 in (0.6 mm)
Throttle valve closed angle (from horizontal plane):	
Primary	9°
Secondary	20°
Throttle valve fully open angle (from horizontal plane):	
Primary and secondary	90°
Fast idle angle with choke valve fully closed (from horizontal plane)	26°
Choke breaker clearance:	
4K with automatic transmission	0.0874 to 0.0913 in (2.22 to 2.32 mm)
Jet sizes – 4K:	
Primary main jet	102
Secondary main jet	168
Power jet	75

Ignition system
Distributor

Static timing – 4K	5° BTDC

Spark plugs

All models	Champion RN11YC or equivalent

Propeller shaft
Torque wrench setting

	lbf ft	Nm
Flange nuts and bolts (black)	31	42

Suspension and steering – 1980 on
Front wheel alignment

Camber	45' ± 20' (left/right error 30')
Castor	2° 00' ± 20' (left/right error 30')
Steering axis inclination	9° 40' ± 20' (left/right error 30')
Toe-in:	
Bias tyre	0.157 ± 0.039 in (4.0 ± 1.0 mm)
Radial tyre	0.079 ± 0.039 in (2.0 ± 1.0 mm)
Inside turning angle	36° 50' ± 1°
Outside turning angle	34° 05'

Steering rack

Pinion preload:	
Maximum	8 to 11 lbf in (10 to 13 kgf cm)
Minimum	5 lbf in (6.0 kgf cm)

Wheels and tyres

	Wheels	Tyres
Starlet 1000	4^1/2J x 13	145 SR 13
Starlet 1200	4^1/2J x 13	145 SR 13
Starlet S	5J x 13	165/70 SR 13
Starlet 1300	4^1/2J x 13	145 SR 13

Note: *for fitting of low profile tyres consult your dealer*

General weights and dimensions – 1983 on
Dimensions

Overall length	148 in (3760 mm)
Overall width	60 in (1525 mm)
Overall height	54.3 in (1380 mm)

Weights

Kerb weight:	
1.0 GL	1529 lb (695 kg)
1.2 GL	1595 lb (725 kg)
1.3 GL	1650 lb (750 kg)

3   Routine maintenance

The routine maintenance operations and recommended intervals given in the preliminary Section of this book still apply, with the following additions:

Weekly: inspect the condition and tension of the fan belt.
6000 miles (10 000 km) or 6 months: check the strength of the antifreeze solution in the cooling system. This is especially important at the onset of winter and where frequent topping-up of the system has been necessary.

View of front underbody

1	Earth lead	5	Clutch control arm
2	Speedometer cable	6	Steering rack
3	Reversing light switch	7	Track rod
4	Gearbox oil drain plug	8	Suspension arm

9	Steering knuckle
10	Anti-roll bar
11	Engine oil drain plug
12	Exhaust

View of rear underbody

1	Fuel tank drain plug	5	Handbrake cable	8	Differential unit oil
2	Rear shock absorber	6	Brake pipeline		drain plug
3	Upper control arm	7	Propeller shaft universal	9	Suspension coil spring
4	Lower control arm		joint	10	Exhaust silencer

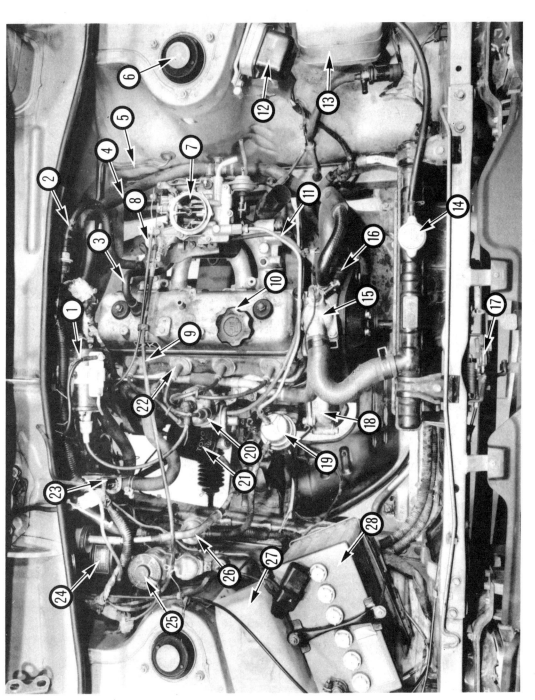

View of engine compartment (air cleaner assembly removed)

1   Coil
2   Brake booster (servo) hose
3   Valve cover breather hose
4   Heater hose
5   Brake pipeline
6   Shock absorber top
    bearing mounting

7   Carburettor
8   Choke cable
9   Throttle cable
10 Engine oil filler cap
11 Fuel supply line
12 Alternator regulator

13 Radiator expansion tank
14 Radiator filler cap
15 Thermostat housing
16 Alternator
17 Bonnet release
    mechanism

18 Water pump
19 Fuel pump
20 Distributor
21 Oil filter
22 Spark plug
23 Heater valve

24 Brake booster (servo)
25 Brake master cylinder
26 Fuel filter
27 Windscreen wash
    reservoir
28 Battery

4 Engine

General

1   The 1290 cc (4K) engine fitted to the 1300 Starlet GL introduced in 1982 – replaced the 1166 cc (3K-H) engine of the 1200 Starlet GL, and was itself discontinued in 1983.

2   The 4K engine was derived from the power unit fitted to the Toyota Corolla, and was basically the same as the 993 cc (2K) and 1166 cc (3K-H) engines, with a different bore and stroke. The 2K engine has continued right through to 1985, when the rear-wheel-drive configuration was discontinued.

3   The 4K engine had several mechanical differences from the 2K, and where these have affected the procedures given in Chapter 1 they are described in the following sub-sections. Most of these modifications have subsequently been used on the 2K engine, and this will also be indicated in the text.

Engine mountings – 1982 on

4   To reduce vibration and engine noise the engine front mountings have been changed from steel to a cast iron forging (photo).

5   The attachment brackets have been changed in profile, which means the mounting bolts are in a different position.

Timing chain and chain tensioner – 1982 to 1984

6   To reduce noise, the timing chain was changed from a double roller to a single roller type.

7   Consequently, the crankshaft sprocket, camshaft sprocket, chain tensioner and chain damper were also modified.

8   This does not affect the procedures given in Chapter 1, but none of the new parts are interchangeable with the old parts, and must be renewed as a complete set.

Timing chain and chain tensioner – 1984 on

9   In 1984 the chain tensioner and chain were again modified, the chain pins and bushes being increased in hardness, and the tensioner modified as shown in Fig. 13.1.

10   The new chain and tensioner may be fitted to an older vehicle (1982 to 1984), but the older chain and tensioner cannot be fitted to a new vehicle.

11   The new tensioner cannot be dismantled and must be renewed as an assembly.

12   Servicing procedures in Chapter 1 are not affected.

Valve lifter – all engines

13   From 1982 the profile of the bottom of the inside of the valve lifter has been modified (Fig. 13.2).

14   This does not affect the servicing procedures, and new lifters may be fitted to older engines, but the older lifters may not be fitted to new engines.

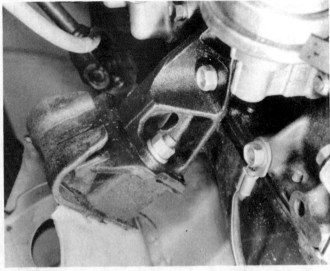

4.4 Forged engine mounting

Exhaust valve and valve guide – all engines

15   From 1982 the carbon relief cut-out, previously made on the valve guide, has been changed to the exhaust valve stem.

16   The new type valves and valve guides may be fitted to an older cylinder head only as a set.

17   Similarly, the new cylinder head, introduced with this modification, may be fitted to earlier engines.

18   Servicing procedures are unaffected.

Crankshaft bearings – 1982 on

19   The oil groove in the lower bearing half has been discontinued.

20   The new type crankshaft bearing caps have two cut-outs for location of the bearing half.

21   When refitting these new bearings, as described in Chapter 1, ensure the bearing half which has no oil groove is installed in the bearing cap, or lubrication problems will occur.

22   These new bearings cannot be fitted to older engines.

Pistons modifications

23   Beginning with production in 1982, the 4K engine had a different shape of piston from previous engines, and the piston diameter and piston-to-bore clearance should be measured as shown in Fig. 13.5.

24   From 1983 on, the piston diameter increased and the piston-to-bore clearance decreased.

25   Also in 1983, the shape of the piston head was changed.

26   In each case the new part may be fitted to older vehicles, and clearances are given in the Specifications.

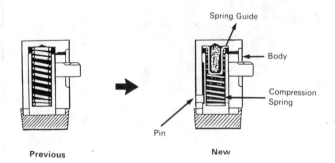

Fig. 13.1 Sectional view of old and new types of timing chain tensioner (Sec 4)

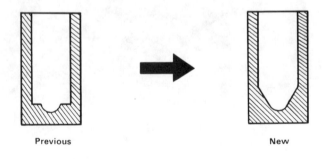

Fig. 13.2 Sectional view of old and new valve lifter (Sec 4)

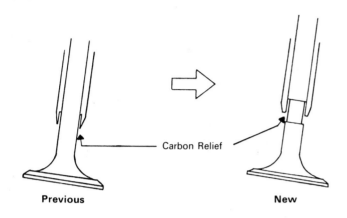

Fig. 13.3 Sectional view of the carbon relief profile on the exhaust valves (Sec 4)

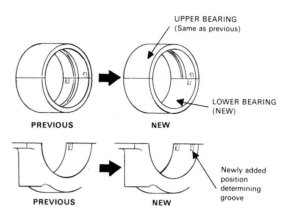

Fig. 13.4 Old and new crankshaft bearings (Sec 4)

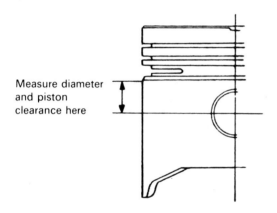

Fig. 13.5 Showing where to measure piston diameter and bore clearance (Sec 4)

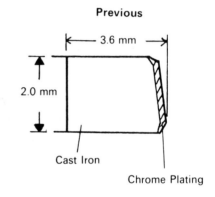

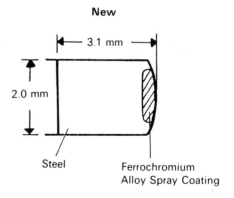

Fig. 13.6 Old and new type piston ring edge profile (Sec 4)

Piston rings – modifications

27 In 1982, for 3K and 4K series, a new piston ring set was introduced with a different edge profile from the previous rings.

28 These rings are also supplied in oversizes.

29 It should be noted that these new piston rings will not fit the new pistons with the increased diameter mentioned in paragraph 24, because the piston ring grooves are too narrow.

30 As from 1984, and pertaining to all engines, the piston ring end gap clearance has been changed, the new values are given in the Specifications.

31 The correct method of measuring the piston ring end gap is to insert the ring into the cylinder bore, and push the ring down with an old piston to just beyond the lowest oil ring travel point.

32 Remove the piston and measure the gap with a feeler gauge.

33 If the gap exceeds the specified maximum, fit new piston rings.

34 If the gap is still exceeded, the cylinders must be rebored and oversize pistons and/or piston rings fitted.

Camshaft bearings – all engines

35 From 1982 the camshaft bearing lubrication holes and grooves have been changed, as shown in Fig. 13.8.

36 When fitting these new bearings, which can also be fitted to older engines, ensure the positioning groove faces the front of the engine, and that the oil holes are in alignment with those in the cylinder head.

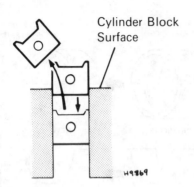

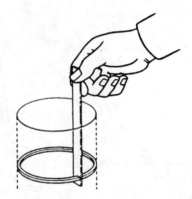

Fig. 13.7 Measuring piston ring end gap (Sec 4)

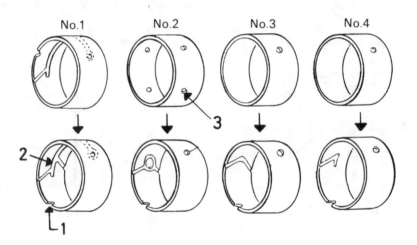

Fig. 13.8 New type camshaft bearings (Sec 4)

1   Positioning groove   2   Oil passage groove   3   Oil hole

Cylinder head bolts – all engines
37 It is no longer necessary to check tighten the cylinder head bolts after 600 miles on new or overhauled engines.

Crankshaft pulley – 1982 on
38 To improve charging performance, the diameter of the crankshaft pulley has been increased from 5.16 to 5.63 in (130 to 142 mm).
39 Consequently the fan belt and alternator pulley have also been changed.
40 Care should be taken that when changing any of these components they remain compatible.

5 Cooling system

Radiator – 1982 on
1 A single new radiator with upper and lower tanks made of a resin material is used, to save weight.
2 The new radiator has different mountings; being held by two lugs and brackets which are a push fit at the bottom edge, and by two bolts at the top (photo).
3 Care should be taken if making repairs to the radiator using direct heat that no damage to the resin tanks occurs.

5.2 Radiator top mounting

Cooling fan

4 A new style cooling fan and shroud are fitted to the new radiator, in much the same way as the previous fan.

Thermostat

5 To improve heater performance, a thermostat having a different opening temperature is fitted.
6 Refer to the Specifications for details.

6 Fuel system

General

1 The fuel system has changed little over the years and the servicing procedures given in Chapter 3 are sufficient to allow the fuel system and carburettor to be adequately serviced.
2 However, one or two minor modifications have been made, in the area of jet sizes and adjustments, and the Specifications in this Supplement should be studied to pinpoint any changes.
3 Where doubt exists as to exact year of manufacture and hence carburettor settings, your dealer should be consulted.
4 The procedures given here apply mainly to the carburettor fitted to the 4K engine, but may also be employed for carburettors fitted to other engines, in conjunction with the Specifications.
5 The throttle and choke valve openings are now set by using angles, and Toyota use a special tool for this purpose.
6 As the angles are given relative to the horizontal plane, the use of a protractor will give reasonably accurate results, but if problems are encountered then the proper tool will have to be obtained, or the work left to your dealer.

Carburettor adjustments – 1981 on

Primary throttle valve opening
7 Remove the carburettor, as described in Chapter 3.
8 Open the primary throttle valve fully.
9 Measure the throttle valve opening angle, which should be as specified.
10 Adjust by bending the throttle lever stopper.

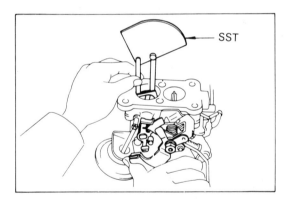

Fig. 13.9 Using special tool to measure throttle valve opening angles (Sec 6)

Secondary throttle valve opening
11 Open the primary throttle valve fully and measure the secondary throttle valve opening angle.
12 Adjust by bending the throttle shaft link rod.
Fast idle adjustment
13 Close the choke valve by turning the choke shaft lever, and hold it closed by using an elastic band.
14 Check the primary throttle valve opening angle in this condition, which should be as specified.
15 Adjust on the fast idle adjustment screw.
16 After adjustment, ensure there is a clearance between the screw and the stop.
Choke breaker (automatic transmission only)
17 Fully close the choke valve.
18 Apply a vacuum to the choke breaker diaphragm and check that the choke flap has opened sufficiently to give the specified clearance.
19 Adjust by bending the connecting rod.

7 Ignition system

Distributor and coil

1 From 1981 a larger, waterproofed distributor was fitted, and the capacity of the coil was increased.
2 Neither of these improvements affect the servicing details in Chapter 4.

Ignition timing – 4K engines

3 The ignition timing advance setting for the 4K (1300 cc) engine is different from that of the 2K (1000 cc) and 3K-H (1166 cc) engines, and is as given in the Specifications.

8 Manual transmission

Modifications

1 The K40 and K50 gearboxes have undergone several minor modifications to improve their performance.
2 These are mainly of a dimensional/profile nature and do not affect the procedures given in Chapter 6.
3 However, in order to ensure the correct parts are obtained during overhaul, it is important to quote the transmission serial number when ordering new parts.

9 Propeller shaft

General

1 The bolts securing the propeller shaft universal joint yoke have changed in material.
2 The new type of bolt can be identified by its colour, which is black, the previous bolts being gold.
3 The tightening torque of the new bolts has changed and is as given in the Specifications.

10 Rear axle – 1982 on

General

1 To improve centering of the wheel and reduce vibration, the rear axleshaft has been flanged, as shown in Fig. 13.10.

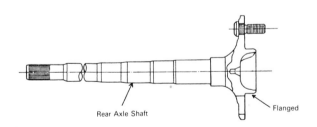

Rear Axle Shaft   Flanged

Fig. 13.10 New type flanged rear axleshaft (Sec 10)

11 Braking system

Master cylinder – cleaning

1 With reference to Section 9 of Chapter 9 and the inspection of the internal bore of the master cylinder, the bore may be cleaned using the following procedure:
2 Wrap a piece of soft lint-free rag around the end of a thin wooden dowel, so that its diameter approximates to the internal bore of the master cylinder.
3 Soak the cloth in clean brake fluid.

4   Insert the cloth and dowel into the bore of the master cylinder and clean the bore using a rotational movement only. Do not push and pull the wadding in and out.

5   Remove the stick and wadding, flush the master cylinder out with clean hydraulic fluid to remove any dust or cloth particles.

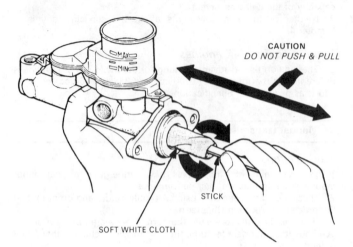

Fig. 13.11 Cleaning the brake master cylinder bore (Sec 11)

12 Electrical system

Part A – General

1   Along with the 1983 facelift, the interior of the vehicle was updated; the dash and instrument panel being completely new. Certain instruments changed position, and the headlights and some auxiliary lamps were changed. The following paragraphs describe these changes where they differ from the main Chapter.

Fusebox

2   The fusebox is situated below the right-hand instrument panel.
3   To gain access to the fuses, remove the plastic cover (photo).
4   Details of the fuses are given on the back of the cover.

Rear wiper – relay

5   The rear wiper relay is positioned inside the tailgate, bolted to the frame (photo).
6   To gain access to it, remove the rear hatch trim panel.

Instrument panel – removal and refitting

7   Remove the four screws securing the instrument panel surround, and remove the surround (photos).
8   Remove the two screws securing the instrument panel (photo).
9   Gently pull the instrument panel forward until the speedometer cable and the electrical connectors can be disconnected, and remove the instrument panel (photos).

10 Further dismantling of the instrument panel is basically as described in Chapter 10.
11 Refitting is a reversal of removal.

Headlamps – 1983 on

Bulb changing

12 The procedure for changing the headlamp bulbs is as described in Chapter 10.

Removal and refitting

13 Remove the front grille, as described in Section 14.
14 Remove the front turn indicator light (see paragraph 20).
15 Remove the two screws securing the headlamp surround to the radiator grille support bracket (photo).
16 Remove the four screws securing the headlamp unit (photo).
17 Refitting is a reversal of removal.

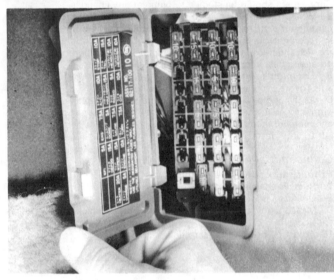

12.3 New type fusebox and cover

Beam alignment

18 The alignment procedure is as given in Chapter 10, although the adjuster screws can be reached with the trim panel in position (photo).
19 There are two adjusting screws for each headlamp, one at the inboard edge, for horizontal plane, and one at the top, for the vertical plane.

Front turn indicator light – removal, refitting and bulb changing

20 Remove the two screws holding the light unit (photo).
21 The bulb holder is a bayonet fix in the light unit, and the bulb a bayonet fix in the holder (photo).
22 Refit in the reverse order.

12.5 Rear wiper relay

12.7A Instrument panel surround lower retaining screw

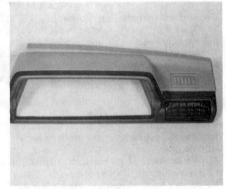

12.7B The surround removed

12.8 Instrument panel right-hand securing screw (arrowed)

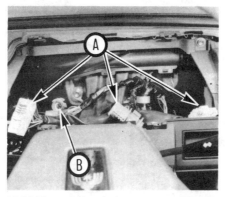

12.9A View of electrical connectors (A) and speedometer cable (B) with instrument panel removed

12.9B Instrument panel removed

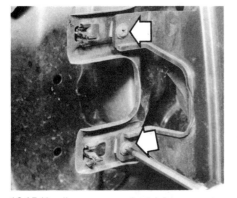

12.15 Headlamp surround retaining screws (arrowed)

12.16 Removing a headlamp unit retaining screw

12.18 Headlamp beam adjuster

12.20 Removing a front turn indicator light screw

12.21 Front turn indicator light unit bulbholder and bulb

Rear foglight – removal, refitting and bulb changing

23 To change the bulb, remove the lens cover, held by two screws (photo).
24 The bulb is a bayonet fix in the holder (photo).
25 Refit the cover.
26 In view of the position of the foglamp, and its susceptibility to damage, should it become necessary to change the lamp unit, remove the cover and bulb, and then drill out the two rivets holding the unit to the bumper.
27 Disconnect the electrical lead and remove the light unit.
28 Refitting is a reversal of removal, although it is suggested that the rivets are renewed with two suitable bolts, to facilitate future renewal of the light unit.

Windscreen wiper drive spindle – modification

29 From 1981 the configuration of the windscreen wiper drive spindle has been altered, as shown in Fig. 13.12.
30 If any of these parts become defective, they are only interchangeable as a set, and a new wiper link arm must also be fitted.

Radio – removal and refitting

31 Remove the centre floor console (Section 14).
32 Remove the instrument panel surround (this Section).
33 Gently pry out the centre face vents (photo).
34 Remove the retaining screws inside the air ducts (photo).
35 Remove the heater control knobs, which pull off, and the choke control knob, which is held by a recessed screw (photo).

12.23 Removing the rear foglight lens

12.24 Bulb is a bayonet fit

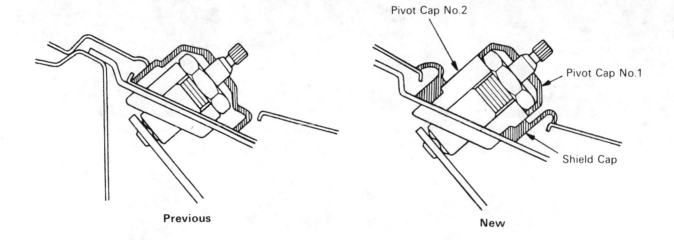

Pivot Cap No.2

Pivot Cap No.1

Shield Cap

Previous

New

Fig. 13.12 Old and new windscreen wiper pivot (Sec 12)

12.33 Removing a centre face vent

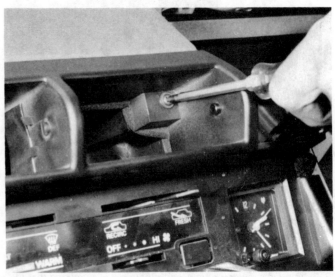

12.34 Removing the retaining screws

12.35 Choke control cable showing knob removed and the retaining screw (arrowed)

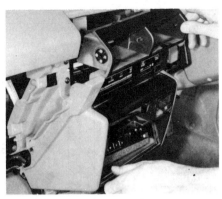

12.37 Lifting the centre panel

12.40 Radio support bracket and screws

12.43 Clock and securing screws

12.46 Prising out a rocker switch

12.47 Pulling out the switch to reveal the connector

36 There are a further four screws holding the centre panel in position, plus a clip to the right-hand side of the clock.
37 Remove these and lift the panel slightly (photo).
38 Disconnect the electrical lead to the cigar lighter.
39 Remove the centre panel.
40 Remove the four screws holding the radio in place (photo), and disconnect the electrical lead and the aerial, then remove the radio.
41 Refitting is a reversal of removal.

Clock – removal and refitting
42 Remove the centre floor console and the centre panel, as described

in the previous sub-section.
43 The clock is held by four screws (photo).
44 Remove these, disconnect the electrical lead, and remove the clock.
45 Refit in the reverse order.

Rocker switches – removal and refitting
46 Prise the switch from the facia panel (photo).
47 Pull the switch out and disconnect the electrical lead (photo).
48 Refit in the reverse order.

Wiring diagrams commence overleaf

For colour code see page 208

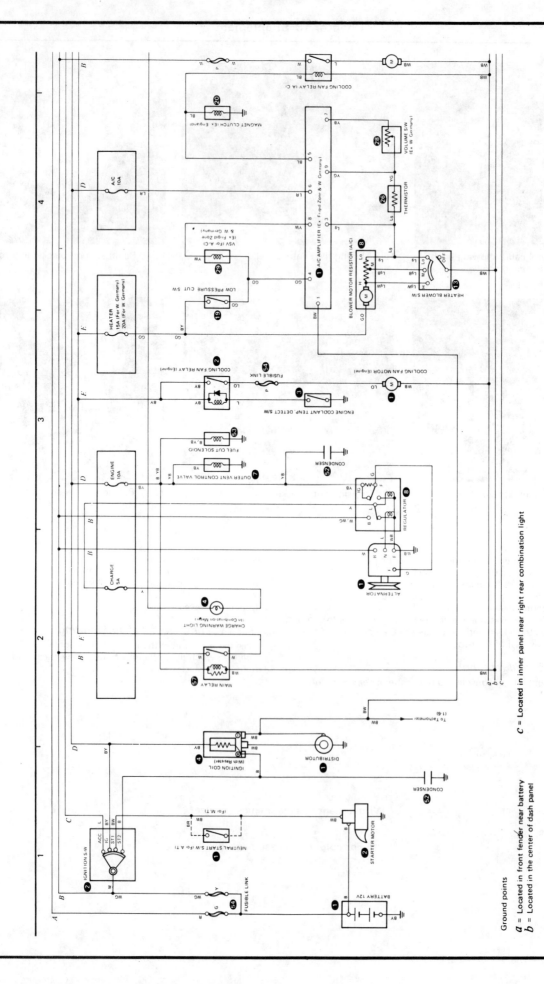

Fig. 13.13 Wiring diagram – later models up to 1982

Ground points

a = Located in front fender near battery
b = Located in the center of dash panel

C = Located in inner panel near right rear combination light

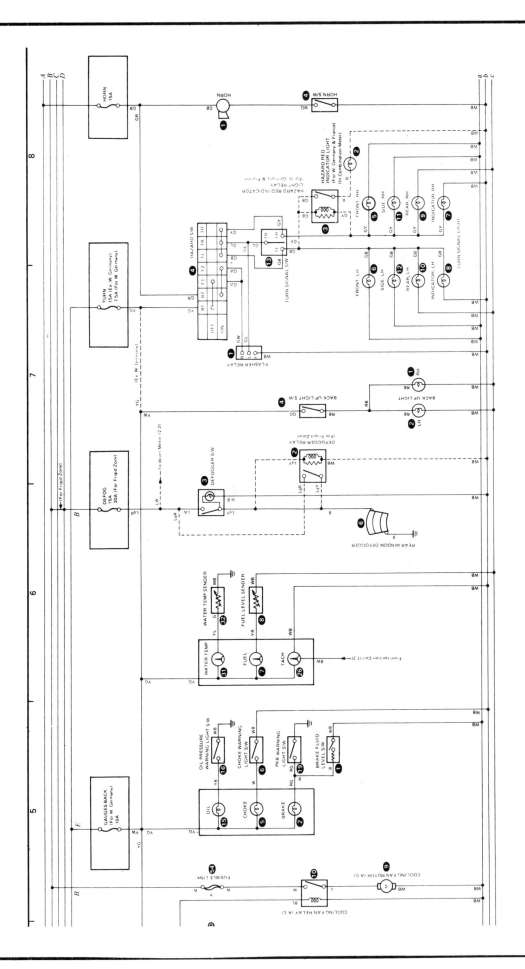

Fig. 13.13 Wiring diagram – later models up to 1982 (continued)

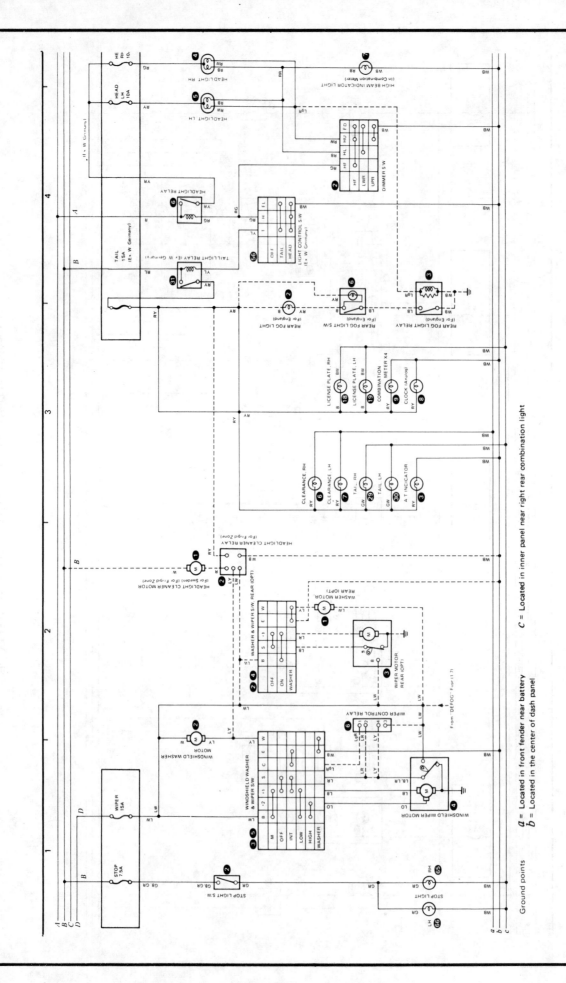

Fig. 13.13 Wiring diagram – later models up to 1982 (continued)

Ground points

a = Located in front fender near battery
b = Located in the center of dash panel
c = Located in inner panel near right rear combination light

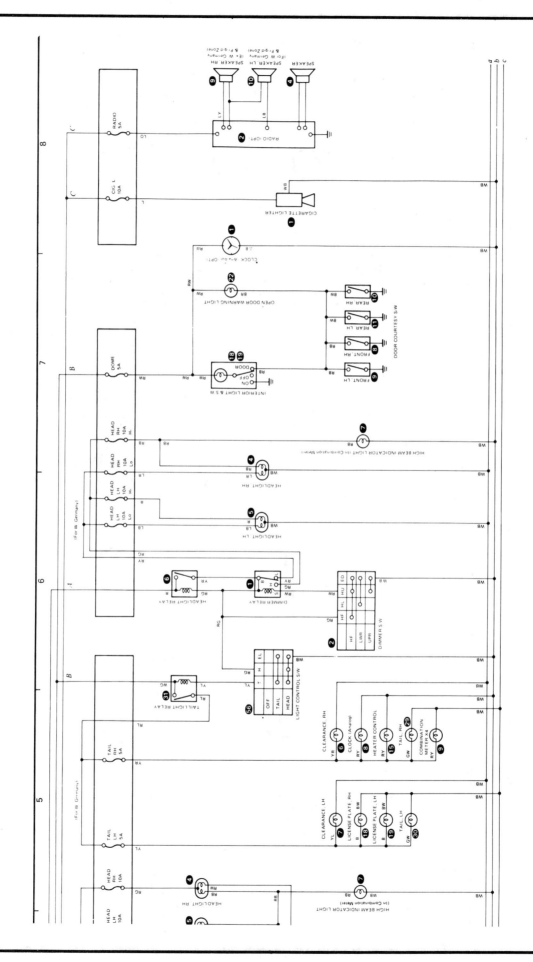

Fig. 13. 13 Wiring diagram – later models up to 1982 (continued)

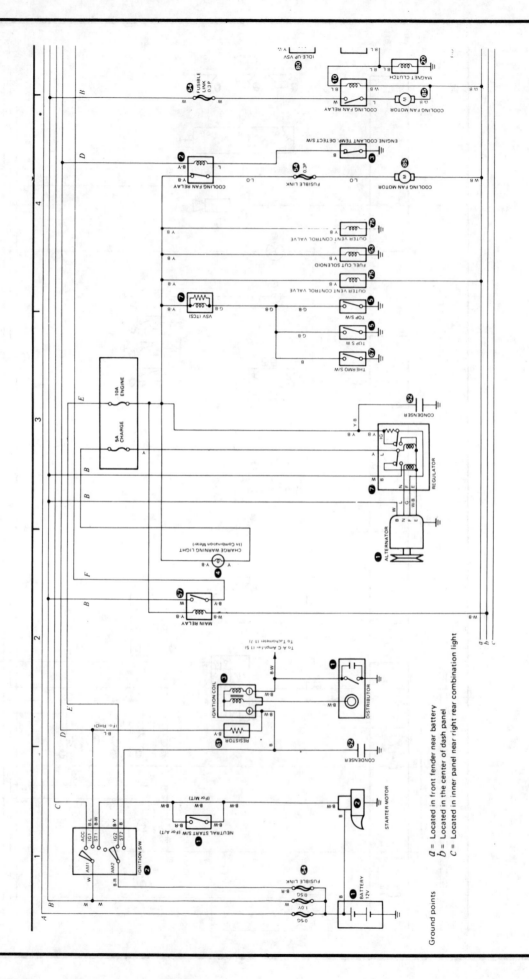

Fig. 13.14 Wiring diagram – all models 1983 on

Ground points

a = Located in front fender near battery
b = Located in the center of dash panel
c = Located in inner panel near right rear combination light

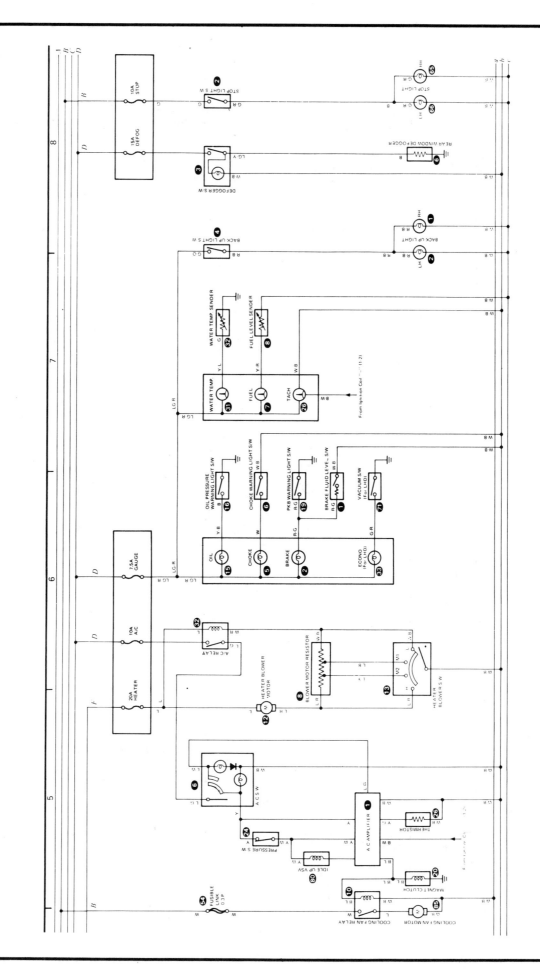

Fig. 13.14 Wiring diagram – all models 1983 on (continued)

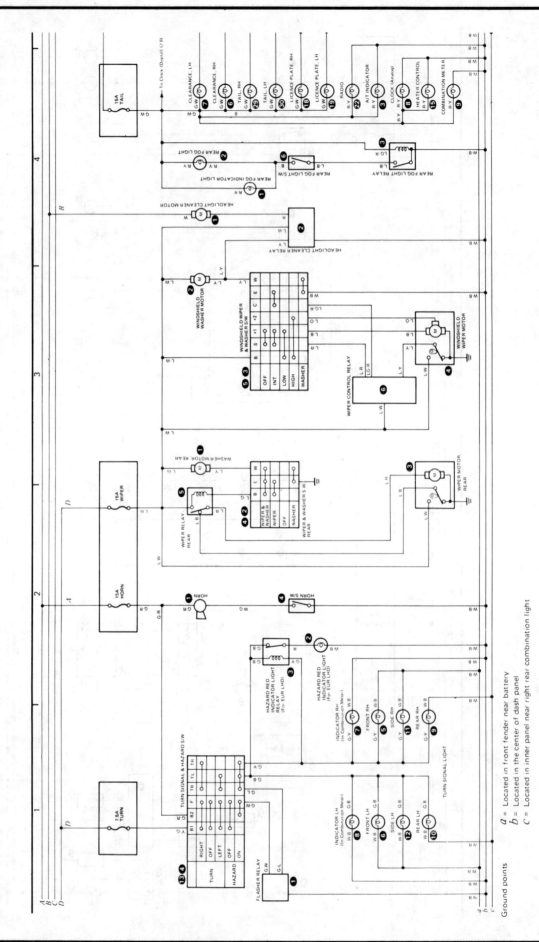

Fig. 13.14 Wiring diagram – all models 1983 on (continued)

Ground points

a = Located in front fender near battery
b = Located in the center of dash panel
c = Located in inner panel near right rear combination light

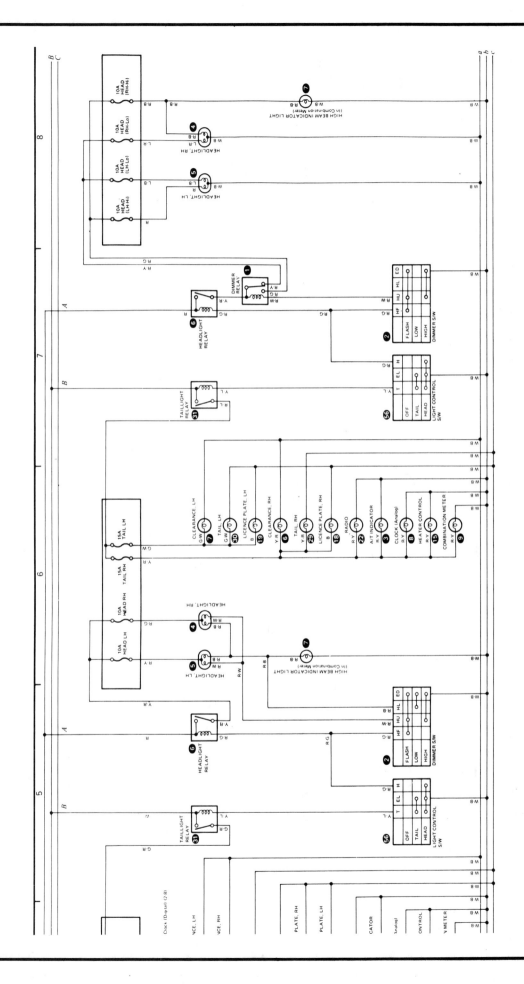

Fig. 13.14 Wiring diagram – all models 1983 on (continued)

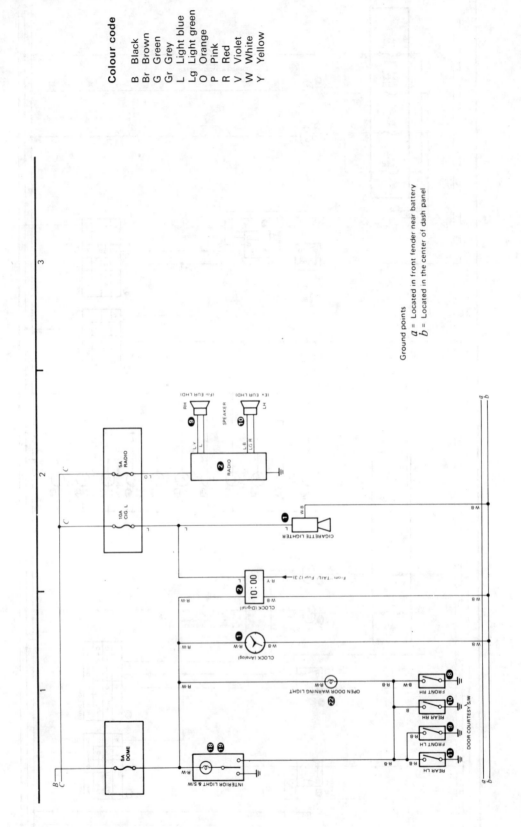

Colour code

B Black
Br Brown
G Green
Gr Grey
L Light blue
Lg Light green
O Orange
P Pink
R Red
V Violet
W White
Y Yellow

Ground points
a = Located in front fender near battery
b = Located in the center of dash panel

Fig. 13.14 Wiring diagram – all models 1983 on (continued)

Part B: Mobile radio equipment – interference-free installation

Aerials – selection and fitting

The choice of aerials is now very wide. It should be realised that the quality has a profound effect on radio performance, and a poor, inefficient aerial can make suppression difficult.

A wing-mounted aerial is regarded as probably the most efficient for signal collection, but a roof aerial is usually better for suppression purposes because it is away from most interference fields. Stick-on wire aerials are available for attachment to the inside of the windscreen, but are not always free from the interference field of the engine and some accessories.

Motorised automatic aerials rise when the equipment is switched on and retract at switch-off. They require more fitting space and supply leads, and can be a source of trouble.

There is no merit in choosing a very long aerial as, for example, the type about three metres in length which hooks or clips on to the rear of the car, since part of this aerial will inevitably be located in an interference field. For VHF/FM radios the best length of aerial is about one metre. Active aerials have a transistor amplifier mounted at the base and this serves to boost the received signal. The aerial rod is sometimes rather shorter than normal passive types.

A large loss of signal can occur in the aerial feeder cable, especially over the Very High Frequency (VHF) bands. The design of feeder cable is invariably in the co-axial form, ie a centre conductor surrounded by a flexible copper braid forming the outer (earth) conductor. Between the inner and outer conductors is an insulator material which can be in solid or stranded form. Apart from insulation, its purpose is to maintain the correct spacing and concentricity. Loss of signal occurs in this insulator, the loss usually being greater in a poor quality cable. The quality of cable used is reflected in the price of the aerial with the attached feeder cable.

The capacitance of the feeder should be within the range 65 to 75 picofarads (pF) approximately (95 to 100 pF for Japanese and American equipment), otherwise the adjustment of the car radio aerial trimmer may not be possible. An extension cable is necessary for a long run between aerial and receiver. If this adds capacitance in excess of the above limits, a connector containing a series capacitor will be required, or an extension which is labelled as 'capacity-compensated'.

Fitting the aerial will normally involve making a $^7/_8$ in (22 mm) diameter hole in the bodywork, but read the instructions that come with the aerial kit. Once the hole position has been selected, use a centre punch to guide the drill. Use sticky masking tape around the area for this helps with marking out and drill location, and gives protection to the paintwork should the drill slip. Three methods of making the hole are in use:

(a) Use a hole saw in the electric drill. This is, in effect, a circular hacksaw blade wrapped round a former with a centre pilot drill.

(b) Use a tank cutter which also has cutting teeth, but is made to shear the metal by tightening with an Allen key.

(c) The hard way of drilling out the circle is using a small drill, say $^1/_8$ in (3 mm), so that the holes overlap. The centre metal drops out and the hole is finished with round and half-round files.

Whichever method is used, the burr is removed from the body metal and paint removed from the underside. The aerial is fitted tightly ensuring that the earth fixing, usually a serrated washer, ring or clamp, is making a solid connection. *This earth connection is important in reducing interference.* Cover any bare metal with primer paint and topcoat, and follow by underseal if desired.

Aerial feeder cable routing should avoid the engine compartment and areas where stress might occur, eg under the carpet where feet will be located. Roof aerials require that the headlining be pulled back and that a path is available down the door pillar. It is wise to check with the vehicle dealer whether roof aerial fitting is recommended.

Loudspeakers

Speakers should be matched to the output stage of the equipment, particularly as regards the recommended impedance. Power transistors used for driving speakers are sensitive to the loading placed on them.

Before choosing a mounting position for speakers, check whether the vehicle manufacturer has provided a location for them. Generally door-mounted speakers give good stereophonic reproduction, but not all doors are able to accept them. The next best position is the rear parcel shelf, and in this case speaker apertures can be cut into the shelf, or pod units may be mounted.

For door mounting, first remove the trim, which is often held on by 'poppers' or press studs, and then select a suitable gap in the inside door assembly. Check that the speaker would not obstruct glass or winder mechanism by winding the window up and down. A template is often provided for marking out the trim panel hole, and then the four fixing holes must be drilled through. Mark out with chalk and cut cleanly with a sharp knife or keyhole saw. Speaker leads are then threaded through the door and door pillar, if necessary drilling 10 mm diameter holes. Fit grommets in the holes and connect to the radio or tape unit correctly. Do not omit a waterproofing cover, usually supplied with door speakers. If the speaker has to be fixed into the metal of the door itself, use self-tapping screws, and if the fixing is to the door trim use self-tapping screws and flat spire nuts.

Rear shelf mounting is somewhat simpler but it is necessary to find gaps in the metalwork underneath the parcel shelf. However, remember that the speakers should be as far apart as possible to give a good stereo effect. Pod-mounted speakers can be screwed into position through the parcel shelf material, but it is worth testing for the best position. Sometimes good results are found by reflecting sound off the rear window.

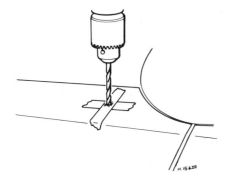

Fig. 13.15 Drilling the bodywork for aerial mounting (Sec 12)

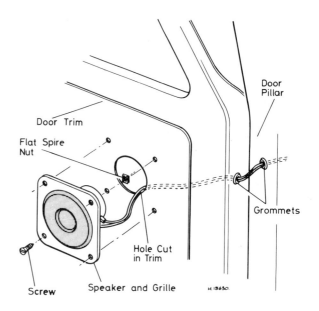

Fig. 13.16 Door-mounted speaker installation (Sec 12)

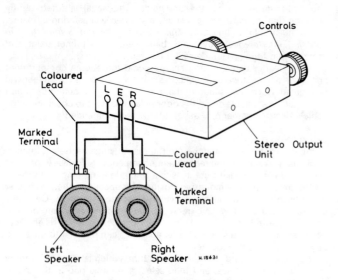

Fig. 13.17 Speaker connections must be correctly made (Sec 12)

Unit installation

Many vehicles have a dash panel aperture to take a radio/audio unit, a recognised international standard being 189.5 mm x 60 mm. Alternatively a console may be a feature of the car interior design and this, mounted below the dashboard, gives more room. If neither facility is available a unit may be mounted on the underside of the parcel shelf; these are frequently non-metallic and an earth wire from the case to a good earth point is necessary. A three-sided cover in the form of a cradle is obtainable from car radio dealers and this gives a professional appearance to the installation; in this case choose a position where the controls can be reached by a driver with his seat belt on.

Installation of the radio/audio unit is basically the same in all cases, and consists of offering it into the aperture after removal of the knobs *(not* push buttons) and the trim plate. In some cases a special mounting plate is required to which the unit is attached. It is worthwhile supporting the rear end in cases where sag or strain may occur, and it is usually possible to use a length of perforated metal strip attached between the unit and a good support point nearby. In general it is recommended that tape equipment should be installed at or nearly horizontal.

Connections to the aerial socket are simply by the standard plug terminating the aerial downlead or its extension cable. Speakers for a stereo system must be matched and correctly connected, as outlined previously.

Note: *While all work is carried out on the power side, it is wise to disconnect the battery earth lead.* Before connection is made to the vehicle electrical system, check that the polarity of the unit is correct. Most vehicles use a negative earth system, but radio/audio units often have a reversible plug to convert the set to either + or – earth. *Incorrect connection may cause serious damage.*

The power lead is often permanently connected inside the unit and terminates with one half of an in-line fuse carrier. The other half is fitted with a suitable fuse (3 or 5 amperes) and a wire which should go to a power point in the electrical system. This may be the accessory terminal on the ignition switch, giving the advantage of power feed with ignition or with the ignition key at the 'accessory' position. Power to the unit stops when the ignition key is removed. Alternatively, the lead may be taken to a live point at the fusebox with the consequence of having to remember to switch off at the unit before leaving the vehicle.

Before switching on for initial test, be sure that the speaker connections have been made, for running without load can damage the output transistors. Switch on next and tune through the bands to ensure that all sections are working, and check the tape unit if applicable. The aerial trimmer should be adjusted to give the strongest reception on a weak signal in the medium wave band, at say 200 metres.

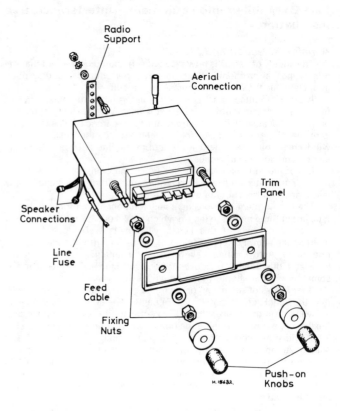

Fig. 13.18 Mounting component details for radio/cassette unit (Sec 12)

Interference

In general, when electric current changes abruptly, unwanted electrical noise is produced. The motor vehicle is filled with electrical devices which change electric current rapidly, the most obvious being the contact breaker.

When the spark plugs operate, the sudden pulse of spark current causes the associated wiring to radiate. Since early radio transmitters used sparks as a basis of operation, it is not surprising that the car radio will pick up ignition spark noise unless steps are taken to reduce it to acceptable levels.

Interference reaches the car radio in two ways:

(a) by conduction through the wiring.
(b) by radiation to the receiving aerial.

Initial checks presuppose that the bonnet is down and fastened, the radio unit has a good earth connection *(not* through the aerial downlead outer), no fluorescent tubes are working near the car, the aerial trimmer has been adjusted, and the vehicle is in a position to receive radio signals, ie not in a metal-clad building.

Switch on the radio and tune it to the middle of the medium wave (MW) band off-station with the volume (gain) control set fairly high. Switch on the ignition (but do not start the engine) and wait to see if irregular clicks or hash noise occurs. Tapping the facia panel may also produce the effects. If so, this will be due to the voltage stabiliser, which is an on-off thermal switch to control instrument voltage. It is located usually on the back of the instrument panel, often attached to the speedometer. Correction is by attachment of a capacitor and, if still troublesome, chokes in the supply wires.

Switch on the engine and listen for interference on the MW band. Depending on the type of interference, the indications are as follows.

A harsh crackle that drops out abruptly at low engine speed or when the headlights are switched on is probably due to a voltage regulator.

A whine varying with engine speed is due to the dynamo or alternator. Try temporarily taking off the fan belt – if the noise goes this is confirmation.

Regular ticking or crackle that varies in rate with the engine speed is due to the ignition system. With this trouble in particular and others in general, check to see if the noise is entering the receiver from the wiring or by radiation. To do this, pull out the aerial plug, (preferably shorting out the input socket or connecting a 62 pF capacitor across it). If the noise disappears it is coming in through the aerial and is *radiation noise*. If the noise persists it is reaching the receiver through the wiring and is said to be *line-borne*.

Interference from wipers, washers, heater blowers, turn-indicators, stop lamps, etc is usually taken to the receiver by wiring, and simple treatment using capacitors and possibly chokes will solve the problem. Switch on each one in turn (wet the screen first for running wipers!) and listen for possible interference with the aerial plug in place and again when removed.

Electric petrol pumps are now finding application again and give rise to an irregular clicking, often giving a burst of clicks when the ignition is on but the engine has not yet been started. It is also possible to receive whining or crackling from the pump.

Note that if most of the vehicle accessories are found to be creating interference all together, the probability is that poor aerial earthing is to blame.

Component terminal markings

Throughout the following sub-sections reference will be found to various terminal markings. These will vary depending on the manufacturer of the relevant component. If terminal markings differ from those mentioned, reference should be made to the following table, where the most commonly encountered variations are listed.

Alternator	Alternator terminal (thick lead)	Exciting winding terminal
DIN/Bosch	B+	DF
Delco Remy	+	EXC
Ducellier	+	EXC
Ford (US)	+	DF
Lucas	+	F
Marelli	+ B	F

Ignition coil	Ignition switch terminal	Contact breaker terminal
DIN/Bosch	15	1
Delco Remy	+	–
Ducellier	BAT	RUP
Ford (US)	B/+	CB/–
Lucas	SW/+	–
Marelli	BAT/+B	D

Voltage regulator	Voltage input terminal	Exciting winding terminal
DIN/Bosch	B+/D+	DF
Delco Remy	BAT/+	EXC
Ducellier	BOB/BAT	EXC
Ford (US)	BAT	DF
Lucas	+/A	F
Marelli		F

Suppression methods – ignition

Suppressed HT cables are supplied as original equipment by manufacturers and will meet regulations as far as interference to neighbouring equipment is concerned. It is illegal to remove such suppression unless an alternative is provided, and this may take the form of resistive spark plug caps in conjunction with plain copper HT cable. For VHF purposes, these and 'in-line' resistors may not be effective, and resistive HT cable is preferred. Check that suppressed cables are actually fitted by observing cable identity lettering, or measuring with an ohmmeter – the value of each plug lead should be 5000 to 10 000 ohms.

A 1 microfarad capacitor connected from the LT supply side of the ignition coil to a good nearby earth point will complete basic ignition interference treatment. *NEVER fit a capacitor to the coil terminal to the contact breaker – the result would be burnt out points in a short time.*

If ignition noise persists despite the treatment above, the following sequence should be followed:

(a) Check the earthing of the ignition coil; remove paint from fixing clamp.

(b) If this does not work, lift the bonnet. Should there be no change in interference level, this may indicate that the bonnet is not electrically connected to the car body. Use a proprietary

braided strap across a bonnet hinge ensuring a first class electrical connection. If, however, lifting the bonnet increases the interference, then fit resistive HT cables of a higher ohms-per-metre value.

(c) If all these measures fail, it is probable that re-radiation from metallic components is taking place. Using a braided strap between metallic points, go round the vehicle systematically – try the following: engine to body, exhaust system to body, front suspension to engine and to body, steering column to body (especially French and Italian cars), gear lever to engine and to body (again especially French and Italian cars), Bowden cable to body, metal parcel shelf to body. When an offending component is located it should be bonded with the strap permanently.

(d) As a next step, the fitting of distributor suppressors to each lead at the distributor end may help.

(e) Beyond this point is involved the possible screening of the distributor and fitting resistive spark plugs, but such advanced treatment is not usually required for vehicles with entertainment equipment.

Electronic ignition systems have built-in suppression components, but this does not relieve the need for using suppressed HT leads. In some cases it is permitted to connect a capacitor to the low tension supply side of the ignition coil, but not in every case. Makers' instructions should be followed carefully, otherwise damage to the ignition semiconductors may result.

Suppression methods – generators

For older vehicles with dynamos a 1 microfarad capacitor from the D (larger) terminal to earth will usually cure dynamo whine. Alternators should be fitted with a 3 microfarad capacitor from the B+ main output terminal (thick cable) to earth. Additional suppression may be obtained by the use of a filter in the supply line to the radio receiver.

It is most important that:

(a) Capacitors are never connected to the field terminals of either a dynamo or alternator.

(b) Alternators must not be run without connection to the battery.

Suppression methods – voltage regulators

Voltage regulators used with DC dynamos should be suppressed by connecting a 1 microfarad capacitor from the control box D terminal to earth.

Alternator regulators come in three types:

(a) Vibrating contact regulators separate from the alternator. Used extensively on continental vehicles.

(b) Electronic regulators separate from the alternator.

(c) Electronic regulators built-in to the alternator.

In case (a) interference may be generated on the AM and FM (VHF) bands. For some cars a replacement suppressed regulator is available. Filter boxes may be used with non-suppressed regulators. But if not available, then for AM equipment a 2 microfarad or 3 microfarad capacitor may be mounted at the voltage terminal marked D+ or B+ of the regulator. FM bands may be treated by a feed-through capacitor of 2 or 3 microfarad.

Electronic voltage regulators are not always troublesome, but where necessary, a 1 microfarad capacitor from the regulator + terminal will help.

Integral electronic voltage regulators do not normally generate much interference, but when encountered this is in combination with alternator noise. A 1 microfarad or 2 microfarad capacitor from the warning lamp (IND) terminal to earth for Lucas ACR alternators and Femsa, Delco and Bosch equivalents should cure the problem.

Suppression methods – other equipment

Wiper motors – Connect the wiper body to earth with a bonding strap. For all motors use a 7 ampere choke assembly inserted in the leads to the motor.

Heater motors – Fit 7 ampere line chokes in both leads, assisted if necessary by a 1 microfarad capacitor to earth from both leads.

Electronic tachometer – The tachometer is a possible source of ignition noise – check by disconnecting at the ignition coil CB terminal. It usually feeds from ignition coil LT pulses at the contact

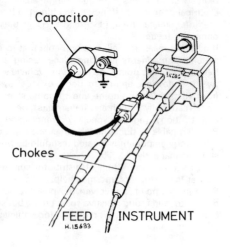

Fig. 13.19 Voltage stabiliser interference suppression
(Sec 12)

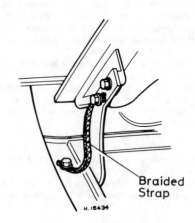

Fig. 13.20 Braided earth strap between bonnet and body
(Sec 12)

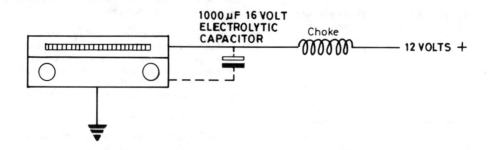

Fig. 13.21 Line-borne interference suppression (Sec 12)

breaker terminal. A 3 ampere line choke should be fitted in the tachometer lead at the coil CB terminal.

Horn – A capacitor and choke combination is effective if the horn is directly connected to the 12 volt supply. The use of a relay is an alternative remedy, as this will reduce the length of the interference-carrying leads.

Electrostatic noise – Characteristics are erratic crackling at the receiver, with disappearance of symptoms in wet weather. Often shocks may be given when touching bodywork. Part of the problem is the build-up of static electricity in non-driven wheels and the acquisition of charge on the body shell. It is possible to fit spring-loaded contacts at the wheels to give good conduction between the rotary wheel parts and the vehicle frame. Changing a tyre sometimes helps – because of tyres' varying resistances. In difficult cases a trailing flex which touches the ground will cure the problem. If this is not acceptable it is worth trying conductive paint on the tyre walls.

Fuel pump – Suppression requires a 1 microfarad capacitor between the supply wire to the pump and a nearby earth point. If this is insufficient a 7 ampere line choke connected in the supply wire near the pump is required.

Fluorescent tubes – Vehicles used for camping/caravanning frequently have fluorescent tube lighting. These tubes require a relatively high voltage for operation and this is provided by an inverter (a form of oscillator) which steps up the vehicle supply voltage. This can give rise to serious interference to radio reception, and the tubes themselves can contribute to this interference by the pulsating nature of the lamp discharge. In such situations it is important to mount the aerial as far away from a fluorescent tube as possible. The interference problem may be alleviated by screening the tube with fine wire turns spaced an inch (25 mm) apart and earthed to the chassis. Suitable chokes should be fitted in both supply wires close to the inverter.

Radio/cassette case breakthrough

Magnetic radiation from dashboard wiring may be sufficiently intense to break through the metal case of the radio/cassette player. Often this is due to a particular cable routed too close and shows up as ignition interference on AM and cassette play and/or alternator whine on cassette play.

The first point to check is that the clips and/or screws are fixing all parts of the radio/cassette case together properly. Assuming good earthing of the case, see if it is possible to re-route the offending cable – the chances of this are not good, however, in most cars.

Next release the radio/cassette player and locate it in different positions with temporary leads. If a point of low interference is found, then if possible fix the equipment in that area. This also confirms that local radiation is causing the trouble. If re-location is not feasible, fit the radio/cassette player back in the original position.

Alternator interference on cassette play is now caused by radiation from the main charging cable which goes from the battery to the output terminal of the alternator, usually via the + terminal of the starter motor relay. In some vehicles this cable is routed under the dashboard, so the solution is to provide a direct cable route. Detach the original cable from the alternator output terminal and make up a new cable of at least 6 mm² cross-sectional area to go from alternator to battery with the shortest possible route. *Remember – do not run the engine with the alternator disconnected from the battery.*

Ignition breakthrough on AM and/or cassette play can be a difficult problem. It is worth wrapping earthed foil round the offending cable run near the equipment, or making up a deflector plate well screwed down to a good earth. Another possibility is the use of a suitable relay to switch on the ignition coil. The relay should be mounted close to the ignition coil; with this arrangement the ignition coil primary current is not taken into the dashboard area and does not flow through the ignition switch. A suitable diode should be used since it is possible that at ignition switch-off the output from the warning lamp alternator terminal could hold the relay on.

Connectors for suppression components

Capacitors are usually supplied with tags on the end of the lead, while the capacitor body has a flange with a slot or hole to fit under a nut or screw with washer.

Connections to feed wires are best achieved by self-stripping connectors. These connectors employ a blade which, when squeezed down by pliers, cuts through cable insulation and makes connection to the copper conductors beneath.

Chokes sometimes come with bullet snap-in connectors fitted to the wires, and also with just bare copper wire. With connectors, suitable female cable connectors may be purchased from an auto-accessory shop together with any extra connectors required for the cable ends after being cut for the choke insertion. For chokes with bare wires, similar connectors may be employed together with insulation sleeving as required.

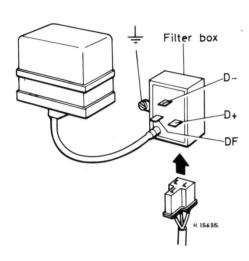

Fig. 13.22 Typical filter box for vibrating contact voltage regulator (alternator equipment) (Sec 12)

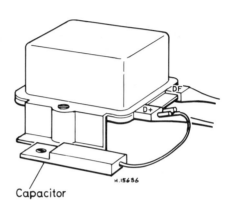

Fig. 13.23 Suppression of AM interference by vibrating contact voltage regulator (alternator equipment) (Sec 12)

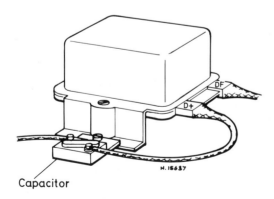

Fig. 13.24 Suppression of FM interference by vibrating contact voltage regulator (alternator equipment) (Sec 12)

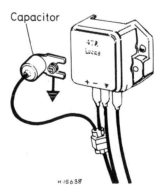

Fig. 13.25 Electronic voltage regulator suppression (Sec 12)

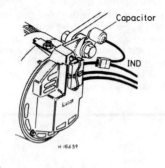

Capacitor

IND

H.15639

Fig. 13.26 Suppression of interference from electronic
voltage regulator when integral with alternator
(Sec 12)

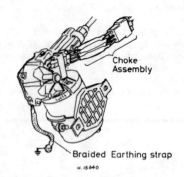

Choke
Assembly

Braided Earthing strap

H.15640

Fig. 13.27 Wiper motor suppression (Sec 12)

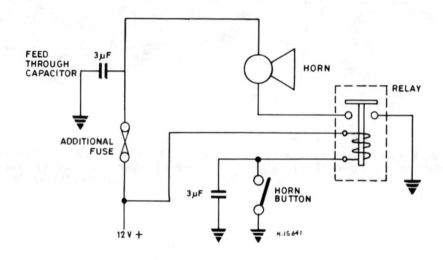

FEED
THROUGH
CAPACITOR

3 µF

HORN

RELAY

ADDITIONAL
FUSE

3 µF

HORN
BUTTON

12 V +

H.15641

Fig. 13.28 Use of relay to reduce horn interference
(Sec 12)

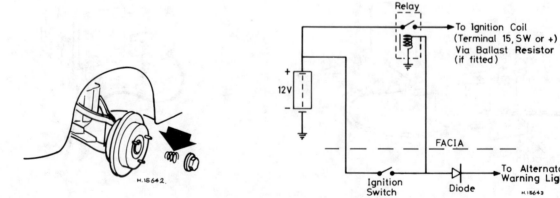

H.15642

Fig. 13.29 Use of spring contacts at wheels (Sec 12)

Relay

To Ignition Coil
(Terminal 15, SW or +)
Via Ballast Resistor
(if fitted)

12V

FACIA

Ignition
Switch

Diode

To Alternator
Warning Light

H.15643

Fig. 13.30 Use of ignition coil relay to suppress case
breakthrough (Sec 12)

VHF/FM broadcasts

Reception of VHF/FM in an automobile is more prone to problems than the medium and long wavebands. Medium/long wave transmitters are capable of covering considerable distances, but VHF transmitters are restricted to line of sight, meaning ranges of 10 to 50 miles, depending upon the terrain, the effects of buildings and the transmitter power.

Because of the limited range it is necessary to retune on a long journey, and it may be better for those habitually travelling long distances or living in areas of poor provision of transmitters to use an AM radio working on medium/long wavebands.

When conditions are poor, interference can arise, and some of the suppression devices described previously fall off in performance at very high frequencies unless specifically designed for the VHF band. Available suppression devices include reactive HT cable, resistive distributor caps, screened plug caps, screened leads and resistive spark plugs.

For VHF/FM receiver installation the following points should be particularly noted:

(a) Earthing of the receiver chassis and the aerial mounting is important. Use a separate earthing wire at the radio, and scrape paint away at the aerial mounting.
(b) If possible, use a good quality roof aerial to obtain maximum height and distance from interference generating devices on the vehicle.
(c) Use of a high quality aerial downlead is important, since losses in cheap cable can be significant.
(d) The polarisation of FM transmissions may be horizontal, vertical, circular or slanted. Because of this the optimum mounting angle is at 45° to the vehicle roof.

Citizens' Band radio (CB)

In the UK, CB transmitter/receivers work within the 27 MHz and 934 MHz bands, using the FM mode. At present interest is concentrated on 27 MHz where the design and manufacture of equipment is less difficult. Maximum transmitted power is 4 watts, and 40 channels spaced 10 kHz apart within the range 27.60125 to 27.99125 MHz are available.

Aerials are the key to effective transmission and reception. Regulations limit the aerial length to 1.65 metres including the loading coil and any associated circuitry, so tuning the aerial is necessary to obtain optimum results. The choice of a CB aerial is dependent on whether it is to be permanently installed or removable, and the performance will hinge on correct tuning and the location point on the vehicle. Common practice is to clip the aerial to the roof gutter or to employ wing mounting where the aerial can be rapidly unscrewed. An alternative is to use the boot rim to render the aerial theftproof, but a popular solution is to use the 'magmount' – a type of mounting having a strong magnetic base clamping to the vehicle at any point, usually the roof.

Aerial location determines the signal distribution for both transmission and reception, but it is wise to choose a point away from the engine compartment to minimise interference from vehicle electrical equipment.

The aerial is subject to considerable wind and acceleration forces. Cheaper units will whip backwards and forwards and in so doing will alter the relationship with the metal surface of the vehicle with which it forms a ground plane aerial system. The radiation pattern will change correspondingly, giving rise to break-up of both incoming and outgoing signals.

Interference problems on the vehicle carrying CB equipment fall into two categories:

(a) Interference to nearby TV and radio receivers when transmitting.
(b) Interference to CB set reception due to electrical equipment on the vehicle.

Problems of break-through to TV and radio are not frequent, but can be difficult to solve. Mostly trouble is not detected or reported because the vehicle is moving and the symptoms rapidly disappear at the TV/radio receiver, but when the CB set is used as a base station any trouble with nearby receivers will soon result in a complaint.

It must not be assumed by the CB operator that his equipment is faultless, for much depends upon the design. Harmonics (that is,

multiples) of 27 MHz may be transmitted unknowingly and these can fall into other user's bands. Where trouble of this nature occurs, low pass filters in the aerial or supply leads can help, and should be fitted in base station aerials as a matter of course. In stubborn cases it may be necessary to call for assistance from the licensing authority, or, if possible, to have the equipment checked by the manufacturers.

Interference received on the CB set from the vehicle equipment is, fortunately, not usually a severe problem. The precautions outlined previously for radio/cassette units apply, but there are some extra points worth noting.

It is common practice to use a slide-mount on CB equipment enabling the set to be easily removed for use as a base station, for example. Care must be taken that the slide mount fittings are properly earthed and that first class connection occurs between the set and slide-mount.

Vehicle manufacturers in the UK are required to provide suppression of electrical equipment to cover 40 to 250 MHz to protect TV and VHF radio bands. Such suppression appears to be adequately effective at 27 MHz, but suppression of individual items such as alternators/dynamos, clocks, stabilisers, flashers, wiper motors, etc, may still be necessary. The suppression capacitors and chokes available from auto-electrical suppliers for entertainment receivers will usually give the required results with CB equipment.

Other vehicle radio transmitters

Besides CB radio already mentioned, a considerable increase in the use of transceivers (ie combined transmitter and receiver units) has taken place in the last decade. Previously this type of equipment was fitted mainly to military, fire, ambulance and police vehicles, but a large business radio and radio telephone usage has developed.

Generally the suppression techniques described previously will suffice, with only a few difficult cases arising. Suppression is carried out to satisfy the 'receive mode', but care must be taken to use heavy duty chokes in the equipment supply cables since the loading on 'transmit' is relatively high.

Glass-fibre bodied vehicles

Such vehicles do not have the advantage of a metal box surrounding the engine as is the case, in effect, of conventional vehicles. It is usually necessary to line the bonnet, bulkhead and wing valances with metal foil, which could well be the aluminium foil available from builders merchants. Bonding of sheets one to another and the whole down to the chassis is essential.

Wiring harness may have to be wrapped in metal foil which again should be earthed to the vehicle chassis. The aerial base and radio chassis must be taken to the vehicle chassis by heavy metal braid. VHF radio suppression in glass-fibre cars may not be a feasible operation.

In addition to all the above, normal suppression components should be employed, but special attention paid to earth bonding. A screen enclosing the entire ignition system usually gives good improvement, and fabrication from fine mesh perforated metal is convenient. Good bonding of the screening boxes to several chassis points is essential.

---

13 Suspension and steering

Front suspension strut – overhaul

1 Should the front suspension shock absorber become defective or develop a leak, a shock absorber insert is available from the manufacturers, which allows the shock absorber to be repaired as opposed to renewing the complete strut.
2 The suspension strut should be removed and dismantled, as described in Chapter 11.
3 During the fitting of strut inserts, all the original parts must be removed and only the new insert and nut refitted.
4 Before fitting the insert into the strut, add a small amount of engine oil to the strut, which will prevent the insert from rattling in service.
5 Tighten the new suspension strut nut to the specified torque on reassembly (Chapter 11).
6 Note that these inserts should be renewed in pairs, as they have a different rebound value from original shock absorbers.
7 Note also that in 1982 the front shock absorber specification was changed, and so the renewing in pairs is also valid even if new suspension struts are being fitted.

Front suspension arm – 1982 on

8   From October 1982, the profile of the front steering knuckle arm has been changed.

9   This does not affect the servicing procedures in Chapter 11, but the steering arms on both sides of the steering assembly should be of the same profile.

Front coil springs

10   The specification of the front suspension coil springs has been changed, in order to improve ride comfort.

11   It is therefore important to renew the coil springs on both sides of the vehicle, should a coil spring become defective.

Rear coil springs

12   The specification of the rear coil springs has also been changed, both in 1981 and again in 1982, and so it is important to ensure that coil springs to the same specification are fitted to both sides of the vehicle.

Rear shock absorber – 1982 on

13   An additional dust seal has been added to the top of the oil seal on the rear shock absorber.

14   Servicing procedures are unaffected.

Steering gear – rack and pinion

15   To eliminate a possible knocking noise from the steering rack when the vehicle is driven over rough terrain, the manufacturers have introduced a new rack guide with a urethane spacer fitted in it, and two kinds of rack end bushing are available to optimise the clearance between the bush and rack.

16   If the steering rack is dismantled for overhaul or repair, the following points should be borne in mind when reassembling the rack.

17   Before inserting the rack into the housing, measure the diameter of the steering rack, (where it contacts the bush).

18   Select the appropriate size rack end bush for fitting to the housing.

19   The rack guide with urethane spacer is shown in Fig. 13.33.

20   Fit the urethane spacer to the new guide without using any grease or sealant.

21   Coat the rack guide face and sliding side surfaces with grease, and pack grease into the recessed back of the guide.

22   Fit the rack guide, spring, cap and locknut to the rack housing.

23   Tighten the guide cap to 18 lbf ft (2.5 kgf m) several times to bed in the urethane spacer.

24   After the final tightening process, loosen the cap through 90°.

25   Now check the force required to turn the rack pinion, and adjust the rack guide so that this force is as specified for the entire range of the rack.

26   Apply liquid sealer to the rack guide spring cap nut and housing, and torque load the locknut to its specified loading.

27   Recheck the pinion load, readjusting if necessary.

Note: *special adaptors are required to tighten the spring cap nut and to check the pinion preload (see Figs. 13.35 to 13.37).*

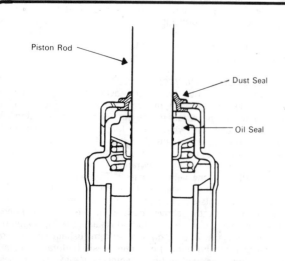

Fig. 13.31 Rear shock absorber dust cap (Sec 13)

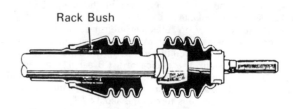

Fig. 13.32 Steering rack end bush (Sec 13)

Steering rack diameter	Bush inner diameter
24.645 to 24.665 mm	24.670 to 24.677 mm
24.660 to 24.680 mm	24.685 to 24.690 mm

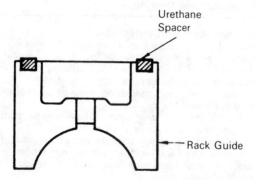

Fig. 13.33 Steering rack guide with urethane spacer (Sec 13)

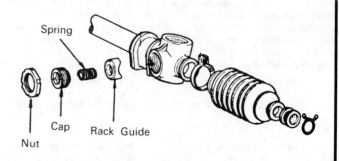

Fig. 13.34 Steering rack guide, cap and locknut assembly (Sec 15)

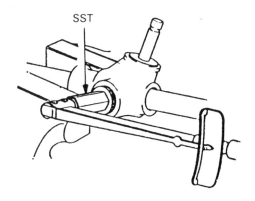

Fig.13.35 Tightening the steering rack guide cap (Sec 13)

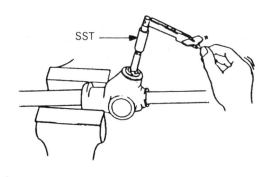

Fig. 13.36 Checking steering rack pinion preload (Sec 13)

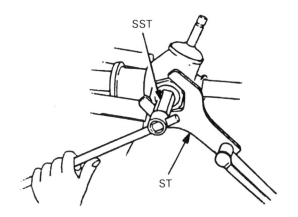

Fig. 13.37 Tightening the guide cap locknut (Sec 13)

14 Bodywork and fittings

Radiator grille – removal and refitting (1983 on)
1 Remove the two screws from the top of the grille (photo).
2 There are five clips, two at each end and one in the centre which hold the grille in place.
3 If you look through the grille at these, you will see a lever in the centre of each clip which must be lowered on the top clips, and raised on the lower ones, to release the clips (photo).
4 Pull the grille forward off the clips.
5 Refit in the reverse order.

Centre floor console – removal and refitting
6 Remove the screws from the sides of the panel.
7 Unscrew and remove the gear lever knob.
8 Lift the centre console up and off the gear lever.
9 The two halves of the console may be separated by removing the three screws and clip (photo).
10 Refit in the reverse order.

14.1 Removing a screw from the radiator grille

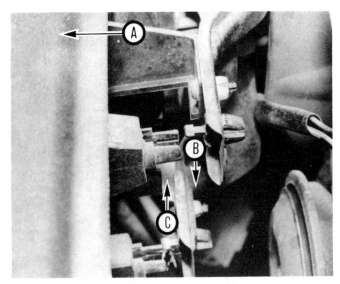

14.3 The grille securing clips

A Front of vehicle
B Lever down
C Lever up

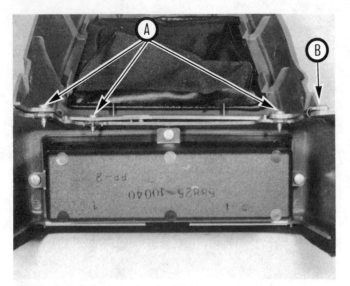

14.9 Three screws (A) and a clip (B)

22 Access to the blower motor can be gained after removing the glovebox (photo) and to the heater unit after removing the centre floor console and centre instrument panel.
23 Limited access to the control lever quadrants is available by removing the instrument panel surround and instrument panel.

Heater control panel – removal and refitting
24 Remove the centre floor console and centre panel.
25 Remove the three screws securing the control panel to the facia panel (photo).
26 The control panel can now be manoeuvred out of the panel.
27 The control cables are a press fit in the lever quadrants, and the cable ends hook into the levers (photo).
28 The blower motor switch should be renewed as a complete unit if it becomes defective (photo).
29 Refitting is a reversal of removal, but ensure the locating spigots on the lever quadrants are properly positioned in the holes in the control panel.
30 The cables should be hooked onto the control flap spigots at the control flap ends, then the cable sheath should be pushed toward the control flap before the cable clamp is locked in position.
31 This will ensure all slackness is taken up.

Door mounted rear view mirrors – removal and refitting
32 Prise off the lower panel (photo).
33 Remove the three retaining screws while supporting the mirror (photo).
34 Lift the mirror away (photo).
35 Refit in the reverse order.

Inertia reel rear seat belts – removal and refitting
36 Later models are fitted with inertia reel seat belts.
37 The inertia reel is situated in the luggage compartment, concealed by a plastic cover (photo).
38 Remove the bolt to release the cover and the reel.
39 Refit in the reverse order.

Remote tailgate release – cable renewal
40 The tailgate release lever is situated by the driver's seat, and actuates the tailgate release mechanism via a cable, which is routed through the vehicle under the trim and rear seat.
41 Should the cable snap and need renewing, unhook the cable at the release mechanism and lever ends, then remove as much of the interior trim as is necessary to feed the cable out of the vehicle.
42 Refit in the reverse order, and adjust the tension of the cable on the lockplate and bolt at the rear end of the release lever support bracket, so that the release mechanism operates smoothly, with no undue tension in the cable when the hatch is closed.

Windscreen wash system – general
43 The windscreen wash reservoir on later models is positioned next to the battery and serves both the front and rear washers (photo).

Facia panel – removal and refitting
11 Remove the centre floor console.
12 Remove the glovebox; held by two screws at its lower edge.
13 Remove the centre console panel and the radio, as described in Section 12.
14 Unscrew the heater control panel.
15 Remove the instrument panel surround and instrument panel, as described in Section 12.
16 Disconnect the rocker switches at the right-hand side of the panel, and disconnect the clock.
17 Disconnect the bonnet release cable from the facia panel.
18 The facia panel retaining screws/bolts are basically as shown in Fig. 12.28 of Chapter 12, but these do seem to vary from model to model, and it is largely a case of working around the panel and undoing each bolt and screw in turn.
19 Lift off the panel gently, and ensure that all electrical leads are disconnected before finally lifting the panel away.
20 Refitting is a reversal of removal, but make sure all electrical connections are made, and that the heating and ventilating ducts are lined up before finally tightening the retaining screws.

Heater – removal and refitting
21 The heater and blower motor are basically the same as fitted to earlier models, and the removal and refitting procedures given in Chapter 12 will suffice.

14.22 View of blower motor with glovebox removed

14.25 Heater control panel securing screws (arrowed)

14.27 Heater control cable quadrant and cable ends

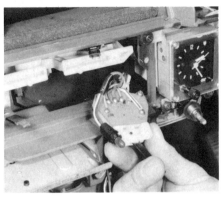
14.28 Blower motor switch and bulb

14.32 Prising off the mirror cover panel

14.33 Removing the screws

14.34 Lifting the mirror away

14.37 Inertia reel rear seat belt mounting bolt (arrowed)

14.43 Filling the windscreen wash reservoir

Plastic components

44 With the use of more and more plastic body components by the vehicle manufacturers (eg bumpers, spoilers, and in some cases major body panels), rectification of damage to such items has become a matter of either entrusting repair work to a specialist in this field, or renewing complete components. Repair by the DIY owner is not really feasible owing to the cost of the equipment and materials required for effecting such repairs. The basic technique involves making a groove along the line of the crack in the plastic using a rotary burr in a power drill. The damaged part is then welded back together by using a hot air gun to heat up and fuse a plastic filler rod into the groove. Any excess plastic is then removed and the area rubbed down to a smooth finish. It is important that a filler rod of the correct plastic is used, as body components can be made of a variety of different types (eg polycarbonate, ABS, polypropylene).

45 If the owner is renewing a complete component himself, he will be left with the problem of finding a suitable paint for finishing which is compatible with the type of plastic used. At one time the use of a universal paint was not possible owing to the complex range of plastics encountered in body component applications. Standard paints, generally speaking, will not bond to plastic or rubber satisfactorily. However, it is now possible to obtain a plastic body parts finishing kit which consists of a pre-primer treatment, a primer and coloured top coat. Full instructions are normally supplied with a kit, but basically the method of use is to first apply the pre-primer to the component concerned and allow it to dry for up to 30 minutes. Then the primer is applied and left to dry for about an hour before finally applying the special coloured top coat. The result is a correctly coloured component where the paint will flex with the plastic or rubber, a property that standard paint does not normally possess.

General repair procedures

Whenever servicing, repair or overhaul work is carried out on the car or its components, it is necessary to observe the following procedures and instructions. This will assist in carrying out the operation efficiently and to a professional standard of workmanship.

Joint mating faces and gaskets

Where a gasket is used between the mating faces of two components, ensure that it is renewed on reassembly, and fit it dry unless otherwise stated in the repair procedure. Make sure that the mating faces are clean and dry with all traces of old gasket removed. When cleaning a joint face, use a tool which is not likely to score or damage the face, and remove any burrs or nicks with an oilstone or fine file.

Make sure that tapped holes are cleaned with a pipe cleaner, and keep them free of jointing compound if this is being used unless specifically instructed otherwise.

Ensure that all orifices, channels or pipes are clear and blow through them, preferably using compressed air.

Oil seals

Whenever an oil seal is removed from its working location, either individually or as part of an assembly, it should be renewed.

The very fine sealing lip of the seal is easily damaged and will not seal if the surface it contacts is not completely clean and free from scratches, nicks or grooves. If the original sealing surface of the component cannot be restored, the component should be renewed.

Protect the lips of the seal from any surface which may damage them in the course of fitting. Use tape or a conical sleeve where possible. Lubricate the seal lips with oil before fitting and, on dual lipped seals, fill the space between the lips with grease.

Unless otherwise stated, oil seals must be fitted with their sealing lips toward the lubricant to be sealed.

Use a tubular drift or block of wood of the appropriate size to install the seal and, if the seal housing is shouldered, drive the seal down to the shoulder. If the seal housing is unshouldered, the seal should be fitted with its face flush with the housing top face.

Screw threads and fastenings

Always ensure that a blind tapped hole is completely free from oil, grease, water or other fluid before installing the bolt or stud. Failure to do this could cause the housing to crack due to the hydraulic action of the bolt or stud as it is screwed in.

When tightening a castellated nut to accept a split pin, tighten the nut to the specified torque, where applicable, and then tighten further to the next split pin hole. Never slacken the nut to align a split pin hole unless stated in the repair procedure.

When checking or retightening a nut or bolt to a specified torque setting, slacken the nut or bolt by a quarter of a turn, and then retighten to the specified setting.

Locknuts, locktabs and washers

Any fastening which will rotate against a component or housing in the course of tightening should always have a washer between it and the relevant component or housing.

Spring or split washers should always be renewed when they are used to lock a critical component such as a big-end bearing retaining nut or bolt.

Locktabs which are folded over to retain a nut or bolt should always be renewed.

Self-locking nuts can be reused in non-critical areas, providing resistance can be felt when the locking portion passes over the bolt or stud thread.

Split pins must always be replaced with new ones of the correct size for the hole.

Special tools

Some repair procedures in this manual entail the use of special tools such as a press, two or three-legged pullers, spring compressors etc. Wherever possible, suitable readily available alternatives to the manufacturer's special tools are described, and are shown in use. In some instances, where no alternative is possible, it has been necessary to resort to the use of a manufacturer's tool and this has been done for reasons of safety as well as the efficient completion of the repair operation. Unless you are highly skilled and have a thorough understanding of the procedure described, never attempt to bypass the use of any special tool when the procedure described specifies its use. Not only is there a very great risk of personal injury, but expensive damage could be caused to the components involved.

Safety first!

Professional motor mechanics are trained in safe working procedures. However enthusiastic you may be about getting on with the job in hand, do take the time to ensure that your safety is not put at risk. A moment's lack of attention can result in an accident, as can failure to observe certain elementary precautions.

There will always be new ways of having accidents, and the following points do not pretend to be a comprehensive list of all dangers; they are intended rather to make you aware of the risks and to encourage a safety-conscious approach to all work you carry out on your vehicle.

Essential DOs and DON'Ts

DON'T rely on a single jack when working underneath the vehicle. Always use reliable additional means of support, such as axle stands, securely placed under a part of the vehicle that you know will not give way.

DON'T attempt to loosen or tighten high-torque nuts (e.g. wheel hub nuts) while the vehicle is on a jack; it may be pulled off.

DON'T start the engine without first ascertaining that the transmission is in neutral (or 'Park' where applicable) and the parking brake applied.

DON'T suddenly remove the filler cap from a hot cooling system – cover it with a cloth and release the pressure gradually first, or you may get scalded by escaping coolant.

DON'T attempt to drain oil until you are sure it has cooled sufficiently to avoid scalding you.

DON'T grasp any part of the engine, exhaust or catalytic converter without first ascertaining that it is sufficiently cool to avoid burning you.

DON'T allow brake fluid or antifreeze to contact vehicle paintwork.

DON'T syphon toxic liquids such as fuel, brake fluid or antifreeze by mouth, or allow them to remain on your skin.

DON'T inhale dust – it may be injurious to health (see *Asbestos* below).

DON'T allow any spilt oil or grease to remain on the floor – wipe it up straight away, before someone slips on it.

DON'T use ill-fitting spanners or other tools which may slip and cause injury.

DON'T attempt to lift a heavy component which may be beyond your capability – get assistance.

DON'T rush to finish a job, or take unverified short cuts.

DON'T allow children or animals in or around an unattended vehicle.

DO wear eye protection when using power tools such as drill, sander, bench grinder etc, and when working under the vehicle.

DO use a barrier cream on your hands prior to undertaking dirty jobs – it will protect your skin from infection as well as making the dirt easier to remove afterwards; but make sure your hands aren't left slippery. Note that long-term contact with used engine oil can be a health hazard.

DO keep loose clothing (cuffs, tie etc) and long hair well out of the way of moving mechanical parts.

DO remove rings, wristwatch etc, before working on the vehicle – especially the electrical system.

DO ensure that any lifting tackle used has a safe working load rating adequate for the job.

DO keep your work area tidy – it is only too easy to fall over articles left lying around.

DO get someone to check periodically that all is well, when working alone on the vehicle.

DO carry out work in a logical sequence and check that everything is correctly assembled and tightened afterwards.

DO remember that your vehicle's safety affects that of yourself and others. If in doubt on any point, get specialist advice.

IF, in spite of following these precautions, you are unfortunate enough to injure yourself, seek medical attention as soon as possible.

Asbestos

Certain friction, insulating, sealing, and other products – such as brake linings, brake bands, clutch linings, torque converters, gaskets, etc – contain asbestos. *Extreme care must be taken to avoid inhalation of dust from such products since it is hazardous to health*. If in doubt, assume that they *do* contain asbestos.

Fire

Remember at all times that petrol (gasoline) is highly flammable. Never smoke, or have any kind of naked flame around, when working on the vehicle. But the risk does not end there – a spark caused by an electrical short-circuit, by two metal surfaces contacting each other, by careless use of tools, or even by static electricity built up in your body under certain conditions, can ignite petrol vapour, which in a confined space is highly explosive.

Always disconnect the battery earth (ground) terminal before working on any part of the fuel or electrical system, and never risk spilling fuel on to a hot engine or exhaust.

It is recommended that a fire extinguisher of a type suitable for fuel and electrical fires is kept handy in the garage or workplace at all times. Never try to extinguish a fuel or electrical fire with water.

Note: *Any reference to a 'torch' appearing in this manual should always be taken to mean a hand-held battery-operated electric lamp or flashlight. It does NOT mean a welding/gas torch or blowlamp.*

Fumes

Certain fumes are highly toxic and can quickly cause unconsciousness and even death if inhaled to any extent. Petrol (gasoline) vapour comes into this category, as do the vapours from certain solvents such as trichloroethylene. Any draining or pouring of such volatile fluids should be done in a well ventilated area.

When using cleaning fluids and solvents, read the instructions carefully. Never use materials from unmarked containers – they may give off poisonous vapours.

Never run the engine of a motor vehicle in an enclosed space such as a garage. Exhaust fumes contain carbon monoxide which is extremely poisonous; if you need to run the engine, always do so in the open air or at least have the rear of the vehicle outside the workplace.

If you are fortunate enough to have the use of an inspection pit, never drain or pour petrol, and never run the engine, while the vehicle is standing over it; the fumes, being heavier than air, will concentrate in the pit with possibly lethal results.

The battery

Never cause a spark, or allow a naked light, near the vehicle's battery. It will normally be giving off a certain amount of hydrogen gas, which is highly explosive.

Always disconnect the battery earth (ground) terminal before working on the fuel or electrical systems.

If possible, loosen the filler plugs or cover when charging the battery from an external source. Do not charge at an excessive rate or the battery may burst.

Take care when topping up and when carrying the battery. The acid electrolyte, even when diluted, is very corrosive and should not be allowed to contact the eyes or skin.

If you ever need to prepare electrolyte yourself, always add the acid slowly to the water, and never the other way round. Protect against splashes by wearing rubber gloves and goggles.

When jump starting a car using a booster battery, for negative earth (ground) vehicles, connect the jump leads in the following sequence: First connect one jump lead between the positive (+) terminals of the two batteries. Then connect the other jump lead first to the negative (–) terminal of the booster battery, and then to a good earthing (ground) point on the vehicle to be started, at least 18 in (45 cm) from the battery if possible. Ensure that hands and jump leads are clear of any moving parts, and that the two vehicles do not touch. Disconnect the leads in the reverse order.

Mains electricity and electrical equipment

When using an electric power tool, inspection light etc, always ensure that the appliance is correctly connected to its plug and that, where necessary, it is properly earthed (grounded). Do not use such appliances in damp conditions and, again, beware of creating a spark or applying excessive heat in the vicinity of fuel or fuel vapour. Also ensure that the appliances meet the relevant national safety standards.

Ignition HT voltage

A severe electric shock can result from touching certain parts of the ignition system, such as the HT leads, when the engine is running or being cranked, particularly if components are damp or the insulation is defective. Where an electronic ignition system is fitted, the HT voltage is much higher and could prove fatal.

Fault diagnosis

Introduction

The vehicle owner who does his or her own maintenance according to the recommended schedules should not have to use this section of the manual very often. Modern component reliability is such that, provided those items subject to wear or deterioration are inspected or renewed at the specified intervals, sudden failure is comparatively rare. Faults do not usually just happen as a result of sudden failure, but develop over a period of time. Major mechanical failures in particular are usually preceded by characteristic symptoms over hundreds or even thousands of miles. Those components which do occasionally fail without warning are often small and easily carried in the vehicle.

With any fault finding, the first step is to decide where to begin investigations. Sometimes this is obvious, but on other occasions a little detective work will be necessary. The owner who makes half a dozen haphazard adjustments or replacements may be successful in curing a fault (or its symptoms), but he will be none the wiser if the fault recurs and he may well have spent more time and money than was necessary. A calm and logical approach will be found to be more satisfactory in the long run. Always take into account any warning signs or abnormalities that may have been noticed in the period preceding the fault – power loss, high or low gauge readings, unusual noises or smells, etc – and remember that failure of components such as fuses or spark plugs may only be pointers to some underlying fault.

The pages which follow here are intended to help in cases of failure to start or breakdown on the road. There is also a Fault Diagnosis Section at the end of each Chapter which should be consulted if the preliminary checks prove unfruitful. Whatever the fault, certain basic principles apply. These are as follows:

Verify the fault. This is simply a matter of being sure that you know what the symptoms are before starting work. This is particularly important if you are investigating a fault for someone else who may not have described it very accurately.

Don't overlook the obvious. For example, if the vehicle won't start, is there petrol in the tank? (Don't take anyone else's word on this particular point, and don't trust the fuel gauge either!) If an electrical fault is indicated, look for loose or broken wires before digging out the test gear.

Cure the disease, not the symptom. Substituting a flat battery with a fully charged one will get you off the hard shoulder, but if the underlying cause is not attended to, the new battery will go the same way. Similarly, changing oil-fouled spark plugs for a new set will get you moving again, but remember that the reason for the fouling (if it wasn't simply an incorrect grade of plug) will have to be established and corrected.

Don't take anything for granted. Particularly, don't forget that a 'new' component may itself be defective (especially if it's been rattling round in the boot for months), and don't leave components out of a fault diagnosis sequence just because they are new or recently fitted. When you do finally diagnose a difficult fault, you'll probably realise that all the evidence was there from the start.

Electrical faults

Electrical faults can be more puzzling than straightforward mechanical failures, but they are no less susceptible to logical analysis if the basic principles of operation are understood. Vehicle electrical wiring exists in extremely unfavourable conditions – heat, vibration and chemical attack – and the first things to look for are loose or corroded connections and broken or chafed wires, especially where the wires pass through holes in the bodywork or are subject to vibration.

All metal-bodied vehicles in current production have one pole of the battery 'earthed', ie connected to the vehicle bodywork, and in nearly all modern vehicles it is the negative (–) terminal. The various electrical components – motors, bulb holders etc – are also connected to earth, either by means of a lead or directly by their mountings. Electric current flows through the component and then back to the battery via the bodywork. If the component mounting is loose or corroded, or if a good path back to the battery is not available, the circuit will be incomplete and malfunction will result. The engine and/or gearbox are also earthed by means of flexible metal straps to the body or subframe; if these straps are loose or missing, starter motor, generator and ignition trouble may result.

Assuming the earth return to be satisfactory, electrical faults will be due either to component malfunction or to defects in the current supply. Individual components are dealt with in Chapter 12. If supply wires are broken or cracked internally this results in an open-circuit, and the easiest way to check for this is to bypass the suspect wire temporarily with a length of wire having a crocodile clip or suitable connector at each end. Alternatively, a 12V test lamp can be used to verify the presence of supply voltage at various points along the wire and the break can be thus isolated.

If a bare portion of a live wire touches the bodywork or other earthed metal part, the electricity will take the low-resistance path thus formed back to the battery: this is known as a short-circuit. Hopefully a short-circuit will blow a fuse, but otherwise it may cause burning of the insulation (and possibly further short-circuits) or even a fire. This is why it is inadvisable to bypass persistently blowing fuses with silver foil or wire.

Spares and tool kit

Most vehicles are supplied only with sufficient tools for wheel changing; the *Maintenance and minor repair* tool kit detailed in *Tools and working facilities,* with the addition of a hammer, is probably sufficient for those repairs that most motorists would consider attempting at the roadside. In addition a few items which can be fitted without too much trouble in the event of a breakdown should be carried. Experience and available space will modify the list below, but the following may save having to call on professional assistance:

Spark plugs, clean and correctly gapped
HT lead and plug cap – long enough to reach the plug furthest from the distributor
Distributor rotor, condenser and contact breaker points (1300 models only)
Drivebelt(s) – emergency type may suffice
Spare fuses
Set of principal light bulbs
Tin of radiator sealer and hose bandage
Exhaust bandage
Roll of insulating tape
Length of soft iron wire
Length of electrical flex
Torch or inspection lamp (can double as test lamp)
Battery jump leads
Tow-rope
Ignition waterproofing aerosol
Litre of engine oil
Sealed can of hydraulic fluid
Worm drive clips
Tube of filler paste

If spare fuel is carried, a can designed for the purpose should be used to minimise risks of leakage and collision damage. A first aid kit and a warning triangle, whilst not at present compulsory in the UK, are obviously sensible items to carry in addition to the above.

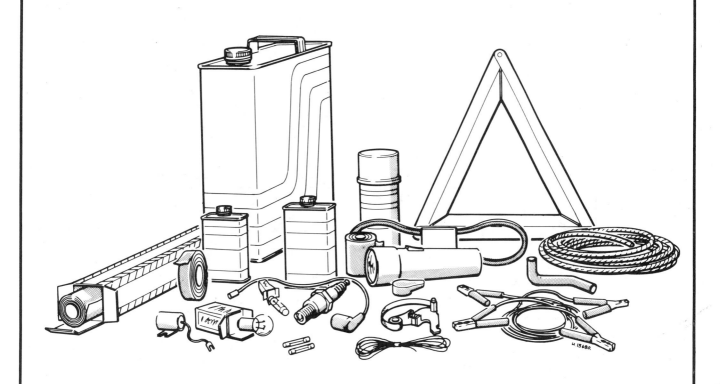

Carrying a few spares can save a long walk

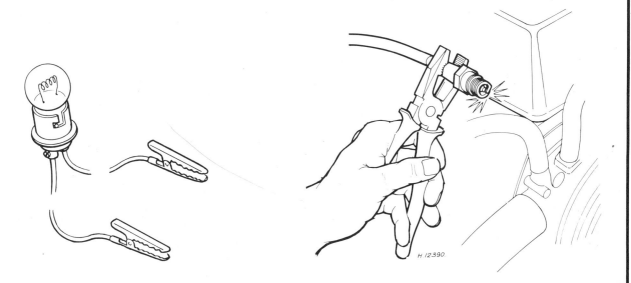

Simple test lamp is useful for tracing electrical faults

Crank engine and check for a spark. Note use of insulated tool

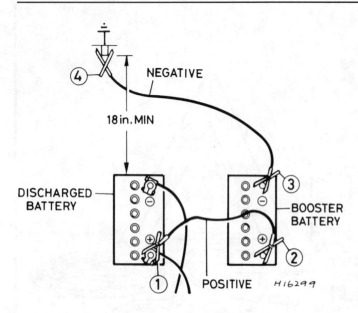

**Jump start lead connections for negative earth vehicles –
connect leads in order shown**

When touring abroad it may be advisable to carry additional spares
which, even if you cannot fit them yourself, could save having to wait
while parts are obtained. The items below may be worth considering:

Clutch and throttle cables
Cylinder head gasket
Alternator brushes
Fuel pump repair kit
Tyre valve core

One of the motoring organisations will be able to advise on
availability of fuel etc in foreign countries.

Engine will not start

Engine fails to turn when starter operated
   Flat battery (recharge, use jump leads, or push start)
   Battery terminals loose or corroded
   Battery earth to body defective
   Engine earth strap loose or broken
   Starter motor (or solenoid) wiring loose or broken
   Automatic transmission selector in wrong position, or inhibitor
   switch faulty
   Ignition/starter switch faulty
   Major mechanical failure (seizure)
   Starter or solenoid internal fault (see Chapter 12)

Starter motor turns engine slowly
   Partially discharged battery (recharge, use jump leads, or push
   start)
   Battery terminals loose or corroded
   Battery earth to body defective
   Engine earth strap loose
   Starter motor (or solenoid) wiring loose
   Starter motor internal fault (see Chapter 12)

Starter motor spins without turning engine
   Flat battery
   Starter motor pinion sticking on sleeve
   Flywheel gear teeth damaged or worn
   Starter motor mounting bolts loose

Engine turns normally but fails to start
   Damp or dirty HT leads and distributor cap (crank engine and
   check for spark)
   No fuel in tank (check for delivery at carburettor)

Excessive choke (hot engine) or insufficient choke (cold engine)
Fouled or incorrectly gapped spark plugs (remove, clean and
regap)
Other ignition system fault (see Chapter 4)
Other fuel system fault (see Chapter 3)
Poor compression (see Chapter 1)
Major mechanical failure (eg camshaft drive)

Engine fires but will not run
   Insufficient choke (cold engine)
   Air leaks at carburettor or inlet manifold
   Fuel starvation (see Chapter 3)
   Ignition fault (see Chapter 4)

Engine cuts out and will not restart

Engine cuts out suddenly – ignition fault
   Loose or disconnected LT wires
   Wet HT leads or distributor cap (after traversing water splash)
   Coil or condenser failure (check for spark)
   Other ignition fault (see Chapter 4)

Engine misfires before cutting out – fuel fault
   Fuel tank empty
   Fuel pump defective or filter blocked (check for delivery)
   Fuel tank filler vent blocked (suction will be evident on releasing
   cap)
   Carburettor needle valve sticking
   Carburettor jets blocked (fuel contaminated)
   Other fuel system fault (see Chapter 3)

Engine cuts out – other causes
   Serious overheating
   Major mechanical failure (eg camshaft drive)

Engine overheats

Ignition (no-charge) warning light illuminated
   Slack or broken drivebelt – retension or renew (Chapter 2)

Ignition warning light not illuminated
   Coolant loss due to internal or external leakage (see Chapter 2)
   Thermostat defective
   Low oil level
   Brakes binding
   Radiator clogged externally or internally
   Electric cooling fan not operating correctly
   Engine waterways clogged
   Ignition timing incorrect or automatic advance malfunctioning
   Mixture too weak

Note: *Do not add cold water to an overheated engine or damage may
result*

Low engine oil pressure

*Gauge reads low or warning light illuminated with engine
running*
   Oil level low or incorrect grade
   Defective gauge or sender unit
   Wire to sender unit earthed
   Engine overheating
   Oil filter clogged or bypass valve defective
   Oil pressure relief valve defective
   Oil pick-up strainer clogged
   Oil pump worn or mountings loose
   Worn main or big-end bearings

Note: *Low oil pressure in a high-mileage engine at tickover is not
necessarily a cause for concern. Sudden pressure loss at speed is far
more significant. In any event, check the gauge or warning light sender
before condemning the engine.*

Engine noises

Pre-ignition (pinking) on acceleration
Incorrect grade of fuel
Ignition timing incorrect
Distributor faulty or worn
Worn or maladjusted carburettor
Excessive carbon build-up in engine

Whistling or wheezing noises
Leaking vacuum hose
Leaking carburettor or manifold gasket
Blowing head gasket

Tapping or rattling
Incorrect valve clearances
Worn valve gear
Worn timing belt
Broken piston ring (ticking noise)

Knocking or thumping
Unintentional mechanical contact (eg fan blades)
Worn drivebelt
Peripheral component fault (generator, water pump etc)
Worn big-end bearings (regular heavy knocking, perhaps less under load)
Worn main bearings (rumbling and knocking, perhaps worsening under load)
Piston slap (most noticeable when cold)

Conversion factors

Length (distance)

Inches (in)	X	25.4	= Millimetres (mm)	X 0.0394	= Inches (in)
Feet (ft)	X	0.305	= Metres (m)	X 3.281	= Feet (ft)
Miles	X	1.609	= Kilometres (km)	X 0.621	= Miles

Volume (capacity)

Cubic inches (cu in; in^3)	X	16.387	= Cubic centimetres (cc; cm^3)	X 0.061	= Cubic inches (cu in; in^3)
Imperial pints (Imp pt)	X	0.568	= Litres (l)	X 1.76	= Imperial pints (Imp pt)
Imperial quarts (Imp qt)	X	1.137	= Litres (l)	X 0.88	= Imperial quarts (Imp qt)
Imperial quarts (Imp qt)	X	1.201	= US quarts (US qt)	X 0.833	= Imperial quarts (Imp qt)
US quarts (US qt)	X	0.946	= Litres (l)	X 1.057	= US quarts (US qt)
Imperial gallons (Imp gal)	X	4.546	= Litres (l)	X 0.22	= Imperial gallons (Imp gal)
Imperial gallons (Imp gal)	X	1.201	= US gallons (US gal)	X 0.833	= Imperial gallons (Imp gal)
US gallons (US gal)	X	3.785	= Litres (l)	X 0.264	= US gallons (US gal)

Mass (weight)

Ounces (oz)	X	28.35	= Grams (g)	X 0.035	= Ounces (oz)
Pounds (lb)	X	0.454	= Kilograms (kg)	X 2.205	= Pounds (lb)

Force

Ounces-force (ozf; oz)	X	0.278	= Newtons (N)	X 3.6	= Ounces-force (ozf; oz)
Pounds-force (lbf; lb)	X	4.448	= Newtons (N)	X 0.225	= Pounds-force (lbf; lb)
Newtons (N)	X	0.1	= Kilograms-force (kgf; kg)	X 9.81	= Newtons (N)

Pressure

Pounds-force per square inch (psi; lbf/in^2; lb/in^2)	X	0.070	= Kilograms-force per square centimetre (kgf/cm^2; kg/cm^2)	X 14.223	= Pounds-force per square inch (psi; lbf/in^2; lb/in^2)
Pounds-force per square inch (psi; lbf/in^2; lb/in^2)	X	0.068	= Atmospheres (atm)	X 14.696	= Pounds-force per square inch (psi; lbf/in^2; lb/in^2)
Pounds-force per square inch (psi; lbf/in^2; lb/in^2)	X	0.069	= Bars	X 14.5	= Pounds-force per square inch (psi; lbf/in^2; lb/in^2)
Pounds-force per square inch (psi; lbf/in^2; lb/in^2)	X	6.895	= Kilopascals (kPa)	X 0.145	= Pounds-force per square inch (psi; lbf/in^2; lb/in^2)
Kilopascals (kPa)	X	0.01	= Kilograms-force per square centimetre (kgf/cm^2; kg/cm^2)	X 98.1	= Kilopascals (kPa)

Torque (moment of force)

Pounds-force inches (lbf in; lb in)	X	1.152	= Kilograms-force centimetre (kgf cm; kg cm)	X 0.868	= Pounds-force inches (lbf in; lb in)
Pounds-force inches (lbf in; lb in)	X	0.113	= Newton metres (Nm)	X 8.85	= Pounds-force inches (lbf in; lb in)
Pounds-force inches (lbf in; lb in)	X	0.083	= Pounds-force feet (lbf ft; lb ft)	X 12	= Pounds-force inches (lbf in; lb in)
Pounds-force feet (lbf ft; lb ft)	X	0.138	= Kilograms-force metres (kgf m; kg m)	X 7.233	= Pounds-force feet (lbf ft; lb ft)
Pounds-force feet (lbf ft; lb ft)	X	1.356	= Newton metres (Nm)	X 0.738	= Pounds-force feet (lbf ft; lb ft)
Newton metres (Nm)	X	0.102	= Kilograms-force metres (kgf m; kg m)	X 9.804	= Newton metres (Nm)

Power

Horsepower (hp)	X	745.7	= Watts (W)	X 0.0013	= Horsepower (hp)

Velocity (speed)

Miles per hour (miles/hr; mph)	X	1.609	= Kilometres per hour (km/hr; kph)	X 0.621	= Miles per hour (miles/hr; mph)

Fuel consumption*

Miles per gallon, Imperial (mpg)	X	0.354	= Kilometres per litre (km/l)	X 2.825	= Miles per gallon, Imperial (mpg)
Miles per gallon, US (mpg)	X	0.425	= Kilometres per litre (km/l)	X 2.352	= Miles per gallon, US (mpg)

Temperature

Degrees Fahrenheit = (°C x 1.8) + 32

Degrees Celsius (Degrees Centigrade; °C) = (°F - 32) x 0.56

*It is common practice to convert from miles per gallon (mpg) to litres/100 kilometres (l/100km),
where mpg (Imperial) x l/100 km = 282 and mpg (US) x l/100 km = 235

Index

Printed by
J H Haynes & Co Ltd
Sparkford Nr Yeovil
Somerset BA22 7JJ England